STUDY GUIDE

Financial Accounting
in an Economic Context

5th Edition

Jamie Pratt
Professor of Accounting
Indiana University, Bloomington

Prepared by

Joseph H. Anthony
Michigan State University

Robin P. Clement
Louisiana State University

John Wiley & Sons, Inc.

To order books or for customer service call 1-800-CALL-WILEY (225-5945).

ISBN 0-471-23895-3

Printed in the United States of America

10 9 8 7 6 5 4 3 2 1

Printed and bound by Bradford & Bigelow, Inc.

TABLE OF CONTENTS

PREFACE

This study guide was prepared to accompany the fifth edition of Pratt's **FINANCIAL ACCOUNTING**. The study guide is intended to both supplement and complement the text. Each chapter contains a ***Review of Key Concepts***. The review expands the discussion of important concepts from the text, offering additional examples to aid student comprehension. Where appropriate, we provide alternative approaches to understanding the concepts presented in the text.

Each chapter also includes a set of multiple choice questions and several short exercises for student review. Answers are provided for the multiple choice questions, as well as, detailed solutions to the exercises.

INSTRUCTIONS TO THE STUDENT

The instructions which follow are intended to allow you to get the most value for your investment in this *STUDY GUIDE*. If used properly, the *STUDY GUIDE* should be of great assistance in learning the materials of introductory financial accounting. Take a few minutes to carefully review the instructions which follow.

1. We recommend reviewing chapters in this *STUDY GUIDE*, only after you have read the assigned materials in your text. The *STUDY GUIDE* provides a review of key concepts. In many instances, these will be presented in an alternative way from that used in the text. In other cases, we follow the text presentation, but provide you with alternative examples.

2. We **DO NOT** recommend using the *STUDY GUIDE* instead of the text. Our Review of Key Concepts is not comprehensive. Rather, we have selected for inclusion **only** those topics, which in our experience, are most troublesome for students. Less difficult topics are excluded.

3. The questions and exercises should provide you with a means of self-testing and practice for examinations in the course. We typically include twenty multiple choice questions and five short exercises/problems per chapter. The following approach is suggested.

   a. Complete all odd-numbered multiple choice questions, before reading the Review of Key Concepts. CIRCLE YOUR RESPONSES. Check your responses against the solutions provided.

   b. Identify your mistakes and the areas which are giving you difficulty. Carefully read the Review of Key Concepts sections where you need additional work.

   c. Complete the short exercises/problems from those topics which you found difficult. You may also want to use these to supplement assignments from the text given by your instructor. We have provided sufficient space for you to work the exercises and problems directly in the *STUDY GUIDE*. All short exercises/problems have detailed solutions provided. You may find it convenient to tear out the completed problems, to allow easier comparison to the solutions.

   d. Use the even-numbered multiple questions to create your own examinations. Prior to your in class examinations, complete these questions. Time yourself. Allow approximately the same time as is available on the scheduled examinations. Multiple choice questions are widely used in introductory accounting classes, due to the large number of students enrolled. This self-testing provides an excellent preparation for actual examinations. Once again, it may be useful to tear out the pages to construct your self-examination.

   Timing yourself carefully, and evaluating your performance on these self-tests, should help to eliminate pre-examination jitters.

ACKNOWLEDGEMENTS

We wish to acknowledge the efforts of Professor Clyde Galbraith of West Chester University in editing the manuscript. We also wish to thank all users of the prior edition who offered comments, corrections and suggestions.

CHAPTER 1

Financial Accounting and Its Economic Context

REVIEW OF KEY CONCEPTS

Your text provides an introduction to the economic role played by financial accounting and reporting. You should carefully read this material. The chapter includes a discussion of the four basic financial statements. Our study guide coverage begins with an introduction to the basic accounting system which produces those financial statements.

The accounting system is an information system used to collect and categorize data used in business decision making. We begin with an introduction to the basic **accounting equation** (sometimes referred to as the accounting model). Our coverage will give you a head start on the material which will appear in the first five chapters of the text. This chapter will define accounting and introduce the major elements of the accounting equation. The simple equation presented here provides the conceptual basis for virtually all of the material to be covered in an introductory financial accounting course.

Accounting Defined

Accounting is the process of identifying, measuring, recording, and communicating information about the production, development, and management of money and other economic resources. This includes the resources of individuals, businesses, or countries. The objective of financial accounting is to provide the suppliers of resources (creditors and owners) with information about how and where managers have invested those resources. Accounting also provides a summary of changes in resources due to the operations of the business.

Businesses obtain resources from **investors** and **creditors**. Investors are the owners of the business. A business may be a small family-owned company or a large modern corporation. The owners of a corporation are the shareholders or stockholders, but we will use the term investors to describe the owners of the business. A business also obtains funds by borrowing from a bank or other lenders. Creditors are those who lend to the business. Investors and creditors use financial accounting information to judge the performance of management over time and to compare investment opportunities across companies.

A major purpose of a business is to increase the wealth of its owners. The accounting system is a collection of rules and definitions designed to measure the total investment (by both investors and creditors) in the business at a point in time as well as changes in the value of the investment over time. The accounting system's rules attempt to measure in a concise and understandable way the events affecting value during a time period. The system represents economic events affecting a business, using assumptions, estimates, and other devices to approximate value and changes in value over time.

The Accounting Equation

The basis of the financial accounting system is the following equation:

$$\text{Assets} = \text{Liabilities} + \text{Owners' Equity}$$

Assets are specific economic resources owned by a business. When owners invest in a business or borrow from creditors, managers choose the specific assets in which to invest the money. As the firm operates its business, it acquires economic resources through selling products or services to customers. The business also consumes economic resources in providing those services or products.

For example, a magazine publisher increases its economic resources when it collects money from subscribers (customers). But the subscribers expect something in return; the publisher must provide the promised magazines. The publisher consumes economic resources to print and distribute the magazines. The publisher must pay for paper and printing supplies, pay employees, and of course pay postage to mail the magazines.

More formally, accounting rules define an asset as a resource:
   (1) having an expected future economic benefit, and
   (2) being the result of a past transaction or event.

The first criterion requires that the item contributes to the process of generating future resources in some way. For example, if the business purchases a building to be used in future operations, it qualifies as an asset. But, if they find the building contaminated with a substance to the point it cannot be repaired, the building's status as an asset becomes questionable. Even though the business legally owns the building, the building is not an asset if its ability to contribute to future wealth is limited or impaired.

The second criterion requires that an asset be the result of a past transaction. A **transaction** is an economic event, that is, the result of performing or doing something. Usually, accountants require an exchange of some sort before recording an item as an asset. Simply entering into a contract to perform a service or provide goods in the future does not create an asset. The business acquires assets as it performs services or delivers products.

Liabilities are probable claims to economic resources or services to be fulfilled at some time in the future. Like an asset, a liability must be the result of a past transaction or event.

Owners' equity is the amount of money or wealth invested by owners at a point in time. It is the amount of assets remaining after satisfying the claims of creditors. Owners' equity is sometimes referred to as the residual claim on assets since it is the difference between assets and the claims of creditors. Rearranging the accounting equation:

$$\text{Assets - Liabilities} = \text{Owners' Equity}$$

Chapter 1

Our focus to this point has been describing economic resources and claims to those resources at a point in time. The **balance sheet** or **statement of financial position** lists the assets and claims to assets (liabilities and owners' equity) at a point in time. It is one of the four basic financial statements included in the financial information provided to investors and creditors.

Accounting for Changes in Financial Position

Investors are also interested in detail regarding how wealth changes over time. Specifically, they are interested in changes in the owners' equity account over time such as from one year-end to another. An owner's investment in the business can change due to three activities: additional investment by owners, withdrawal of investment by the owners, and the successful operation of the business. The **statement of owners' equity** provides information regarding these three activities.

Since a primary motive for investing in a company is to increase wealth from the business's operation, a summary of operating transactions called the **income statement** provides more detail to investors about changes in their investment value due to operating activities of the business. Accountants separate the change due to operations into transactions which increase value, called **revenues and gains**, and those decreasing value, called **expenses and losses**.

Revenues arise when, in exchange for the business's services or products, the company receives an asset (usually cash or a promise to pay cash which is called a receivable) or reduces a liability. As an example of the latter, assume a customer pays in advance for a service. Cash increases, and the business incurs a liability. Owners' wealth is unaffected because the cash received has not been earned yet. When the business provides the service, the accountant reduces or eliminates the liability because the owner has earned the cash previously received. Thus, revenues are increases in owners' wealth due to providing services or goods.

Expenses reduce owners' equity. Expenses represent the costs of providing services or goods to customers. Either the business consumes an asset or incurs a liability when performing the service or selling the product. For example, when a department store sells a shirt, it reduces its inventory. The inventory is an asset. The store also employs sales people to help customers. Their salaries may be paid, immediately reducing assets, or may be paid in the future, increasing liabilities. The net affect is a reduction in owners' wealth.

For a business to operate successfully, in the long-run, revenues or increases in owners' wealth due to operations must exceed expenses or decreases in owners' wealth. The difference between revenues and expenses is called **net income** or profit. Investors find the listing of types of revenues and expenses on the income statement useful in assessing the management of resources across time and in comparing companies' abilities to increase owners' wealth.

A Comprehensive Example

The following example illustrates some of the important basic concepts underlying the use of the accounting system to develop financial statements for a business.

Jewelbox, is a small jewelry store owned by Karrie Webb. The following events took place during June 2003, the store's first month of business. For each item presented, we discuss the effect on the accounting equation. Following that discussion, we illustrate how to prepare the financial statements.

Transactions and Analysis (in chronological order)

1. The business opens a checking account depositing the $100,000 original investment of Ms. Webb. The business's resources are increased, and the claimant to those resources is Ms. Webb.

Account Type	Specific Account Affected
Assets	**Cash** increases by $100,000
Liabilities	No account affected
Owner's Equity	**K. Webb, Capital** increases by $100,000

2. The business purchases land for $10,000 and a building for $50,000. These are **assets** because the business will be conducted from this site now and in the future. Current and future years' operations will likely benefit from this purchase.

    The business purchased these resources by exchanging other resources (Cash, $20,000) and entering into a loan contract with the bank. Thus, total resources or assets increase by $40,000 ($10,000 + $50,000 - $20,000), and the claims on the total resources of the business increase by $40,000. The claimant is not the owner, but the bank that provided the loan of $40,000.

Account Type	Specific Account Affected
Assets	**Cash** decreases by $20,000
	Land increases by $10,000
	Building increases by $50,000
	Net change: Assets increase by $40,000
Liabilities	**Notes Payable** increases by $40,000
Owner's Equity	No account affected

3. The business purchases a display case for $4,000 cash. The business expects to use the display case for several years. The purchase represents the exchange of one economic resource, Cash, for another, Equipment.

Account Type	Specific Account Affected
Assets	**Cash** decreases by $4,000 **Equipment** increases by $4,000 Net change is zero
Liabilities	No account affected
Owner's Equity	No account affected

4. Leta Lindley is hired as a sales clerk. A contract exists between Ms. Lindley and Jewelbox. However, this type of event is usually not recorded in the accounting records because the accounting equation is unaffected. Since Ms. Lindley has not performed services yet, she does not have a claim on the business's resources. When Ms. Lindley actually begins to work, the company will record as revenues the sales price received for merchandise sold to customers. The company will record as expenses the cost of purchasing merchandise sold and the cost of Ms. Lindley's salary. The change in owner's equity for the period is the difference between revenue and expense (**net income**).

5. The business purchases $10,000 of jewelry from GEMS R US, Inc., on account. Jewelbox intends to resell the jewelry to its customers. We classify merchandise intended for resale (retailers) or raw materials to be used to produce products for sale (manufacturers) in **Inventory** accounts.

   When a firm purchases or sells **on account**, they create a contract promising to pay the amount owed in the future. Businesses usually have a group of suppliers they purchase inventory from on a regular basis, and record amounts owed such suppliers in **Accounts Payable**.

Account Type	Specific Account Affected
Assets	**Inventory** increases by $10,000
Liabilities	**Accounts Payable** increases by $10,000
Owner's Equity	No account affected

6. Jewelbox sells jewelry for $4,000 cash. The jewelry cost $3,000. This transaction includes an outflow of an economic resource, the jewelry which cost Jewelbox $3,000. The $4,000 cash received from the customer represents an inflow of resources. Assets have increased by $1,000 (Cash increased by $4,000 and Inventory decreased by $3,000). The owner is the claimant to the increase in resources. Jewelbox records the change in owner's equity in two accounts, Jewelry Revenue increases by $4,000 and Cost of Goods Sold Expense increases by $3,000, representing the inflow and outflow of resources resulting from the transaction.

Account Type	Specific Account Affected
Assets	**Cash** increases by $4,000 **Inventory** decreases by $3,000 Net change: Assets increase by $1,000
Liabilities	No account affected
Owner's Equity	**Revenues** increase by $4,000 **Expenses** increase by $3,000 Net change: Owner's Equity increases by $1,000

7. Jewelbox sells jewelry for $3,000 which cost $4,000. The sale was on account. As mentioned in 5, sales of merchandise to customers or purchases of merchandise from suppliers can be **on account**. The customer is contracting with Jewelbox to pay the $3,000 in the future. Obviously, Jewelbox sells on credit only if the customer has a good credit history. The promise to pay for the jewelry in the future is an asset since Jewelbox expects to receive cash in the future.

   Like transaction 6, Jewelbox increases assets by the difference between the assets received and assets given up, or $2,000 ($6,000 - $4,000). Owner's equity also increases by $2,000. Jewelbox records the change in owner's equity as an increase in Jewelry Revenue of $6,000 and an increase in Cost of Goods Sold of $4,000.

Account Type	Specific Account Affected
Assets	**Accounts Receivable** increases by $6,000 **Inventory** decreases by $4,000 Net change: Assets increase by $2,000
Liabilities	No account affected
Owner's Equity	**Revenues** increase by $6,000 **Expenses** increase by $4,000 Net change: Owner's Equity increases by $2,000

8. The business pays GEMS R US, Inc. for item purchased in 5. The $10,000 claim settles the creditor's, GEM R US, Inc., claim. Both assets and liabilities decrease. Owner's equity is not affected.

Account Type	Specific Account Affected
Assets	**Cash** decreases by $10,000
Liabilities	**Accounts Payable** decreases by $10,000
Owner's Equity	No account affected

9. The business pays Ms. Lindley's salary, $1,000. Cash decreases by $1,000, and the owner is charged for Ms. Lindley's work for the month.

Account Type	Specific Account Affected
Assets	**Cash** decreases by $1,000
Liabilities	No account affected
Owner's Equity	**Salary Expense** increases by $1,000 Net change: Owner's Equity decreases by $1,000

From the above analysis, Jewelbox determines the resources and claims to resources the end of the month.

Assets

Cash changes due to transactions 1, 2, 3, 6, 8, and 9.
   $100,000 [1] - $20,000 [2] - $4,000 [3] + $4,000 [6] - $10,000 [8] - $1,000 [9]
   = $69,000.
Jewelbox's accounting records indicate it has $69,000 of cash at end of month.

Accounts Receivable changes due to transaction 7 only. It has a $6,000 balance at end of month.

Inventory changes due to transactions 5, 6, and 7.
   $10,000 [5] - $3,000 [6] - $4,000 [7] = $3,000.

Land's balance is $10,000 from transaction [2].

Building's balance is $50,000 from transaction [2].

Equipment's balance is $4,000 due to transaction [3].

Assets total **$142,000** [$69,000 + $6,000 + $3,000 + $10,000 + $50,000 + $4,000].

Claims to Resources: Liabilities + Owner's Equity

Liabilities: Notes Payable balance is $40,000 due to transaction [2].

Owners Equity:

K. Webb, Capital balance changes due to transactions 1, 6, 7, and 9.
   $100,000 [1] + $4,000 [6] - $3,000 [6] + $6,000 [7] - $4,000 [7] - $1,000 [9] = $102,000.

Claims to Resources total **$142,000** [Liabilities, $40,000 + Owner's Equity, $102,000].

Financial Statements: The formal financial statements presented below highlight how the statements interrelate.

Jewelbox
Income Statement
For the Month Ended June 30, 2003

Revenues			$10,000
Expenses:	Cost of goods sold	$ 7,000	
	Salaries	1,000	8,000
Net income			$ 2,000

Jewelbox
Statement of Owner's Equity
For the Month Ended June 30, 2003

K. Webb, capital June 1, 2003		$ 0
Add: Contribution by owner	$100,000	
Net income for June	2,000	102,000
K. Webb, capital June 30, 2003		$102,000

Jewelbox
Balance Sheet
June 30, 2003

Assets:		**Liabilities:**	
Cash	$ 69,000	**Notes payable**	$ 40,000
Accounts receivable	6,000		
Inventory	3,000		
Land	10,000	**Owner's Equity:**	
Building	50,000	**K. Webb, capital**	102,000
Equipment	4,000		
		Total liabilities	
Total assets	$142,000	**and owner's equity**	$142,000

QUESTIONS FOR YOUR REVIEW

1. Which financial statement shows the assets and claims to those assets at a point in time?
   a. income statement
   b. balance sheet
   c. statement of retained earnings
   d. statement of cash flows

2. Suzie's Nuts paid $40,000 cash for a new refrigerated display case. What effect did the above transaction have on assets, liabilities, and owner's equity?

	Assets	Liabilities	Owner's Equity
a.	none	none	none
b.	lower	lower	none
c.	lower	lower	lower
d.	lower	none	lower

3. A balance sheet:
   a. presents assets and claims to those assets during a period of time.
   b. shows the changes in owner's equity during a period of time.
   c. shows revenues earned and the expenses used to earn them over a period of time.
   d. presents assets and claims to those assets at a point in time.

4. A transaction which decreases both total assets and total owner's equity is:
   a. payment of rent for the month.
   b. payment of principal on a bank loan.
   c. the purchase of inventory on account.
   d. collection of an account receivable.

5. Barkely Stores purchases inventory for $25,000. In return, Barkely promises to pay the seller in 60 days. This transaction:
   a. increases total assets and decreases total liabilities.
   b. increases total assets and increases total liabilities.
   c. is a "wash." Total assets are unaffected.
   d. is not recorded since no cash is involved.

6. A user of accounting information with a direct financial interest in the business is a(n):
   a. owner.
   b. taxing authority.
   c. regulatory agency.
   d. labor union.

7. Most business enterprises in the United States are:
   a. sole proprietorships.
   b. partnerships.
   c. corporations.
   d. governmental units.

Questions 8 through 12 refer to the following information. Gill Decorating Company had the following balance sheet accounts and balances:

Accounts Payable	$32,000	Equipment	$28,000
Accounts Receivable	4,000	S. Gill, Capital	?
Building	?	Land	28,000
Cash	12,000		

8. If the balance in the Capital account is $88,000, the Building account's balance is:
    a. $ 8,000.
    b. $28,000.
    c. $48,000.
    d. $96,000.

9. If the Building account's balance is $60,000, the total of liabilities and owner's equity is:
    a. $ 60,000.
    b. $100,000.
    c. $120,000.
    d. $132,000.

10. If the Building account's balance is $80,000 and if the equipment is sold for $28,000, the balance in owner's equity is:
    a. $ 80,000.
    b. $ 84,000.
    c. $120,000.
    d. $152,000.

11. If the Building account's balance is $40,000 and $12,000 of Accounts Payable is paid using cash, the balance in owner's equity is:
    a. $ 68,000.
    b. $ 80,000.
    c. $112,000.
    d. $120,000.

12. If equipment is sold for $28,000, the owner's equity balance is:
    a. increased by $28,000.
    b. decreased by $28,000.
    c. increased by $56,000.
    d. unchanged.

Questions 13 through 16 are independent and refer to the following information. The total assets and liabilities at the beginning and end of the year for Carter Corporation are as follows:

	Assets	Liabilities
Beginning of the year	$ 14,000	$ 6,000
End of the year	20,000	10,000

13. Assuming Carter received no additional investments in the business and no owner withdrawals occurred, net income for the year is:
    a. $10,000.
    b. $ 2,000.
    c. $18,000.
    d. $ 6,000.

14. Assuming Carter received no additional investments in the business and the owner withdrew $8,800, net income for the year is:
    a. $14,400.
    b. $ 5,600.
    c. $10,800.
    d. $ 1,600.

15. Assuming Carter received an additional investment of $2,000 in the business and no owner withdrawals occurred, net income for the year is:
    a. $ 4,000.
    b. $ 8,000.
    c. $20,000.
    d. $0.

16. Assuming Carter received an additional investment of $2,000 in the business and the owner withdrew $4,400, net income for the year is:
    a. $ 4,400.
    b. $12,400.
    c. $ 7,600.
    d. ($400).

17. Campus Bookstore's beginning of the year account balances are:
    Total assets $120,000
    Total owner's equity   60,000
    During the year, total assets increased by $54,000, and total liabilities increased by $36,000. The owner withdrew $12,000 from the business. Net income for the year is:
    a. $42,000.
    b. $30,000.
    c. $90,000.
    d. not determinable using the available information.

18. A revenue:
    a. increases both assets and liabilities.
    b. increases both assets and owner's equity.
    c. increases assets and decreases owner's equity.
    d. affects only the income statement.

19. Animal Kingdom purchased twenty black cats for $500 cash. This transaction:
    a. does not affect total assets.
    b. increases total assets by $500.
    c. decreases total assets by $500.
    d. increases total assets by $1,000.

20. Spartan Sports Stores reported the following amounts:

	June 1	June 30
Total assets	$ 750,000	$ 930,000
Total liabilities	600,000	640,000

    During the month, the owners withdrew $50,000 in cash from the business. There were no additional investments by the owners. What is Spartan's net income for the month?
    a. $ 140,000
    b. $ 240,000
    c. $ 190,000
    d. It cannot be determined without additional information.

21. Identify each of the following transactions as either an owner's investment, withdrawal, revenue, or expense. Briefly explain your response.

    (a) Received cash from a customer for providing a service.

    (b) Owner transferred personal assets to the business.

    (c) Paid service station for gasoline.

21. (d)   Paid cash to employee for services performed.

Questions 22 through 25 refer to the following. Show all required calculations to support your answers.

On September 30, 2003, Tony Paco's Hot Dog Company had the following account balances:

Cash	$ 6,900
Accounts Payable	2,900
Accounts Receivable	11,340
Tony, Capital (Sept. 1, 2003)	23,040
Sales Revenue	4,400
Wage Expense	1,500
Hot Dog Inventory	3,400
Restaurant Equipment	6,800
Rent Expense	400

22. What are the total assets for Tony Paco's Hot Dog Company?

23. What are the total liabilities for Tony Paco's Hot Dog Company?

24. What is the net income for Tony Paco's Hot Dog Company for the period?

25. What is the total owner's equity at September 30, 2003?

CHAPTER 1 - SOLUTIONS

1.	b	6.	a	11.	b	16.	a
2.	a	7.	a	12.	d	17.	b
3.	d	8.	c	13.	b	18.	b
4.	a	9.	d	14.	c	19.	a
5.	b	10.	c	15.	d	20.	c

21. a.   **Revenue**. The sale of products increases the owners' claims on the business resources. We record an increase in the revenue accounts.

    b.   **Investment**. The additional investment amount increases the owners' claims on the business resources.

    c.   **Expense**. Gasoline is used to deliver goods which are sold to customers. This is a cost incurred to earn revenue. Owners are charged for the use of this resource.

    d.   **Expense**. Employees help to conduct business, including the production of revenue. Their wages are a cost incurred to earn revenue. Owners are charged for the use of this resource.

22. The assets are:

Cash	$ 6,900
Accounts Receivable	11,340
Hot Dog Inventory	3,400
Restaurant Equipment	6,800
Total	$ 28,440

23. Liabilities consist of Accounts Payable only. Therefore, total liabilities are $2,900.

24. Net income is $2,500. Net income is the change in owners' wealth during a time period due to business operations. Revenues represent increases in owners' wealth and expenses represent decreases in owners' wealth. Net income is calculated as follows:

Sales revenues		$ 4,400
Expenses:		
Wage expense	$ 1,500	
Rent expense	400	1,900
Net income		$ 2,500

25. The balance is $25,540. Tony's capital at September 30, 2003, is computed as follows:

Tony, capital (September 1, 2003)	$ 23,040
Add net income	2,500
Tony, capital (September 30, 2003)	$ 25,540

CHAPTER 2

The Financial Statements

REVIEW OF KEY CONCEPTS

This chapter provides more detail regarding the basic financial statements provided to owners and creditors to help them assess the performance of the business and as a basis for comparison to other businesses. After completing this chapter, you should be able to describe each of the four basic financial statements. Your description should include a discussion of the type of information each provides and the names and definitions of each statement's basic elements.

The Financial Statements

The information contained in the annual report to investors consists of several statements:
(a) balance sheet
(b) income statement
(c) statement of cash flows
(d) statement of retained earnings

Footnotes accompany the four statements and summarize information considered important in fully understanding the financial statements. Footnotes may contain more detail regarding information summarized in the body of the financial statements.

The notes always contain a **summary of significant accounting procedures**. This footnote summarizes the rules and assumptions used in preparing the financial statements. Since companies can select from a variety of different assumptions, rules, and procedures within Generally Accepted Accounting Principles (GAAP), the investor comparing companies' financial performance must factor in differences in accounting choices in their computations of ratios. Only then can the investor make a valid comparison of financial statements. The notes aid in this task.

In preparing financial statements, accountants analyze economic events using the set of assumptions, rules, and procedures selected by the business from GAAP. Accountants formally record the result of this analysis using the mechanical process to be discussed in Chapter 4. The accountant prepares financial statements from the data collected during this analysis and recording process.

As discussed in Chapter 1, the basic financial accounting equation (which serves as the foundation for GAAP) is:

Assets = Liabilities + Owners' Equity
- or -
Economic Resources = Claims to Resources

People use the financial statements to evaluate investment opportunities. A business's primary objective is to create wealth for its owners. We can use financial statements to assess how well businesses manage the invested wealth. Criteria used to assess the health of the business include:

1. the ability to pay off business obligations as they come due, which is called **solvency**.

2. the ability to use business resources in such a way that the inflows from their use (the **revenues**) exceed the outflows of resources made to earn those revenues (the **expenses**). Investors are also

interested in the effectiveness of the business's managers in managing resources compared to their competitors. This is called **operational efficiency**.

3.   the ability to capitalize on the existing regulatory and financial environment so that the maximum can be earned on each dollar invested by the owners (the **profitability** of the business).

The financial statements are a raw material in the production of conclusions regarding a business's health. Analysts and investors add labor, tools (such as computers and related software) and information from the financial press to reach conclusions regarding a business's current and future performance. These conclusions assist investors in deciding how to allocate their investment dollars.

While the gross dollar and percentage changes in financial statement numbers over time are a part of financial statement analysis, analysts widely use **ratio analysis** as well. Ratios represent the relation between financial account balances and can be used to assess the solvency, operational efficiency, and profitability of the business over time and compared to other businesses. We will discuss the specific ratios and their formulas in chapter 5.

The Financial Statements

Accountants organize the financial statements to assist investors and creditors in **financial statement analysis**. We discuss the organization of the financial statements and its relation to ratio analysis below.

Classified Balance Sheet

The **balance sheet** lists the assets, liabilities, and owners' equity of the firm at a point in time. Typically, accountants list the balances of these accounts for the current year and one or two prior years. The reader can compute percentage changes across time using this format. The listing order for the accounts is usually comparable across companies since GAAP requires most companies to present **classified** balance sheets.

The accounting principle which defines the dollar amount at which to initially record assets is the **historical cost principle**. **Historical cost** is the cash equivalent price at which the business acquires economic resources and readies them for their intended use. Cash equivalent price means that accountants usually exclude interest from the cost of an asset. For example, if the business buys a delivery truck for $20,000 using a bank loan to be repaid over 3 years at 10% interest, $20,000 is the historical cost of the asset. Accountants charge the interest paid over the three years to finance the truck to owners' equity using the Interest Expense account as the interest accumulates.

The second aspect of the historical cost principle is that accountants include all additional costs incurred to prepare the asset for its intended use in the cost of the asset. For example, if the delivery truck's operation required special training, we include the cost of training the initial driver to operate the truck in the truck's cost. Typical additional costs which may be included in an asset's historical cost are brokerage fees paid when purchasing investments and delivery costs for purchased inventory and plant assets.

Assets

The balance sheet asset classifications are **current assets**; **long-term investments**; **plant, property, and equipment**; and **intangibles**. A **current asset** is an asset expected to be converted into cash or consumed within one year or the **operating cycle**, whichever is longer.

The **operating cycle** is the amount of time required to invest cash in the product which the business plans to sell, sell the product and turn the asset back into cash. For a manufacturing firm, the steps of the **operating cycle** can be represented as:

1. Invest cash.
2. Buy raw materials.
3. Convert raw materials to the finished good to be offered to customers by adding labor and machine effort.
4. Market the product.
5. Deliver the product to a customer and receive in return either cash or a promise to pay cash in the future.
6. Collect cash.

The operating cycle for most businesses is less than one year. For some businesses, such as whiskey distillers, the operating cycle can be several years. The assets which may exist at a point in time related to the operating cycle are Cash, Accounts Receivable, Raw Materials Inventory, Work-in-Process Inventory, and Finished Goods Inventory.

A well-managed company will attempt to shorten the various steps in the operating cycle without sacrificing quality or the ability to meet customer demand. A shorter operating cycle means that the business can serve customers with a smaller average investment in economic resources. This means more money is available for other investments, meeting debt obligations, and paying dividends. The ratios constructed from financial statement elements related to various aspects of the operating cycle can be used to assess changes in this aspect of management performance over time.

The current asset section also includes assets which are not directly related to the operations, but which are either expected to be converted into cash or used up within one year or the operating cycle, whichever is longer. Other types of current assets include Temporary Investments and Prepaid Expenses. The former are investments of cash which is not needed immediately to pay bills, but will be needed in the future. Instead of earning no interest or a lower interest rate from a checking account, the business invests excess cash in low risk but higher yielding securities such as U.S. Treasury Bills or the common stock of other businesses. Prepaid Items are assets whose benefits will be received in the future. Accountants consider Prepaid Expenses assets because they benefit future operations. Examples are prepayment of insurance or rent. For example, an insurance company typically requires that policy premiums be paid one year in advance. A landlord may require prepayment of three months rent when leasing an office.

The current asset section lists assets in order of decreasing liquidity (the ability to be quickly converted into cash) or closeness to cash or time to be converted into cash. Accountants list Cash first, then Temporary Investments, Accounts Receivable, Inventory (Raw Material, Work-in-Process, and Finished Goods) and Prepaid Items.

Long-term investments follow current assets on the balance sheet. Long-term investments are investments of economic resources which do not directly relate to the operations of the business. For example, idle plant or land held for future use are typically listed here. They do not contribute to the main production or operating activities of the business. Other examples include long-term investments in another company's stock.

Plant, property, and equipment represent the assets which house the production and which the business uses to manufacture and sell the product. These are **long-lived assets** because the business typically uses them in operations for a number of years.

Intangibles are assets without a physical existence. They generally represent **purchased** rights or value of some type. **Goodwill** is the difference between the price paid for another company and the market value of identifiable assets at the purchase date. Thus, to be recorded on the financial statements, goodwill must be purchased. Other examples include the price paid to people outside the business for costs related to patent development.

Liabilities

Like assets, accountants classify liabilities as **current** and **long-term**. Current liabilities are obligations to be paid with current assets or services to be rendered, or to be replaced with other current liabilities within one year or the operating cycle, whichever is longer. Current liabilities include **Accounts Payable**, which is the amount due on purchases of material which becomes a part of Inventory.

Long-term liabilities are due in more than one year or the operating cycle, whichever is longer. Mortgage Payable, Bonds Payable, and Lease Obligations are examples of long-term liabilities. The mortgage loan is used to purchase long-lived assets such as buildings. The loan is secured by the asset which is being purchased with its proceeds. If a company fails to meet its mortgage payments, the creditor can take possession of the asset being purchased by the loan. This process is called foreclosure. Mortgage payments due within one year are reclassified as a current liability - the current portion of long-term debt.

A Bond Payable is actually several individual loans made by creditors. Unlike most loans, bonds are traded in a market in a fashion similar to stock. Each bond of a particular issue is identical regarding the cash payments to be made to repay the loan and the maturity date. Companies issue bonds when they need large amounts of money to finance projects.

A Lease Obligation is a contract to use a particular long-lived asset in operations in exchange for rental payments. Accounting rules distinguish between leases which are effectively purchases of long-lived assets and those which are not. If leases are deemed in effect purchases of long-lived assets with long-term debt, the Lease Obligation and the leased asset are included in the balance sheet as liabilities and assets, respectively. If a lease term is of a relatively short duration, the lease is not considered a purchase and the asset and liability are not recorded.

Owners' Equity

The owners' equity section of the balance sheet reflects the legal organization of ownership. If a business is formed as a sole proprietorship or partnership, the accounting system measures and records owners' wealth in **capital** accounts.

If the business is formed as a corporation, accountants record the amount originally invested by owners when the stock was sold in the **contributed capital** section. If the stock sold has a **par value**, then the contributed capital has two parts: par value and paid-in-capital in excess of par. Par value represents the minimum amount for which stock can sell in order for owners to enjoy limited liability, an appealing legal feature of the corporation. If stock sells initially at less than par, owners can be liable for the difference between par value and the amount paid if the firm goes bankrupt. State laws governing incorporation establish par value requirements. If the corporation sells stock above par value, the stockholder is not liable to pay anything more.

The other section of a corporation's owners' equity is **retained earnings**. The balance in Retained Earnings represents the cumulative earnings less distributions to owners from the date of incorporation. As the name implies, the retained earnings balance represents the increase in owners' wealth due to operations which is reinvested or retained in the business.

Owners of a corporation are the owners of its common stock. Since the owners are stockholders, this section of the corporate balance sheet is also known as the **stockholders' equity**.

Income Statement

The income statement provides detail about the change in owners' equity due to business operations during a time period. As mentioned in Chapter 1, revenues represent increases in the owners' share of the total economic resources of the business resulting from inflows of resources from business operations. Expenses are decreases in the owners' share of total economic resources of the business resulting from outflows of resources due to business operations.

In addition to revenues and expenses, the income statement includes changes in owners' wealth from activities outside the normal operations of the business. For example, if the business sells land for more than its historical cost, the excess increases total economic resources. The difference is called a **gain on disposal of assets**, and belongs to the owners. If total economic resources decline, (the land is sold for less than its cost) a **loss on the disposal of assets** reduces the owners' wealth.

The **revenue realization** and **matching** principles determine when and at what amount accountants record revenues and expenses in the accounting database. The **revenue realization criteria** are:
1. the earnings process must be substantially complete, and
2. the net amount to be ultimately received must be reasonably estimable.

The first criterion indicates when the owners of the business have provided sufficient services or products to be able to claim an increase in wealth. We do not record revenue upon signing a contract to provide services in the future because the business has not yet provided a service or product. Accountants record revenue when the business actually provides products or services.

The second criterion requires that we can reasonably estimate the net increase in owners' wealth. If uncertainties exist regarding the collectibility of the contracted amount or future services to be rendered by the business to fulfill the contract, then we must delay the recording of revenue. For example, if a contract includes a warranty and we cannot reasonably estimate future warranty costs, accountants dely the recording of revenue until this uncertainty is reduced to a tolerable level.

The **matching principle** determines when accountants record expenses. The net increase or decrease in owners' wealth due to the goods or services provided by the business is relevant for decision making. Accordingly, if possible, accountants record expenses in the same period in which they record the related revenue.

Accountants call costs directly traceable to the good or service provided to customers **product costs**. When the providing the good or service, we include the product cost in the income statement as **Cost of Goods Sold** or **Cost of Sales**.

Unfortunately, matching cannot be applied to all expenses. Some expenses cannot be directly traced to the individual good or service being provided. Office staff salaries and advertising are examples of costs necessary to conduct business. However, they are not a direct cost of the good or service being provided.

Accountants also organize the income statement's elements to aid investors' analysis. A **multi-step** income statement groups elements which result from operations together and then lists the other elements. Accountants list Sales Revenues (from sale of products) or Service Revenues (from providing services) first within the operating section, net of any returns or discounts. They list **Cost of Goods Sold** (the cost directly traceable to such sales) after Sales Revenue. They deduct Cost of Goods Sold from Sales Revenue to arrive at the **Gross Profit** subtotal. Cost of Goods Sold is the cost per unit of the items sold multiplied by the quantity sold. Thus, gross profit is the amount available to cover all the other costs necessary to produce and sell the good and generate a profit.

Accountants deduct operating expenses from gross profit to arrive at income from operations. The other **operating expenses** (or period costs) include the cost of marketing the good, and administrative costs. We include commissions and advertising as marketing costs. Administrative costs include the accounting department, purchasing department, and other support functions within the business.

After income from operations, we list the other items which are not directly related to operations but which affect owners' wealth. Interest Expense, Interest Revenue and Gains and Losses on Disposal of Assets are examples of these nonoperating items.

Finally, accountants deduct Income Tax Expense to arrive at the net income or net loss for the period. Accountants include net income in the **statement of stockholders' equity** because it represents the portion of the change in owners' equity during the period related to business operations. Other components of the Statement of Stockholders' Equity include additional contributions by owners and withdrawals by owners. The withdrawals by the stockholders (the owners of the corporation) are known as **Dividends**.

The Statement of Cash Flows

The statement of cash flows provides a detailed summary of the transactions affecting the asset account which has the most transactions affecting it during the year. Cash can be viewed as the life's blood of the business since ultimately all transactions have cash consequences. If a company is unable to maintain sufficient Cash balances to meet obligations as they come due, the business will fail.

The statement of cash flows divides the transactions affecting Cash into three categories. **Cash from operations** is the amount that Cash increased or decreased during the period as a result of the business's on-going operations. Examples of sources of Cash from operations are Cash collections on Sales and Accounts Receivable. Examples of uses or outlays of Cash from operations include paying for inventory or paying salaries and utilities.

Cash from investing activities is the amount that Cash increased or decreased due to the acquisition or disposal of noncurrent assets. Examples include the purchase of buildings or sale of equipment.

Cash from financing activities is the amount that Cash increased due to the issuance of stocks or bonds and additional contributions of owners or decreased due to the repayment of debt or withdrawals by owners.

The Statement of Retained Earnings

The statement of retained earnings provides a summary of the current period transactions affecting the earnings reinvested in the company. Net income increases retained earnings. Net losses and dividends reduce retained earnings.

Summary

Historical cost, revenue realization, and the matching principle are the accounting concepts followed to determine when and at what amount accountants record assets, revenues, and expenses. The chapter explained the format of the balance sheet, income statement, and statement of cash flows.

QUESTIONS FOR YOUR REVIEW

Use the following information to answer questions 1 and 2.

King Corporation began business in January of 2003. The following transactions occurred during January. King issued common stock for $60,000 in cash. King $20,000 from the bank (the loan will be repaid in two years). King purchased inventory for $40,000 (the bill will be paid next month). King sold inventory which cost $30,000 for $50,000. The customer paid $44,000 in cash immediately and will pay $6,000 next month. King bought a parcel of land for $20,000 and also paid a $20,000 dividend.

1. The total current assets at January 31, 2003 are:
    a. $120,000.
    b. $104,000.
    c. $106,000.
    d. $100,000.

2. What is net income (loss)?
    a. $20,000
    b. $24,000
    c. $0
    d. ($20,000)

3. Expense(s) is (are):
    a. another word for a liability.
    b. cash payments for costs incurred to earn revenues.
    c. costs (whether paid or not) incurred to produce revenues.
    d. decreases in assets.

4. Profitable operations are evident when:
    a. assets increase.
    b. the difference between assets and liabilities increases.
    c. common stock increases.
    d. retained earnings increases.

5. An important legal benefit of a corporation compared to a partnership or proprietorship is:
    a. the owners are directly involved in the day-to-day operations of the company.
    b. dividend income is taxable.
    c. the stockholder is generally only liable for his initial investment.
    d. only the corporation allows distributions of earnings to its owners.

6. Accountants would record the amount of cash received from the sale a building on the:
    a. income statement.
    b. balance sheet.
    c. statement of cash flows.
    d. statement of retained earnings.

7. The sum of the average time period required to collect Accounts Receivable and the average time to sell Inventory is an estimate of:
    a. the company's operating cycle.
    b. the company's revenue cycle.
    c. the company's production cycle.
    d. nothing.

Use the following information for questions 8 through 11.

The Turner Company engaged in the following transactions during 2003:
(1)   Sales totalled $150,000. All but $15,000 was collected during the year. The goods sold cost $105,000. All the goods sold were bought and paid for by Turner during 2003.
(2)   Turner issued 30,000 shares of common stock for $750,000.
(3)   Turner borrowed $60,000 from the bank.
(4)   Turner sold a parcel of land for $180,000.
(5)   Turner purchased a building for $150,000 cash.
(6)   Turner paid dividends of $18,000.
(7)   Turner paid employees $9,000.

8. What is Turner's net income (loss) for 2003?
    a. $45,000
    b. $36,000
    c. $30,000
    d. $18,000

9. What is net cash from (used in) operations for 2003?
    a. $45,000
    b. $36,000
    c. $21,000
    d. $ 3,000

10. Net cash from (used in) investing activities during 2003 is:
    a. $ 180,000.
    b. $ 30,000.
    c. $(30,000).
    d. $(150,000).

11. Net cash from (used in) financing activities during 2003 is:
    a. $810,000.
    b. $792,000.
    c. $732,000.
    d. $ 60,000.

Questions 12 and 13 use the following information.

The Harry Potter Company began business in 2003. The following are Harry's revenues, expenses, and dividends from 2003 to 2005.

	Revenues	Expenses	Dividends
2003	$300,000	$360,000	$ 0
2004	600,000	450,000	30,000
2005	750,000	540,000	90,000

12. Compute Harry's net income for each of the years 2003 through 2005.

    2003

    2004

    2005

13. Compute Harry's Retained Earnings balance for 2003 through 2005.

2003

2004

2005

CHAPTER 2 - SOLUTIONS

1.	d	5.	c	9.	c
2.	a	6.	c	10.	b
3.	c	7.	a	11.	b
4.	d	8.	b		

12. Net income for Harry for:

	2003	2004	2005
Revenues	$300,000	$600,000	$750,000
Less Expenses	(360,000)	(450,000)	(540,000)
Net Income (Loss)	$ (60,000)	$150,000	$210,000

13. Ending Retained Earnings balance for Harry:

	2003	2004	2005
Beginning retained earnings	$ 0	$ (60,000)	$ 60,000
+/- Net Income (Loss)	(60,000)	150,000	210,000
- Dividends	0	(30,000)	(90,000)
Ending retained earnings	$(60,000)	$ 60,000	$180,000

CHAPTER 3

The Measurement Fundamentals of Financial Accounting

REVIEW OF KEY CONCEPTS

This chapter introduces the concepts underlying the measurement of economic events reported in the financial statements. Accountants usually categorize concepts as assumptions, principles, and exceptions. In addition, the text discusses the valuation bases used to account for economic events and, in particular, the effect of an unstable monetary unit in interpreting financial statements prepared under a stable monetary unit assumption. If the dollar is stable across time, it can purchase the same quantity of every good at all points in time. If the dollar is unstable, interpreting changes in operating results must include factoring the effect of changing prices.

We present a discussion of measurement valuation bases and the effect of inflation in interpreting financial statements below. After completing this chapter, you should be familiar with the concepts underlying accounting and the relation between these concepts and the rules followed to account for transactions. You should also be able to describe the valuation basis for items on the balance sheet and the effect of inflation on the interpretation of financial statement data.

The Basis of Accrual Accounting: Revenue Recognition and Matching Principle

Revenue recognition is the process involving the measurement and timing of recording revenues. Recall that revenues are increases in stockholders' equity resulting from the inflow of economic resources (typically cash or accounts receivable) accompanying selling the products or providing the services that represent the company's core business.

Accountants record revenue when (1) the earnings process is substantially complete and (2) the net amount to be received from the transaction can be reasonably estimated. Notice that the actual receipt of cash from the customer is not required. The company can record revenue if they receive a promise to pay from the customer, and if they can estimate any uncollectible portion (product returns and bad debts). The company must also be able to estimate costs incurred subsequent to the actual exchange (for example, if the product sold includes a warranty, the company estimates any future payments to repair or replace the item).

The **matching principle** determines timing of recording expenses. Recall that expenses are decreases in stockholders' equity resulting from the assets used or liabilities incurred when selling the products or providing the services that represent the company's core business.

Ideally, accountants record expenses in the same time period that they record related revenues. Notice that a cash payment is NOT required in order to record an expense. Expenses represent the using up of assets such as cash or inventory or plant and equipment or the incurring of liabilities such as wage expense in order to earn revenue. Expense recognition may follow the payment of cash (for example, inventory purchased earlier is sold) or precede payment of cash (for example, when the company pays employees after they have provided the service). **Expense recognition follows revenue recognition, not the payment of cash.**

Example: Hercules sells weight-lifting equipment, and includes a one-year warranty for repairs. Assume that Hercules sells 100 sets of weights for $300 each and that each set cost Hercules $200. Customers pay half the money immediately and the remaining half will be collected in six months. Hercules estimates no sets will be returned, but $500 will not be collected. Hercules also estimates that there will be $750 of warranty-related repair costs.

Because Hercules has delivered the equipment and estimated uncollectible accounts and warranty-related repairs costs, Hercules can record the $30,000 as sales. The journal entries to record the sale is:

Cash (+A)	15,000	
Accounts Receivable (+A)	15,000	
Sales (R,+SE)		30,000
To record the sale.		
Cost of Goods Sold (E,-SE)	20,000	
Inventory (-A)		20,000
Bad Debt Expense (E,-SE)	500	
Allowance for Bad Debts (-A)		500
Warranty Expense (E,-SE)	750	
Warranty Liability (+L)		750
To record the sale related expenses.		

The company reports net income of $8,750 on the sale (revenues - expenses).

Measurement Valuation Bases

Fair Market Value

Businesses operate in both input and output markets. The company markets and sells the goods or services that it produces in output markets. They record the price received for goods and services sold by the business as revenue. The selling price is the fair market value. Businesses purchase the raw materials and the labor required to produce goods and services in input markets. Businesses typically receive cash, accounts receivable, or notes receivable in exchange for the good or service sold to customers. Typically, the accounts receivable contract is informal, requiring payment of the amount due within 30 days. Usually, accounts receivable do not include interest if they are paid within the grace period. The amount due is the same amount that would have been due if cash had been paid.

Present Value

Notes receivable are formal contracts specifying the exact timing of payment and the amount to be paid, including interest. Unlike a cash sale or sale on account, the amount recorded initially as an asset is not the total that will be paid by the customer over the life of the contract. A portion of the final payment amount is interest, which is the additional amount the customer pays for delaying payment. A business earns interest as time passes. When initially signing the contract, no time has passed, and therefore no interest is earned. The amount recorded at the contract signing, is the total contract payments less any interest included in the contract payments, or **the present value of the contract payments**. Alternatively, the present value of the contract payments is the amount that would be paid today in cash instead of signing the contract. The present value of the contract payments is the cash equivalent price of the good or service.

Example. Ron Mason purchases a minivan from a local dealer. The payment terms are $2,000 down and 24 payments of $612 each, beginning in one month. The interest rate charged for loans of similar risk and duration is 12% per year, or 1% per month. The total cash that Mr. Mason will pay for the car is $16,688 [$2,000 + ($612 x 24)]. However, a portion of the total cash paid is interest, which is the dealer earns over the 24 month period. The amount earned by the dealer when he delivers the minivan to Mr. Mason is the $16,688 less the total interest included in the $16,688. To determine the amount earned at delivery, calculate the present value of the cash flow stream using the techniques discussed in Appendix B in your textbook. This amount is $15,000 [$2,000 + ($612 x present value factor for an ordinary annuity), where i=1 and n=24]. (This factor is 21.2434). Mr. Mason could purchase the car for $15,000 in cash instead of the contracted payment terms. Mr. Mason pays interest of $1,688 ($16,688 - $15,000). This is the cost of choosing this contract.

The dealer records sales revenue of $15,000 when he delivers the car to Mr. Mason. The dealer will record interest revenue of $1,688 over the life of the contract. The dealer determines the exact amount to record each month using the **effective interest method**, which will be discussed in Chapter 11 of your textbook.

The present value is the basis for valuing most long-term liabilities. The payments made by the company to honor these contracts include repayment of the amount originally borrowed plus interest. At any point in time, the accounting records reflect the total amount owed, which includes the amount originally borrowed and interest which is owed according to the terms of the contract, but unpaid to that date. The present value of the future cash flow payments required by the contract represents the amount owed at that point in time. Mortgages, leases, bonds, and pensions are examples of long-term liabilities which accountants value using present value concepts.

Historical Cost

Businesses acquire labor, materials, equipment, buildings, and other factors used to produce goods and services in **input markets**. Like the price received for goods and services sold in the output market, the price paid for these **factors of production** depends upon the market mechanism.

The company can acquire these input factors by paying cash, exchanging other assets, incurring liabilities, or issuing common stock. The company uses up some factors immediately in earning revenues and immediately record these as expenses. The business records other factors acquired for use in earning revenues in future time periods as assets.

Businesses may use different valuation bases to account for an asset at various points in time before using the asset to earn revenues. Initially, we record assets using the historical cost principle. We include all costs necessary to ready the asset for its intended use in the cost of the asset on the balance sheet. The asset account is increased when incurring these costs. Some assets such as self-constructed buildings may take an extended period of time to complete. Several transactions may increase the value of the asset over time.

There are exceptions to the historical cost principle for valuing assets. Occasionally firms acquire and finance assets using long-term liabilities. As mentioned for notes receivable, the long-term contracts specify the timing and amount of all future cash payments. The total of the cash payments satisfies the purchase obligation and interest incurred due to purchasing the asset on a long-term liability contract. Like the notes receivable case, the present value of the promised cash payments represents the initial cost of the asset. Interest is not considered part of the original cost of an asset. Accountants value assets in such a case using the present value of the future cash payments.

Example. Lex Luther purchases land exchange for a long-term note. The note requires payment of $20,000 per year for four years, with the first payment due in one year. The total cash payments to satisfy the note's terms are $80,000 ($20,000 x 4). A portion of the $80,000 is payment for the land itself and a portion is the interest incurred from choosing this specific form of financing. If notes of similar risk and duration require a 10% interest rate, the present value of the note payments is $63,400 [20,000 x (the present value factor for an annuity where i=10 and n=4). (The factor is 3.17)]. The analysis suggests that the business could have paid cash of $63,400 instead of signing the long-term obligation. The business pays $16,600 ($80,000 - $63,400) in interest expense over the note's term. Interest payments do not increase the land's book value under the historical cost principle. Accountants record the interest as an expense as it is incurred with the passage of time.

After acquiring an asset in either the input or output market, accountants periodically evaluate its book value to ensure that the asset is not overvalued. The diverse nature of assets requires using different methods for this evaluation. This periodic review is an application of the **conservatism** concept. Conservatism states that when in doubt, financial statements should understate assets, overstate liabilities, accelerate recognition of losses, and delay recognition of gains.

Accountants evaluate accounts receivable by applying the **net realizable value** concept. They periodically review the collectibility of accounts receivable, and reduce the book value by the estimated uncollectible amount.

Accountants apply the **lower of cost or market** method to evaluate inventories. If the current price purchase the inventory in the input market (its **replacement cost**) is below its book value, the accountant reduces the inventory's book value to replacement cost.

The book value of long-term productive assets, such as plant and equipment and intangibles, is typically not compared to fair market values because these assets often are not directly sold in input markets. Businesses use these assets to produce other assets (inventory) or services which are then sold in output markets. Accountants value these assets at historical cost reduced by accumulated depreciation and amortization. Depreciation and amortization are unrelated to changes in the fair market value of the assets. Depreciation and amortization are allocations of cost over time.

Periodically, accountants review long-term productive assets' book values to determine if obsolescence has occurred. For example, as new technologies improve the efficiency of a production process, some older plant assets may be replaced by the new technology. The company may choose to discard the assets by selling or scrapping them, or may use the assets in other production processes. In either case, there is an impairment of asset's value to the company's operations. If the book value exceeds the impaired value, we write the asset down.

Inflation and Financial Statement Data Interpretation

The dollar's value to an individual depends upon the quantity of goods that the dollar can purchase. A stable dollar can purchase the same quantity of every good at all points in time. An underlying assumption of financial accounting is that the dollar is stable with respect to purchasing power. Unfortunately, this assumption is not a very good representation of the real world. The implication of this poor assumption is that the financial statement reader must factor in the effect of inflation when interpreting changes in the reported economic condition of the business.

For example, businesses sell products in output markets. The price received is determined by the operating mechanism in that market. If the dollar's value deteriorates during a year, each dollar purchases less of the good or service. In order to acquire a unit of the good or service, more dollars must be exchanged.

The business either reinvests the dollars received in goods or services from customers or distributes the dollars as dividends to stockholders. The dollars received or distributed can each purchase less of every good in the economy. The business and its owners are not as well off as they appear according to the financial statements, because the purchasing power of every dollar is less.

Example. Tiger Golf, Inc. reports sales of $3 million in 2003, $3.5 million in 2004, and $4 million in 2005. Tiger appears to be doing well. Growth in sales is 16.7% from 2003 to 2004, and 14.3% from 2004 to 2005. Assuming inflation is 10% in 2004, and 25% from 2003 to 2005, 2004 sales of $3.5 million expressed in 2003 purchasing power are only $3.18 million [$3.5 million / (1 + .10) (2004 inflation)]. 2005 sales expressed in 2003 purchasing power are only $3.2 million [$4 million / (1 + .25)].

The real sales changes, after accounting for inflation, are 6.1% from 2003 to 2004, [($3.18 million - $3 million) / $3 million] and .6% from 2004 to 2005 [($3.2 million - $3.18 million) / $3.18 million].

Inflation-adjusted 2005 sales growth is relatively worse than when inflation is not accounted for. Financial statement users must be aware of the effects of inflation so that they can make the necessary adjustments to arrive at comparable numbers across time.

QUESTIONS FOR YOUR REVIEW

1. The Hannah Corporation purchases 20,000 units of inventory for $1 each from various wholesalers on January 1, 2003. The inventory can be sold to customers for $1.50 each. If Hannah valued the inventory on its books at $30,000, what valuation basis was used?
   a. Historical cost
   b. Replacement cost
   c. Fair market value
   d. Present value

2. Referring to question 1, on January 1, 2004, 2,000 units of the 2003 purchase remain in inventory. If purchased from wholesalers today these units would cost $1.20, the inflation rate from 2003 to 2004 on the inventory is:
   a. 20% [(1.20-1.00) / 1.00].
   b. -20% [(1.20-1.50) / 1.50].
   c. - 4%. Average cost in 2003 [(1.00 + 1.50) / 2 = 1.25]. Inflation from 2003 to 2004 = [(1.20 - 1.25) / 1.25].
   d. 0%.

3. Referring to questions 1 and 2, if Hannah was very efficient during 2004 and held all other costs equal to 2003 levels, how much would Hannah need to charge per unit to earn the same gross profit in 2004 as was earned in 2003? (Gross profit = Selling price - Cost).
   a. $ 1.40
   b. $ 1.50
   c. $ 1.70
   d. $ 1.80

4. Duval Products owns land originally purchased in 2000 for $20,000 cash. In 2003, Duval purchased another tract of land for $20,000 cash. Assume that prices in general increased by 30 percent from 2000 to 2003. After the 2003 purchase, the *total* book value in the Land account, using the stable dollar assumption, is:
   a. $ 20,000.
   b. $ 40,000.
   c. $ 46,000.
   d. $ 52,000.

5. Referring to question 4, and relaxing the stable dollar assumption, the Land account balance should be:
   a. $ 20,000.
   b. $ 40,000.
   c. $ 46,000.
   d. $ 52,000.

6.   The Alcott Company reported sales as follows:

2003	2004	2005
$200,000	$260,000	$320,000

Assuming the general inflation rate for 2003 through 2005 is 20%, what was the real increase in sales from 2003 to 2005?
a.   20 percent
b.   33 percent
c.   40 percent
d.   60 percent

7.   An example of an asset whose initial book value is determined by the output markets in which the business operates is:
a.   inventory.
b.   plant and equipment.
c.   accounts receivable.
d.   goodwill.

8.   Net income can be thought of as:
a.   the difference between cash received for goods or services sold and the cash paid to provide those goods or services.
b.   the difference between the prices received for goods or services in output markets and prices paid in input markets for factors of production used to create those goods and services.
c.   the increase in stockholders' equity during a fiscal period.
d.   the increase in the difference between assets and liabilities during a fiscal period.

9.   An accounting process or principle justified by the fiscal period assumption is (are):
a.   accrual and deferral adjusting entries.
b.   conservatism.
c.   historical cost principle.
d.   stable monetary unit assumption.

10.   What is the principal reason that accountants use some form of historical cost to value most assets subsequent to acquisition?
a.   The replacement cost, fair market value, or present value bases are generally difficult to objectively determine compared to historical cost.
b.   The other valuation bases generally result in amounts close to historical cost, and historical cost is appropriate because the differences are not material.
c.   Matching and revenue recognition are only possible if historical cost is used.
d.   Accruals and deferrals are only possible if historical cost is used.

11.   Accountants recognize (record) revenue when:
a.   it is earned.
b.   it can be measured.
c.   all material benefits given up (expenses) to earn revenue can be measured.
d.   all of the above.

12.   An example of applying conservatism is:
a.   the lower of cost or market rule applied to inventories.
b.   the matching principle.
c.   the recognition of accumulated depreciation.
d.   the recording of accrual and deferral adjusting journal entries.

13. Expenses are usually recorded when:
    a. paid for.
    b. related revenues have been recorded.
    c. the tax law indicates that they are deductible.
    d. the fiscal period ends.

14. Most companies' fiscal year ends on December 31. Some companies choose non December 31 year-ends because:
    a. the fiscal year-end is determined by the tax law.
    b. accruals and deferrals are not possible otherwise.
    c. their operating cycle is seasonal and financial reports are more meaningful if the entire operating cycle is included.
    d. the SEC determines a company's fiscal year-end.

15. Annika Corporation purchased land using a long-term contract. Annika promises to pay $45,000 each year for the next 10 years. How should Annika record the land's acquisition?
    a. No entry should be made because no cash payment has been made.
    b. The land should be recorded at $450,000, since this is the total amount that Annika will pay to satisfy the purchase agreement's terms.
    c. The land should be recorded at some amount less than $450,000, since the future payments include interest. The land's book value should not include interest.
    d. At some amount greater than $450,000, since real estate market prices will likely increase in the future.

For questions 16-18, refer to the Time Value of Money Tables in your text.

16. What is the present value of $15,000, due in five years, discounted at 8%, compounded annually?
    a. $ 22,039
    b. $ 10,209
    c. $ 10,134
    d. $ 10,095

17. John is saving to purchase a new SUV four years from today. The bank pays interest at 6%, compounded annually. John is able to save $8,000 each year. John will make his first deposit at the end of the current year. How much will John accumulate at the end of the four years?
    a. $ 30,000
    b. $ 32,000
    c. $ 35,000
    d. $ 36,000

18. John purchases a new car today for $14,000. The bank charges interest at 12%, compounded quarterly. John makes a cash down payment of $3,000 today. His first payment is due at the end of the current quarter. The bank offers John a thirty quarter loan. What will be the amount of John's quarterly payments?
    a. $ 231
    b. $ 294
    c. $ 561
    d. $ 714

19. Amber Corporation purchased a piece of land on January 1, 2003, for $100,000. On December 31, 2003, Amber sold the land for $250,000.

    Required:

    a. Prepare the journal entries to record the purchase and sale of the land, assuming Amber follows generally accepted accounting principles.

    b. Assuming the general inflation rate from January 1, 2003 to December 31, 2003, is 15%, how much would Amber need to receive on the land's sale for the business to maintain the same level of purchasing power at the end of 2003 as it had at the beginning of 2003?

    c. Compute the return on investment in the land, assuming you use the reported gain.

d. What is the return on investment in the land, after accounting for general inflation?

e. Mr. Amber notices the reported gain and suggests paying it out as a dividend. Given your analysis in parts (b), (c), and (d), and Mr. Amber's intention to maintain the same level of real investment in the business, how much of the gain is available for distribution as dividends?

20. Maroon Corporation is evaluating its policy of allowing customers to issue notes receivable in exchange for Maroon's products, which initially cost Maroon $500 each. Maroon charges the customers an annual interest rate of 4%, plus expected general inflation. The 4% is selected because that is how much Maroon typically earns on its assets over a year when inflation is zero.

Tarragon Corporation purchased some of Maroon's merchandise on January 1, 2003, in exchange for a one-year note due December 31, 2003. Maroon anticipated inflation of 6% for 2003, so Maroon set the interest rate on the note at 10%. If Tarragon paid cash for the merchandise, it would have paid $1,000.

a. Prepare the journal entries for 2003 related to the Tarragon sale and the payment of the note receivable by Tarragon on December 31, 2003.

b. If the general inflation rate is 15% during 2003, how much would Maroon need to receive from Tarragon on December 31 to maintain the same purchasing power that was available on January 1?

c. If the general inflation rate is 15% during 2003, considering that Maroon could have earned 4% on the $1,000 if Tarragon had paid cash for the sale, what interest rate would fully compensate Maroon for delaying receipt of the payment? Given this interest rate, what dollar amount would Tarragon pay Maroon at December 31, 2003?

d. Given that Tarragon actually paid Maroon $1,100 at the end of 2003, is the interest revenue reported on the income statement an accurate reflection of the economic substance of the transactions? In real terms, did stockholder wealth increase or decrease?

CHAPTER 3 - SOLUTIONS

1.	c	7.	c	13.	b
2.	a	8.	b	14.	c
3.	d	9.	a	15.	c
4.	b	10.	a	16.	b
5.	c	11.	d	17.	c
6.	b	12.	a	18.	c

19. a. 1/1/03   Land (+A)   100,000
                    Cash (-A)   100,000
                Record the land purchase.

    12/31/03 Cash (+A)   250,000
                    Land (-A)   100,000
                    Gain on Sale of Land (Ga,+SE)   150,000
                Record the land sale.

    b. $100,000 + ($100,000 x .15) = $100,000 + $15,000 = $115,000. To maintain the same purchasing power at the end of the year as the business invested in the land at the beginning, the land's value needs to increase by $15,000.

    c. Return on investment using the reported gain:

       [$150,000 (reported gain) / $100,000 (investment in the land)] x 100 = 150%.

    d. Return on investment controlling for general inflation:
       Revised gain based upon investment in land adjusted for inflation:

       $250,000 - $115,000 = $135,000.

       Return on investment, controlling for general inflation:

       ($135,000 / $115,000) x 100 = 117%.

       While the return is still sizable, the return on investment is overstated if the financial statement gain is used.

    e. In order for Mr. Amber to maintain the real investment in the business, the reported gain cannot be paid out as dividends. The company can pay $135,000, the gain on the land sale after controlling for general inflation, in dividends and maintain its purchasing power.

20. a. 1/1/03   Note Receivable (+A)   1,000
                        Sales (R,+SE)   1,000

                      Cost of Goods Sold (E,-SE)   500
                        Inventory (-A)   500

          12/31/03   Cash (+A)   1,100
                        Note Receivable (-A)   1,000
                        Interest Revenue (R,+SE)   100

b. $1,000 + ($1,000 x .15) = $1,000 + $150 = $1,150.

c. If Maroon correctly estimated general inflation, the interest charged Tarragon would have been .15 + .04 = .19. Maroon would receive $1,190 at the end of the year ($1,000 + ($1,000 x .19)).

d. Maroon did not even maintain its purchasing power. In real terms, Maroon is worse off at the end of the period than at the beginning since it received only $1,100 instead of the $1,150 needed to increase its purchasing power. Yet, its financial statements indicate that stockholders' wealth increased by $100.

Investors might believe the $100 is available for dividends. Clearly, if the reported income of $100 was paid in dividends, the company's real investment would continue to deteriorate.

When inflation is particularly high and difficult to estimate, businesses which allow customers to issue notes in exchange for merchandise run the risk of deteriorating real investment.

CHAPTER 4

The Mechanics of Financial Accounting

REVIEW OF KEY CONCEPTS

A modern business engages in thousands of economic events each day. The formal accounting system introduced in this chapter provides an organized and rational approach to analyzing the transactions using the **accounting equation** and documenting the analysis. Information regarding the financial condition of the business at any point in time is available with relatively little extra effort when using a formal accounting system. A well-designed, formal accounting system also reduces the possibility of undetected errors in recording the transactions.

We discuss three critical points in the **accounting cycle** in detail below: (1) the **analysis of transactions** and the application of debit and credit rules to the analysis; (2) the **periodic adjustment process**; and (3) the **closing process**. A comprehensive problem appears at the end of this chapter, providing an opportunity for you to review the entire accounting cycle, including preparation of the financial statements. After completing the comprehensive problem, you will be more at ease with the mechanics of the formal accounting system and you will improve your understanding of financial accounting.

The Double-Entry Accounting System

The most widely used system of organizing economic transactions is the double-entry accounting system. The accounting equation is the basis of the system:

$$\textbf{Assets = Liabilities + Owners' Equity}$$

Owners' equity includes two basic components, the owners' original investments (common stock for a corporation) and the earnings retained in the business from successful past operations (retained earnings). Retained earnings equals revenues earned less expenses incurred less any dividends paid to the stockholders (the owners). We can expand the accounting equation to include additional detail on these changes in owners' equity as follows:

$$\textbf{Assets = Liabilities + Common Stock + Retained Earnings + Revenues - Expenses - Dividends}$$

Since this is an arithmetical relation, we can rearrange the elements by adding expenses and dividends to both sides:

$$\textbf{Assets + Expenses + Dividends = Liabilities + Common Stock + Retained Earnings + Revenues}$$

Notice that now all of the elements of the equation are positive. Assets, expenses, and dividends appear on the left-hand side of the equation, and liabilities, common stock, retained earnings, and revenues appear on the right-hand side.

At any point in time, the total of assets, expenses, and dividends equals the total of liabilities, common stock, retained earnings, and revenues. The economic interpretation of this relation is that the total of existing economic resources (assets), resources used thus far in the accounting period to earn revenues (expenses), and resources distributed to stockholders during the accounting period (dividends) must equal the sources of those existing, expired and distributed resources (liabilities, common stock, retained earnings, and revenues).

The accounting system uses this expanded accounting model as the basis for recording transactions. The Latin terms debit and credit (translated left and right) describe the physical writing of changes in account balances. Accountants record increases in assets, expenses, and dividends with left-hand side entries or debits. They record decreases in assets, expenses, and dividends with right-hand side entries, credits. Assets, expenses and dividends normally have debit or left-hand side balances because the balances are usually positive.

Accountants record increases in liabilities, common stock, retained earnings, and revenues with right-hand side entries or credits. They record decreases in liabilities, common stock, and retained earnings with left-hand side entries or debits. The normal balance in liabilities, common stock, retained earnings, and revenues are credit balances because their balances are usually positive.

At any point in time, the sum of the balances of the accounts on the left-hand (debit) side of the equation (assets, expenses, and dividends) equals the sum of the balances on the right-hand (credit) side of the equation (liabilities, common stock, retained earnings, and revenues). An illustration which continues the Jewelbox, Inc. example from Chapter 1 follows:

Jewelbox, Inc.
Accounting Equation
August 1, 2003

Cash ($40,000) + Accounts Receivable ($60,000) + Inventory ($90,000) + Land ($80,000) + Expenses ($0) + Dividends ($0) =

Accounts Payable ($50,000) + Notes Payable ($60,000) + Common Stock ($60,000) + Retained earnings ($100,000) + Revenues ($0)

At August 1, 2003, revenues, expenses, and dividends all have zero account balances, since no operating events have yet occurred. The following transactions take place during August of 2003.

1. Sold inventory which cost $30,000 for $44,000 cash.
2. Collected $20,000 on accounts receivable.
3. Paid $1,000 of wages earned during the first two weeks of the month.
4. Sold inventory which cost $20,000 for $34,000 on account.
5. Purchased $60,000 of inventory on account.

The analysis of transactions uses the accounting equation and a few simple rules.

Assets + Expenses = Liabilities + Common Stock + Retained Earnings + Revenues

Rules to Conform with the Accounting System

1. Record increases in assets, expenses, and dividends with debits (left-side entries). Record decreases in assets, expenses, and dividends with credits (right-side entries).

2. Record increases in liabilities, common stock, retained earnings, and revenues with credits (right-side entries). Record decreases in liabilities, common stock, retained earnings, and revenues with debits (left-side entries).

	Account	Category	Effect
1a.	Cash	Asset	+ 44,000 debit
	Sales	Revenue	+ 44,000 credit
1b.	Cost of Goods Sold	Expense	+ 30,000 debit
	Inventory	Asset	- 30,000 credit
2.	Cash	Asset	+ 20,000 debit
	Accounts Receivable	Asset	- 20,000 credit
3.	Wage Expense	Expense	+ 1,000 debit
	Cash	Asset	- 1,000 credit
4a.	Accounts Receivable	Asset	+ 34,000 debit
	Sales	Revenue	+ 34,000 credit
4b.	Cost of Goods Sold	Expense	+ 20,000 debit
	Inventory	Asset	- 20,000 credit
5.	Inventory	Asset	+ 60,000 debit
	Accounts Payable	Liability	+ 60,000 credit

You can formally record the results of the analysis in the **general journal**. Record all transactions in the journal in chronological order. The general journal follows the format shown below.

	Account Title and Explanation	Debit	Credit
1a.	Cash (+A)	44,000	
	Sales (R,+SE)		44,000
1b.	Cost of Goods Sold (E,-SE)	30,000	
	Inventory (-A)		30,000
2.	Cash (+A)	20,000	
	Accounts Receivable (-A)		20,000
3.	Wage Expense (E,-SE)	1,000	
	Cash (-A)		1,000
4a.	Accounts Receivable (+A)	34,000	
	Sales (R,+SE)		34,000
4b.	Cost of Goods Sold (E,-SE)	20,000	
	Inventory (-A)		20,000
5.	Inventory (+A)	60,000	
	Accounts Payable (+L)		60,000

After we record the transactions in the journal, we can compute the effect on individual accounts by **posting** the journal entries to the **general ledger** accounts. We then total the debits and credits of each account and the difference between the totals is the balance at that point in time. If the debit total exceeds the credit total, a debit balance exists. If the credit total exceeds the debit total, a credit balance exists. We next prepare the **unadjusted trial balance** which lists and totals the debit and credit balance accounts separately to ensure that (1) we have recorded the same dollar value of debits and credits in the ledger and (2) have made no obvious errors (i.e., an asset or expense account has a credit balance or a liability, common stock, retained earnings or revenue account has a debit balance). Typically, accountants use an unadjusted trial balance worksheet when many accounts exist. An example of such a worksheet appears on the next page.

Periodic Adjustments

The **accrual basis of accounting** provides a long-term perspective of the company's operating performance. Under accrual accounting, we measure benefits with revenues, and measure efforts with expenses. The net income (revenues minus expenses) provides a measure of the profitability of the company's operating activities.

Accrual accounting **records revenues when they are earned**. The company earns revenues by providing goods or services to its customers. Accrual accounting uses the **matching principle** to determine when to record expenses. Expenses measure of the efforts employed to earn revenues. Under the matching principle, we record expenses during the same accounting period in which we record the related, earned revenues.

Jewelbox, Inc.
Unadjusted Trial Balance
August 31, 2003

Accounts	Debit	Credit
Cash	103,000	
Accounts Receivable	74,000	
Inventory	100,000	
Land	80,000	
Cost of Goods Sold	50,000	
Wage Expense	1,000	
Dividends	0	
Accounts Payable		110,000
Notes Payable		60,000
Common Stock		60,000
Retained Earnings		100,000
Sales		78,000
	408,000	408,000

The difference between the performance measures provided by the cash and accrual bases is a matter of timing. Eventually, receipts from customers and payments to the company's employees and suppliers will be settled in cash. If all cash settlements were made in the same period during which revenues were earned and expenses incurred, the change in the company's cash position would equal its net income.

Preparing Periodic Adjustments

A company prepares its balance sheet and income statement using the accrual basis of accounting. Recall from the text that the company periodically records external exchange transactions as they occur. These journal entries include both cash and noncash transactions. However, these entries do not reflect the full accrual basis of accounting. We must update the accounting records to a full accrual basis by **preparing adjusting journal entries** at the end of the accounting period.

Adjusting journal entries record revenues earned or expenses incurred which are not the direct result of external transactions. We can summarize these into two general categories: **accrual adjustments** and **cost expiration adjustments** (sometimes referred to as **deferral adjustments**). Accruals and deferrals can arise relative to either revenues or expenses.

An accrual adjustment is necessary when revenue is earned (or expense is incurred) through the passage of time. For example, a bank earns Interest Revenue each day for which it lends money to its customers (even though payments by customers are typically made on a less frequent basis).

Similarly, the customer (borrower) incurs an Interest Expense with the passage of time. It may be useful for you to think of an accrual as a case where the cash receipt (cash payment) **follows** the revenue earning process (incurs an expense).

Deferrals (cost expirations) arise when the cash receipt or payment **precedes** the revenue or expense recognition. Magazine subscriptions provide a good example. The customer typically pays the publisher in advance for a one year or longer subscription. The customer has an asset, the right to receive future editions of the magazine, for which cash payment has been made. The customer cannot use the magazines until they are received; therefore, the cost only becomes an expense in future periods, when customers receive and use the magazines. The publisher has an obligation (a liability) to deliver future editions to the customer. The publisher received a cash prepayment, but only earns revenue by providing its product to the customer during future time periods.

Recall from the text the following three characteristics of all adjusting journal entries:
1.   We enter them in the books at the end of the accounting period to achieve a matching of revenues and expenses in that and future time periods.
2.   They always include at least one temporary (revenue, expense, or dividend) account and at least one permanent (asset or liability) account.
3.   They never involve the Cash account.

Answering the following three basic questions facilitates the preparation of adjusting entries:
1.   What is the correct revenue or expense amount under the accrual basis of accounting?
2.   What amounts, if any, have previously been recorded? This requires an investigation of revenue and expense account balances, as well as any related asset and liability accounts.
3.   What entry will bring the accounting records to the correct accrual basis amounts?

Example of a Cost Expiration Adjusting Entry for Revenues

The following example illustrates this three-step approach for a cost expiration adjusting entry. Inquiring Minds Magazine sells subscriptions to customers. During 2003, Inquiring Minds collected $48,000 from customers for advance payments on subscriptions. Inquiring Minds records cash collections for subscriptions as Unearned Subscriptions Revenue (a liability). By the end of the year, Inquiring Minds had mailed to customers monthly magazines having a total selling price of $27,000. The adjusting entry required for Inquiring Minds Magazine follows.

1. Inquiring Minds earned revenue of $27,000 by providing magazines to customers under its subscription obligations. Since $27,000 worth of magazines were provided to customers, the liability for future deliveries should now be only $21,000.

2. Inquiring Minds previously recorded a related liability (Unearned Subscriptions Revenue) of $48,000. To date, Inquiring Minds has recorded no revenue from these transactions.

3. Revenue must be increased (credited) for $27,000. The liability must be reduced (debited) for $27,000. The adjusting entry below leaves the correct balances in the revenue and liability accounts.

Unearned Subscriptions Revenue (+L)	27,000	
Subscriptions Revenue (R,+SE)		27,000

Example of a Cost Expiration Adjusting Entry for Expenses

Let's use the same transaction from the customer's perspective as an example illustrating the approach for a cost expiration expense adjustment. Assume Big City Hospital buys a subscription to place in its waiting room. In June 2003, Big City paid $480 for a one-year subscription. Big City records the cash payment for subscriptions as Prepaid Subscriptions Expense (an asset). By the end of the year, Big City received one-half of the magazines under its subscription. The adjusting entry on Big City's records is as follows.

1. Big City incurred expense of $240 when it received magazines under its subscription. Since $240 worth of magazines were received, the asset for future deliveries should now be only $240.
2. Big City previously recorded a related asset (Prepaid Subscriptions Expense) of $480. To date, Big City Hospital has recorded no expense from these transactions.
3. Expense must be increased (debited) for $240. The asset must be reduced (credited) for $240. The adjusting entry below leaves the correct balances in the expense and asset accounts.

Subscriptions Expense (E,-SE)	240	
Prepaid Subscriptions Expense (-A)		240

Example of an Accrual Adjusting Entry for Expenses

The Hall Corporation borrows $300,000 from the Last National Bank on July 1, 2003. The note requires Hall to repay the entire principal plus accumulated interest on June 30, 2005. The interest rate is 12% per year. You can prepare the required adjusting entry for Hall Corporation on December 31, 2003 as follows.

1. Hall borrowed funds for a period of six months, thereby incurring an expense, even though cash payment was not required during the current year. The expense (the cost of borrowing) on an accrual basis is $18,000. You calculate this by multiplying the interest rate (12%) times the amount borrowed ($300,000) times the period of time covered (6/12 of one year). Since an expense has been incurred and the amount has not yet been paid, Hall's accrual basis accounting records should include Interest Expense of $18,000 and a liability for Interest Payable of $18,000.

2. Hall originally recorded the borrowing by debiting Cash account and crediting a liability for Notes Payable, in the amount of $300,000. Hall recorded no entry for the interest expense incurred.

3. Interest Expense must be increased (debited) by $18,000. Interest Payable must also be increased (credited) by $18,000. The adjusting entry places the correct accrual balances (as determined in step 1) on Hall's records.

Interest Expense (E,-SE)	18,000	
Interest Payable (+L)		18,000

Example of an Accrual Adjusting Entry for Revenues

The records of Last National Bank provide an example of a revenue accrual. The required adjusting entry for Last National on December 31, 2003 follows.

1. Last National has lent funds for a period of six months, thereby earning interest revenue, even though the cash receipt will not occur until June 30, 2004. The revenue on an accrual basis would be $18,000. Since a revenue has been earned and the amount has not yet been paid, Last National's accrual basis accounting records should include Interest Revenue of $18,000 and an asset for Interest Receivable of $18,000.

2. Last National originally recorded the borrowing by debiting the Note Receivable asset account and crediting the Cash account in the amount of $300,000. Last National has recorded no entry for the interest revenue earned.

3. Interest Revenue must be increased (credited) by $18,000. Interest Receivable must also be increased (debited) by $18,000. The adjusting entry places the correct accrual balances (as determined in step 1) on Last National's records.

Interest Receivable (+A)	18,000	
Interest Revenue (R,+SE)		18,000

Completion of the Accounting Cycle

Periodic adjustments represent entries which "fine tune" the account balances to ensure that all the accounts fairly present the financial position of the business at the end of the accounting period. Accountants record adjustments in the same way as any other transaction, preparing journal entries and posting them to the general ledger accounts.

You prepare an adjusted trial balance after posting the adjusting journal entries to ensure that the debit balance and credit balance accounts total the same number.

You prepare the financial statements after completing the adjusted trial balance. If the business uses a manual system, the accountant prepares the income statement, which includes revenues and expenses, the statement of stockholders' equity, which lists changes in common stock and retained earnings due to additional investments, dividends (withdrawals by owners), and net income (loss) for the period. Finally, you prepare the balance sheet, by copying the asset, liability, and stock account balances from the ledger balances. Copy the balance in retained earnings from the statement of stockholders' equity. The beginning retained earnings balance plus net income (revenues minus expenses) minus dividends equals the ending retained earnings balance.

Closing Entries

After completing the financial statements, you prepare **closing entries**. These are journal entries which transfer the revenue, expense, and dividend balances into the Retained Earnings account. After the transfer, the revenue, expense, and dividend accounts' balances are zero. Transactions related to operations for the next period can now be recorded and an income statement summarizing the operating results for that period alone can be prepared. This process facilitates presenting comparative income statements to be used in financial statement analysis.

Since temporary accounts require zero balances, the closing process requires credit entries to debit balance accounts and an offsetting debit to the **Income Summary** account. Credit balance accounts require debit entries and offsetting credits to the Income Summary account.

The Income Summary account has a credit balance if credits (revenues) exceed debits (expenses). Obviously, a net income exists in this circumstance. The income summary account has a debit balance if debits (expenses) exceed credits (revenues), a net loss situation.

Next close the Income Summary by debiting it in the event of income, and crediting Retained Earnings. The reverse is true in the event of a loss.

Close the Dividend account directly into Retained Earnings without an intermediate step. Recall that dividends differ from expenses. Expenses represent resources consumed in the process of earning revenues. The difference between revenues and expenses represents the change in stockholders' wealth due to operations. Dividends do not represent consumption of resources, but a distribution of the business resources to the stockholders. Dividends reduce the wealth invested in the business, but individual stockholder wealth remains the same. The stockholders' investment in the company declines, but they receive cash which can be used for whatever purpose the stockholders wish.

After completing the closing process, the balance in the general ledger Retained Earnings account should agree with the balance sheet Retained Earnings account.

QUESTIONS FOR YOUR REVIEW

1. The purpose of a trial balance is to:
   a. make certain the accounts have correct balances.
   b. make certain the debits equal the credits.
   c. meet a legal requirement.
   d. replace the income statement and balance sheet.

2. Which of the following accounts usually has a nonzero balance after posting closing entries to the general ledger account?
   a. Retained Earnings
   b. Dividends
   c. Income Summary
   d. Salaries Expense

3. Accountants close the revenue, expense, gain, and loss accounts at the end of the financial statement time interval because:
   a. they would incorrectly present assets on the balance sheet otherwise.
   b. they could not prepare income statement otherwise.
   c. they could not easily prepare next period's income statement otherwise.
   d. they could not prepare the balance sheet for the current period since the calculating the ending retained earnings balance without closing entries.

4. Amy's Pet Store sold 25 parrots for $200 cash each. The parrots initially cost Amy $140 each. The journal entry(ies) to record the sale is (are):

   a. Cash (+A)   5,000
         Sales (R,+SE)   5,000
      Cost of Goods Sold (E,-SE)   3,500
         Inventory (-A)   3,500

   b. Cash (+A)   5,000
         Revenue (R,+SE)   1,500
         Inventory (-A)   3,500

   c. Cash (+A)   5,000
         Gain on Parrot Sale (Ga,+SE)   1,500
         Inventory (-A)   3,500

   d. Cash (+A)   5,000
         Sales (R,+SE)   5,000
      Cost of Goods Sold (E,-SE)   3,500
         Accounts Payable (+L)   3,500

5. A debit balance in which of the following accounts indicates an error has occurred in either analyzing or recording a transaction?
   a. Retained Earnings
   b. Income Summary
   c. Dividends
   d. Sales Revenue

6. The journal entry to record the sale of land for $24,000 cash that initially cost the company $30,000 is:

a. Retained Earnings (-SE)	6,000	
Cash (+A)	24,000	
Land (-A)		30,000
b. Cash (+A)	24,000	
Land (-A)		24,000
c. Cash (+A)	24,000	
Sales Expense (E,-SE)	6,000	
Land (-A)		30,000
d. Cash (+A)	24,000	
Loss on Sale of Land (Lo,-SE)	6,000	
Land (-A)		30,000

Questions 7 and 8 refer to the following information.

Proust Brewery, Inc.'s ledger at December 31, 2003, the company's fiscal year-end, reports the following accounts and balances. All accounts have normal balances.

Cash	$ 14,500	Equipment	$ 25,000
Beer sales	300,000	Notes payable	15,000
Accounts receivable	37,500	Prepaid expenses	1,500
Dividends	5,000	Retained earnings	30,000
Cost of goods sold	225,000	Salary expense	35,000
Interest expense	2,000	Land	4,500

7. Net income for 2003 is:
   a. $31,500.
   b. $33,000.
   c. $36,500.
   d. $38,000.

8. Total assets on the balance sheet are:
   a. $88,000.
   b. $86,5000.
   c. $83,000.
   d. $81,500.

9. Which of the following transactions is normally recorded as a capital expenditure?
   a. Wages paid to manufacturing employees
   b. Wages paid to management employees
   c. Electric utility charges
   d. Purchase of a new delivery vehicle

10. Which of the following transactions is normally recorded as an expense?
    a. Purchase of merchandise for resale
    b. Wages paid to management employees
    c. A twelve-month prepayment on a fire insurance policy
    d. Purchase of a new delivery vehicle

11. Which of the following items is most properly classified as an accrual?
    a. Depreciation expense
    b. Expiration of prepaid insurance
    c. Interest expense
    d. Usage of office supplies

12. Which of the following items is most properly classified as a cost expiration?
    a. Depreciation expense
    b. Wage expense
    c. Interest expense
    d. Purchase of a new delivery vehicle

13. InSync, Inc. reported accounts receivable on January 1 of $66,000 and $80,000 on January 31. Sales revenues during January were $200,000. How much cash was collected from InSync's customers during January?
    a. $200,000
    b. $ 14,000
    c. $266,000
    d. $186,000

14. Sam's Sandwich Shop reported prepaid rent of $210,000 at the beginning of 2003 and a zero balance in this account at the end of the year. During 2003, Sam paid $660,000 in cash for rent. What is Sam's rent expense for 2003?
    a. $870,000
    b. $660,000
    c. $450,000
    d. $210,000

15. Office supplies on hand were $12,000 at the end of the year. Purchases during the year totaled $18,000. Supplies used during the year were $22,500. What was the amount of office supplies on hand at the beginning of the year?
    a. $22,500
    b. $18,000
    c. $16,500
    d. $12,000

16. Jim's Hardware pays for all merchandise purchases in cash. Jim's inventory on July 1 was $42,000, and $46,000 on July 31. Jim recorded cost of goods sold during July of $86,500. How much did Jim pay for purchases in July?
    a. $132,500
    b. $128,500
    c. $ 90,500
    d. $ 88,000

17. The following comprehensive problem set will allow you to review the entire accounting cycle (excluding periodic adjusting entries). You will analyze transactions, prepare journal entries, post those entries to ledger accounts, prepare a trial balance, prepare the financial statements, prepare the closing entries and post those to the ledger, and prepare the final trial balance. When you successfully finish this problem, your understanding of the mechanics of the formal accounting system will be considerably improved.

    Suggestion: We recommend tearing out this section of the study guide to enable you to freely move through the steps with all of the schedules readily available to you.

    Step One. On the following page is the final trial balance at August 31, 2003, for Sorenstam Sporting Goods, Inc. Use the T-accounts provided and record the beginning balances for September (which are the ending balances of August). Notice that the only types of accounts with balances are Assets, Liabilities, Common Stock, and Retained Earnings. August's revenue, expense, and dividend accounts have been closed into Retained Earnings.

    Step Two. Prepare the analysis and journal entries for each of the transactions listed below using the analysis and journal entry schedules provided. We suggest writing down on a separate piece of paper or index card the debit and credit rules. Refer to these rules as you fill out the analysis schedule.

    Step Three. Post the journal entries to the T-accounts. Use the blank T-accounts provided for any accounts included in the journal entries, but not in the final trial balance for August.

    Step Four. After posting all of the entries to the T-accounts, determine each account's balance by adding debit (left-hand side) entries together and credit (right-hand side) entries together. Subtract the debit total from the credit total. Draw a line across the T-account after the last entry and enter the balance on the appropriate side. If the debit total exceeds the credit total, a debit balance for the difference exists. The opposite is true if credits exceed debits.

Step Five. Using the account balances from step four, prepare the trial balance in the space provided. Are the debit and credit side totals equal? Do the balances appear correct? Do asset and expense accounts have debit balances? Do liabilities, common stock, retained earnings, and revenues have credit balances? If you answer no to any of these questions, recheck the analysis, journal entries, and posting to T-accounts to identify your mistake.

Step Six. Prepare the income statement, statement of retained earnings, and balance sheet from the trial balance. You must select the accounts which are appropriately included in each.

Step Seven.
a.   Using the trial balance, identify the Revenue, Expense, and Dividend accounts. Prepare the closing journal entries using the account titles and balances identified.
b.   Post the closing journal entries to the T-accounts.
c.   Using the T-account balances after closing, prepare the final trial balance.

Sorenstam Sporting Goods, Inc.
Final Trial Balance
August 31, 2003

	Debit	Credit
Cash	200,000	
Accounts Receivable	500,000	
Inventory	800,000	
Land	150,000	
Accounts Payable		600,000
Notes Payable		100,000
Common Stock		400,000
Retained Earnings		550,000
Totals	1,650,000	1,650,000

The following transactions occurred during September 2003:

1.   9/1   Inventory which cost $50,000 is sold for $70,000 cash.
2.   9/1   Accounts receivable collected, $40,000.
3.   9/1   Bought land for $60,000, $20,000 cash and $40,000 note payable, due in one year. The interest rate on this note and the $100,000 note outstanding at the beginning of the month is 12% annually, 1% paid at the end of each month.
4.   9/10   Declared and paid dividends of $20,000. A dividend account is used as discussed in the chapter in the textbook.
5.   9/15   Inventory which cost $150,000 is sold for $240,000; $120,000 cash and a $120,000 accounts receivable are received.
6.   9/15   Paid K. Webb, sales clerk, $4,000 salary and commission for the first half of September.
7.   9/20   Paid accounts payable, $50,000.
8.   9/25   Collected accounts receivable, $150,000.

9. 9/30 Interest on the notes paid, $1,400. [($100,000 + $40,000) x .01.].

10. 9/30 K. Webb, sales clerk, is owed $4,000 for the second half of September, but this amount is unpaid at September 30.

11. 9/30 A telephone bill of $2,000 is owed but unpaid at September 30.

Transaction Analysis

	Account	Category	Effect
1a.			
1b.			
2.			
3.			
4.			
5a.			
5b.			
6.			
7.			
8.			

9.			
10.			
11.			

General Journal

	Account Title	Debit	Credit
1a.			
1b.			
2.			
3.			
4a.			
4b.			
5.			
6.			
7.			
8.			
9.			

10.			
11.			

Cash

Accounts Receivable

Inventory

Land

Accounts Payable

Notes Payable

Common Stock

Retained Earnings

Sorenstam Sporting Goods, Inc.
Trial Balance
September 30, 2003

<u>Debit</u>   <u>Credit</u>

Sorenstam Sporting Goods, Inc.
Income Statement
For the Month Ended September 30, 2003

Sorenstam Sporting Goods, Inc.
Statement of Retained Earnings
For the Month Ended September 30, 2003

Sorenstam Sporting Goods, Inc.
Balance Sheet
September 30, 2003

General Journal (Closing entries)

	Account Title and Explanation	Debit	Credit

Sorenstam Sporting Goods, Inc.
Final Trial Balance
September 30, 2003

<u>Debit</u>   <u>Credit</u>

18. Presented below is an unadjusted trial balance for Colonel Ward's Fried Chicken, Inc., as of December 31, 2003. Using the additional information provided, prepare any required adjusting journal entries.

Accounts	Debit	Credit
Cash	40,000	
Accounts Receivable	90,000	
Chicken and Cole Slaw Inventory	130,000	
Prepaid Rent	8,000	
Restaurant Supplies	16,000	
Restaurant Fixtures and Equipment	550,000	
Accumulated Depreciation		165,000
Accounts Payable		100,000
Long-term Note Payable		160,000
Common Stock		200,000
Retained Earnings		211,000
Sales		510,000
Cost of Goods Sold	310,000	
Supplies Expense	32,000	
Salary Expense	88,000	
Advertising Expense	48,000	
Interest Expense	0	
Utilities and Other Operating Expense	24,000	
Dividends	10,000	
	1,346,000	1,346,000

a. On December 1, Colonel Ward paid $48,000 to a local television station for some new advertising spots. The advertising was to be equally spaced and aired throughout the months of December and January. The cost was expensed when paid.

b. On May 1, Colonel Ward signed a lease for storage space in an adjoining building. Colonel Ward paid $8,000 to cover the first ten months rent, and capitalized this amount.

18. c. Ward depreciates the restaurant fixtures and equipment on a straight-line basis over a 20-year useful life.

    d. Colonel Ward borrowed $160,000 on January 1, 2001. The interest rate is 12%, and payments of interest only are to be made on January 1 of each year. The original borrowing plus the final year's interest is due on January 1, 2007.

    e. All restaurant supplies purchased during the year were charged to Supplies Expense. A physical count revealed that $6,400 in restaurant supplies were on hand at December 31.

    f. Employees were owed $2,080 in unpaid wages for work performed since the last payroll date on December 28.

19. Using the information in question 18, prepare an income statement for Colonel Ward's Fried Chicken, Inc., for the year ended December 31, 2003.

20. Prepare adjusting journal entries, as required, for each of the following independent situations. In all cases, the fiscal year ends on December 31.

    a. Fixed assets costing $150,000 have an estimated life of 15 years. The company uses the straight-line method of depreciation.

    b. On July 1, the company purchased a three-year fire insurance policy for $72,000 in cash. The $72,000 was charged to insurance expense.

    c. The company's supplies inventory balance was $15,000 on January 1. Supplies purchased during the year totaled $24,000. These amounts were capitalized throughout the year. A count at year end reveals that $15,750 are still on hand.

    d. The company pays rent at the end of every three months, in the amount of $2,000 per month. The rent was last paid on October 31.

    e. The company borrowed $30,000 on September 1 at a rate of 6% per year. The entire balance, including interest, is due to be repaid in March of next year.

CHAPTER 4 - SOLUTIONS

1.	b	6.	d	11.	c
2.	a	7.	d	12.	a
3.	c	8.	c	13.	d
4.	a	9.	d	14.	a
5.	d	10.	b	15.	c
				16.	c

17.   **Steps 1 and 2.**   **Transaction Analysis**

	Account	Category	Effect	
1a.	Cash	Asset	+ 70,000	debit
	Sales	Revenue	+ 70,000	credit
1b.	Inventory	Asset	- 50,000	credit
	Cost of Goods Sold	Expense	+ 50,000	debit
2.	Cash	Asset	+ 40,000	debit
	Accounts Receivable	Asset	- 40,000	credit
3.	Land	Asset	+ 60,000	debit
	Cash	Asset	- 20,000	credit
	Notes Payable	Liability	+ 40,000	credit
4.	Cash	Asset	- 20,000	credit
	Dividend	Dividend	+ 20,000	debit
5a.	Cash	Asset	+ 120,000	debit
	Accounts Receivable	Asset	+ 120,000	debit
5b.	Inventory	Asset	- 150,000	credit
	Cost of Goods Sold	Expense	+ 150,000	debit
	Sales	Revenue	+240,000	credit

	Account	Category	Effect	
6.	Cash	Asset	- 4,000	credit
	Salaries Expense	Expense	+ 4,000	debit
7.	Cash	Asset	- 50,000	credit
	Accounts Payable	Liability	- 50,000	debit
8.	Cash	Asset	+ 150,000	debit
	Accounts Receivable	Asset	- 150,000	credit
9.	Cash	Asset	- 1,400	credit
	Interest Expense	Expense	+ 1,400	debit
10.	Salary Expense	Expense	+ 4,000	debit
	Salary Payable	Liability	+ 4,000	credit
11.	Utility Expense	Expense	+ 2,000	debit
	Utility Payable	Liability	+ 2,000	credit

General Journal

	Account Title	Debit	Credit
1a.	Cash (+A)	70,000	
	Sales (R,+SE)		70,000
1b.	Cost of Goods Sold (E,-SE)	50,000	
	Inventory (-A)		50,000
2.	Cash (+A)	40,000	
	Accounts Receivable (-A)		40,000
3.	Land (+A)	60,000	
	Cash (-A)		20,000
	Notes Payable (+L)		40,000
4.	Dividends (-SE)	20,000	
	Cash (-A)		20,000
5a.	Cash (+A)	120,000	
	Accounts Receivable (+A)	120,000	
	Sales (R,+SE)		240,000
5b.	Cost of Goods Sold (E,-SE)	150,000	
	Inventory (-A)		150,000

6.	Salary Expense (E,-SE)		4,000		
	Cash (-A)			4,000	
7.	Accounts Payable (-L)		50,000		
	Cash (-A)			50,000	
8.	Cash (+A)		150,000		
	Accounts Receivable (-A)			150,000	
9.	Interest Expense (E,-SE)		1,400		
	Cash (-A)			1,400	
10.	Salary Expense (E,-SE)		4,000		
	Salary Payable (+L)			4,000	
11.	Utility Expense (E,-SE)		2,000		
	Utility Payable (+L)			2,000	

Steps 3, 4, and 7b. Posting to the T-accounts (ledger accounts).

Cash						Accounts Receivable				
B.B.	200,000		(3)	20,000		B.B.	500,000		(2)	40,000
(1a)	70,000		(4)	20,000		(5a)	120,000		(8)	150,000
(2)	40,000		(6)	4,000						
(5a)	120,000		(7)	50,000						
(8)	150,000		(9)	1,400		E.B.	430,000			
E.B.	484,600									

Inventory						Land			
B.B.	800,000		(1b)	50,000		B.B.	150,000		
			(5b)	150,000		(3)	60,000		
E.B.	600,000					E.B.	210,000		

Accounts Payable						Notes Payable			
(7)	50,000		B.B.	600,000				B.B.	100,000
								(3)	40,000
			E.B.	550,000				E.B.	140,000

Common Stock		
	B.B.	400,000
	E.B.	400,000

Retained Earnings		
Div. 20,000	B.B.	550,000
	Inc.	98,600
	E.B.	628,600

Sales		
	(1a)	70,000
	(5a)	240,000
	E.B.	310,000
To		
close 310,000	Post-closing	
	balance	0

Cost of Goods Sold		
(1b)	50,000	
(5b)	150,000	
E.B.	200,000	To
		close 200,000
Post-closing		
balance	0	

Interest Expense		
(9)	1,400	
E.B.	1,400	To
		close 1,400
Post-closing		
balance	0	

Salary Expense		
(6)	4,000	
(10)	4,000	
E.B.	8,000	To
		close 8,000
Post-closing		
balance	0	

Utility Expense		
(11)	2,000	
E.B.	2,000	
		To
Post-closing		close 2,000
balance	0	

Dividends		
(4)	20,000	
E.B.	20,000	To
		close 20,000
Post-closing		
balance	0	

Salary Payable				Utility Payable		
		(10)	4,000			(11)	2,000
		E.B.	4,000			E.B.	2,000

Income Summary			
CGS	200,000	Sales	310,000
Int. Exp.	1,400		
Sal. Exp.	8,000		
Util.Exp.	2,000		
		E.B.	98,600
To close	98,600		
		Post-closing balance	0

Step 5. Preparation of the trial balance.

Sorenstam Sporting Goods, Inc.
Trial Balance
September 30, 2003

	Debit	Credit
Cash	484,600	
Accounts Receivable	430,000	
Inventory	600,000	
Land	210,000	
Accounts Payable		550,000
Notes Payable		140,000
Common Stock		400,000
Retained Earnings		550,000
Sales		310,000
Cost of Goods Sold	200,000	
Interest Expense	1,400	
Salary Expense	8,000	
Utility Expense	2,000	
Dividends	20,000	
Salary Payable		4,000
Utility Payable		2,000
	1,956,000	1,956,000

Step 6. Preparation of the financial statements.

Sorenstam Sporting Goods, Inc.
Income Statement
For the Month Ended September 30, 2003

Sales		$310,000
Less expenses:		
Cost of goods sold	$200,000	
Salary expense	8,000	
Utility expense	2,000	
Interest expense	1,400	211,400
Net income		$ 98,600

Sorenstam Sporting Goods, Inc.
Statement of Retained Earnings
For the Month Ended September 30, 2003

Retained earnings - August 31, 2003	$550,000
Add: Net income for September	98,600
Less: Dividends	(20,000)
Retained earnings - September 30, 2003	$628,600

Sorenstam Sporting Goods, Inc.
Balance Sheet
September 30, 2003

Assets		**Liabilities and Stockholders' Equity**	
Cash	$ 484,600	Notes payable	$ 140,000
Accounts receivable	430,000	Accounts payable	550,000
Inventory	600,000	Utility payable	2,000
Land	210,000	Salary payable	4,000
		Total liabilities	$ 696,000
		Common stock	$ 400,000
		Retained earnings	628,600
		Total stockholders' equity	$1,028,600
		Total liabilities and	
Total assets	$1,724,600	stockholders' equity	$1,724,600

Step 7.a.

General Journal (Closing Entries)

Account Title and Explanation	Debit	Credit
Sales	310,000	
Income Summary		310,000
Close revenue accounts.		
Income Summary	211,400	
Cost of Goods Sold		200,000
Salary Expense		8,000
Utility Expense		2,000
Interest Expense		1,400
Close expense accounts.		
Income Summary	98,600	
Retained Earnings		98,600
Close income summary.		
Retained Earnings	20,000	
Dividends		20,000
Close dividends.		

Step 7. c.

Sorenstam Sporting Goods, Inc.
Final Trial Balance
September 30, 2003

	Debit	Credit
Cash	484,600	
Accounts Receivable	430,000	
Inventory	600,000	
Land	210,000	
Accounts Payable		550,000
Notes Payable		140,000
Salary Payable		4,000
Utility Payable		2,000
Common Stock		400,000
Retained Earnings		628,600
	1,724,600	1,724,600

18. a. Prepaid Advertising (+A) 24,000
       Advertising Expense (E,-SE) 24,000

    b. Rent Expense (E,-SE) 6,400
       Prepaid Rent (-A) 6,400

    c. Depreciation Expense (E,-SE) 27,500
       Accumulated Depreciation (-A) 27,500

    d. Interest Expense (E,-SE) 19,200
       Interest Payable (+L) 19,200

    e. Supplies Expense (E,-SE) 9,600
       Restaurant Supplies (-A) 9,600

    f. Salary Expense (E,-SE) 2,080
       Salary Payable (+L) 2,080

19. You may wish to begin by preparing an adjusted trial balance. Post the adjusting entries made in question 18. The accounts highlighted in bold type were added during the adjustment process.

Colonel Ward's Fried Chicken, Inc.
Adjusted Trial Balance
December 31, 2003

	Debit	Credit
Cash	40,000	
Accounts Receivable	90,000	
Chicken and Cole Slaw Inventory	130,000	
Prepaid Rent	1,600	
Prepaid Advertising	**24,000**	
Restaurant Supplies	6,400	
Restaurant Fixtures and Equipment	550,000	
Accumulated Depreciation		192,500
Accounts Payable		100,000
Salary Payable	**2,080**	
Interest Payable		**19,200**
Long-term Note Payable		160,000
Common Stock		200,000
Retained Earnings		211,000
Sales		510,000
Cost of Goods Sold	310,000	
Supplies Expense	41,600	
Salary Expense	90,080	
Advertising Expense	24,000	
Interest Expense	19,200	
Rent Expense	**6,400**	
Depreciation Expense	**27,500**	
Utilities and Other Operating Expense	24,000	
Dividends	10,000	
	1,394,780	1,394,780

Colonel Ward's Fried Chicken, Inc.
Income Statement
For the Year Ended December 31, 2003

Sales	$510,000
Less: Cost of goods sold	310,000
Gross margin	$200,000
Less expenses:	
Supplies expense	$ 41,600
Salary and wage expense	90,080
Advertising expense	24,000
Interest expense	19,200
Rent expense	6,400
Depreciation expense	27,500
Utilities and other operating expenses	24,000
Total expenses	$232,780
Net income (loss)	$(32,780)

20.   a.

Depreciation Expense (E,-SE)	10,000	
Accumulated Depreciation (-A)		10,000
b. Prepaid Insurance (+A)	60,000	
Insurance Expense (E,-SE)		60,000
c. Supplies Expense (E,-SE)	23,250	
Supplies Inventory (-A)		23,250
d. Rent Expense (E,-SE)	4,000	
Rent Payable (+L)		4,000
e. Interest Expense (E,-SE)	600	
Interest Payable (+L)		600

CHAPTER 5

Using Financial Statement Information

REVIEW OF KEY CONCEPTS

This chapter discusses how to use financial accounting numbers in business decision-making. The chapter also reviews technical procedures involved in the analysis of financial statements and focuses on how to use the output of these analyses.

Control and Prediction

The two major uses of financial accounting information are **control** and **prediction**. Investors and creditors attempt to assess the future cash flows to be provided by a business. It is the future cash flows which give value to the investment. Historical data provided in the financial statements is useful in predicting future cash flows. Financial data is also useful in monitoring or controlling the performance of company management.

The financial statements report historical accounting data concerning past operating performance. The financial statements do not attempt to directly measure future cash flows. However, research results indicate that historical data is useful in predicting future performance. Specifically, financial accounting numbers are useful in assessing the **solvency** and **profitability** of a company.

Solvency is the company's ability to pay liabilities as they come due. Profitability is the company's ability to generate future cash flows and increases in wealth through business operations. Profitability is a measure of a company's earning power. There is a close relation between solvency and profitability. Operating activities are a primary source of the cash used to meet obligations and liabilities as they come due. An insolvent company cannot survive. An insolvent company cannot maintain earning power or profitability. Profitability measures the company's ability to generate the cash flows needed to meet obligations.

Also closely related to profitability is the concept of **earnings persistence**. Earnings persistence is a measure of the likelihood that reported income numbers will persist, or continue in future periods. For example, a large gain from the sale of a portion of the business's assets has low earnings persistence. The assets have already been sold. This gain will not appear again in future years. On the other hand, income earned from long-term service contracts will continue for at least the term of the existing contracts. Such income has a higher earnings persistence.

Financial accounting numbers are also used to monitor and control the decisions of company management. Shareholders might directly use the numbers, assess past performance, and simply vote to change management, when performance does not meet expectations. While this has occurred in the past, control is usually accomplished in another way. Financial accounting measures and numbers are included as **contracting** variables.

For example, **creditors** include financial ratios and other accounting numbers as covenants in the debt contracts. Such covenants serve to limit the flexibility of management and provide additional protection for the financial interests of the creditors. Typical debt covenants are restrictions on the payment of dividends to shareholders, requiring a company to maintain a minimum level of the current ratio, or a maximum level for the debt/equity ratio.

Shareholders want management to act in their own best interests as a means of maximizing shareholder wealth. One way to accomplish this is to contract with managers to base compensation, at least in part, on the operating performance of the company. It is common to observe compensation contracts that base a significant portion of management's total compensation on the company's reported net income.

Assessing Profitability and Solvency

There are four primary tools used to assess profitability and solvency. Investors and creditors should include a careful review of (1) the **audit report**, (2) **significant transactions**, (3) **financial statement analysis**, and (4) the company's **credit rating**.

The certified public accountant hired by the Board of Directors as the company's external auditor prepares the audit report. Company management prepares the financial statements. Companies hire independent external auditors to review the company's financial records and provide additional assurance to the users of the financial statements. The auditor normally indicates that the financial statements **fairly present** the **operations** and **financial position** of the company. The report also indicates that the auditors conducted all necessary tests and audit procedures. The audit report also states that the company prepared the financial statements in accordance with generally accepted accounting principles. When all of the above conditions have been met, the audit report is referred to as a **standard audit report**.

When some conditions are not met, the auditor issues a departure from the standard report. The following are reasons for issuing a non-standard report.
- One or more necessary audit tests could not be completed, known as a scope limitation.
- The auditor has relied on another auditor to perform a portion of the work.
- The financial statements do not fully conform to generally accepted accounting principles.
- Major accounting principles or methods have been changed during the current reporting period.
- The future outcome of uncertainties affecting the statements cannot be reasonably estimated.
- There is extreme uncertainty. The company's ability to continue as a going concern is in question.

Significant transactions are also important in assessing the profitability and solvency. It is important for investors and creditors to recognize that single, large transactions may often distort the numbers presented in the financial statements. Normally, the footnotes which accompany the financial statements discuss such single significant transactions.

Professional credit rating agencies provide additional reports useful to both investors and creditors. These agencies base the reports in part on financial statement analysis. The credit rating agencies provide formal ratings or rankings on the riskiness of a company's outstanding debt issues.

The final important step is to conduct financial statement analysis. Financial statement analysis normally includes vertical analysis, horizontal analysis, and ratio analysis. **Vertical analysis** techniques convert the financial statements to percentages, and are also known as **common-size financial statements**. This is especially useful in comparing a company's operating performance to others in the same industry. It is unlikely that two companies will have exactly the same numbers appear in their financial statements. However, companies in an industry have similar technologies and face similar costs in material and labor input markets. Therefore, companies within an industry should have similar operating performances.

Horizontal analysis compares a company's performance over time. **Ratio analysis** focuses on key relationships of financial statement items. Professional analysts combine the three types of analysis in their review of a company. The next section discusses technical procedures for the analyses.

Assessing Solvency

In order to survive, a company must remain solvent. **Insolvency**, or **bankruptcy**, imposes significant costs on investors, creditors, and the economy as a whole. As noted previously, the goal of solvency assessment is to determine whether the company can generate sufficient future cash flows to meet liabilities and obligations as they come due. Analysts base evaluation of future cash flows on consideration of **operating performance**, **financial flexibility**, and **liquidity**.

Operating performance measures the company's ability to increase net assets from normal operating activities. Companies provide goods and/or services to customers. A company can only increase net assets if operating activities are profitable. Profitable operating activities are the primary source of a company's cash inflows and outflows.

Financial flexibility measures the company's ability to generate cash flows from sources other than operating activities. Other sources are an important secondary source of cash flows to the company. Debt and equity markets are the most important other sources for cash flows. A company has less financial flexibility if it has exhausted its ability to borrow. A company has less financial flexibility if recent stock market prices for its shares are depressed.

Liquidity measures how quickly a company can convert its existing assets into cash. Current assets are more liquid than operating assets such as property and equipment. For example, there is a ready market for a company's investments in marketable securities. The company can normally convert these into cash as the need arises by a simple call to the company's broker. On the other hand, it may be difficult to find a buyer for certain types of specialized production machinery and equipment. While the productive assets may be sold, considerable time may elapse before these can be converted to cash. Higher liquidity indicates a lower risk of insolvency.

Financial Statement Analysis Techniques

Financial statement analysis is an important skill for managers, investors, creditors, and others interested in assessing the financial performance of a company. Three primary tools (horizontal, vertical, and ratio analyses) form the basis of financial statement analysis.

Horizontal analysis compares a company's financial statement data across two or more time periods. Vertical analysis (also known as common-size financial statements) converts raw dollar amounts in the financial statements to percentages to facilitate comparisons. For example, all balance sheet amounts are divided by total assets. Vertical analysis emphasizes the interrelation of the various financial statement numbers. **Ratio analysis** places an even greater emphasis on financial statement interrelations. Ratios are fractions using one (or more) account balances in the numerator and another account balance (or more) in the denominator.

Analysts frequently combine horizontal and vertical analyses. For example, analysts often first prepare common-size financial statements and then analyze the percentage-changes in the common-size amounts from year to year. They also prepare analyses by computing ratios and then investigating trends for percentage-changes over time. You will have an opportunity to do some combined analyses of your own in completing the comprehensive review problem at the end of this chapter.

It is worth your time to reinforce the concepts presented in Chapter 5 with additional practice. Presented below (question 39) is a comprehensive review problem. Once you have completed the problem, you should be comfortable with the various calculations, and will have gained a greater appreciation of the techniques employed in financial statement analysis.

Before turning to the review problem, take a few minutes to read the paragraphs below which should refresh your memory on completing the various financial statement analysis procedures. You should also carefully read those sections in your text which deal with interpreting the results of ratio analyses.

Preparing Common-Size Financial Statements

Common-size financial statements facilitate direct comparisons from one period to another. Difficulties due to differences in reported financial statement balances because of inflation and overall growth in the company are mitigated when the comparisons use common-size amounts. Normally, an analyst prepares both common-size income statements and balance sheets, referred to as vertical analysis.

Preparation of common-size statements converts all dollar amounts into percentages. A common-size balance sheet uses total assets as the denominator in calculating the percentages. A common-size income statement uses net sales as the denominator in calculating the percentages.

Preparing Comparisons Across Time

Comparisons across time are another useful tool for financial statement analysis. Intertemporal comparisons are also known as horizontal analysis or trend analysis. It is typical to see such analyses prepared on the basis of both changes in dollar amounts from one year to the next, and in percentage change format.

Ratio Analysis

Your text presents a wide variety of ratios used by financial analysts. Here we discuss a few frequently used ratios from each category and offer of exercises to practice the computations.

Solvency Ratios

As discussed earlier, solvency is a criterion used by investors to assess the health of a business. Analysts use several ratios to assess the ability of the company to meet obligations as they come due.

The **quick ratio** or **acid-test ratio** divides the total of cash, temporary securities, and accounts receivable by the total current liabilities. In other words, the ratio is the number of dollars of highly liquid assets per dollar of obligations due in the near future. The higher the quick ratio, the better the ability to meet obligations as they come due.

The **current ratio** or **working capital ratio** divides current assets by current liabilities. Since the numerator includes more types of assets, the current ratio will be higher than the quick ratio. The assets added are inventory and prepaid expenses. According to the operating cycle, inventory is farther away from being converted into cash than accounts receivable. In economic downturns, companies may have more inventory on hand than at other times because they cannot sell it. An increase in the current ratio may not be a positive signal in such a situation. An investor must determine the reason for changes in inventory before interpreting this ratio.

The **interest coverage ratio** equals Net income + Interest expense + Income tax expense / Interest expense. It measures the average number of times that the company earns interest during the period. This ratio assesses the long-term ability of the business to meet its interest payments.

Leverage Ratios

The **debt/equity ratio** is the ratio of average total liabilities to average stockholders' equity. This ratio provides the investor with a measure of the relative claims on economic resources by creditors and investors. Since the tax law allows deductibility of interest but not dividends, some degree of debt or leverage is advisable; however, too much debt may result in risk of bankruptcy.

Analysts compute a **capital structure leverage ratio** by dividing average total assets by average stockholders' equity. The measure provides an indication of a company's reliance on borrowed funds. High levels of this ratio inform investors that the relies heavily on borrowings to finance its assets, and also exhibits higher levels of risk.

Asset Turnover Ratios

Receivables turnover is net credit sales divided by average accounts receivable. You calculate average accounts receivable by adding beginning and ending accounts receivable together and dividing by 2. This ratio measures the average speed with which the company collects its receivables. It measures the efficiency of collection. For a company to remain solvent, the collection process must be efficient.

Inventory turnover is cost of goods sold divided by average inventory. You calculate average inventory by adding together beginning and ending inventory and dividing by 2. The inventory turnover measures the average liquidity in inventory.

The receivables turnover ratio can be converted into the average number of days sales in the accounts receivable by dividing 365 days by the receivables turnover ratio. The resulting number represents the average time period to collect accounts receivable after the sale. You can also compute average number of days sales in inventory dividing 365 days by the inventory turnover ratio. The resulting number represents the average time period until inventory is sold. The sum of the two days sales numbers is an estimate of the operating cycle. For example, if a company has an average of 20 days sales in inventory and another 30 days in accounts receivable, its operating cycle is approximately 50 days.

Profitability

Return on sales (profit margin) is net income plus after-tax interest expense divided by sales. It measures the residual amount of each sales dollar attributed to owners.

Return on assets is net income plus after-tax interest expense divided by average total assets. Average total assets is the beginning total assets plus ending total assets divided by 2. Return on assets measures resources generated from using all of the resources invested in the business.

Return on equity is net income divided by average stockholders' equity. Return on equity can be used by owners to compare alternative investments.

Other Ratios

Earnings per share is the ratio of net income available to common stockholders divided by the average number of shares outstanding. The individual shareholder can determine the increase in his personal wealth according to the accounting model during the time period.

The **price/earnings ratio (P/E ratio)** expresses the market price as a multiple of the current year's earnings. Analysts calculate the ratio by dividing the market price per share by the earnings per share for the period. It is often compared to the P/E ratio of other firms in the industry as a rough gauge of whether the stock is over- or under-valued.

Analysts calculate the **dividend yield ratio** by dividing dividends received during the year by the market price per share. It measures the cash return on the investment during the year, similar to the rate of interest earned on savings or other investment in interest bearing securities.

Stock price return is a market price-based version of return on equity. Analysts calculate this ratio by dividing the change in stock price for the year, plus dividends by the beginning of year stock price.

Limitations of Financial Accounting Information

The primary limitation of financial accounting information is that it does not provide a direct measure of the variable of interest in investment and credit decision-making. Investors and creditors are interested in the **future performance** of the company. The true value of a company is the present value of its future cash flows. The financial accounting numbers are the result of past transactions and events. As such, the financial statements provide book values, which are only imperfect measures of a company's true value.

Companies prepare financial statements in accordance with generally accepted accounting principles, which are inherently limited because they do not include all relevant information about a company. It takes time to prepare and audit financial statements, rendering financial accounting information as deficient in not being available on a timely basis. Management prepares financial statements. As such, the application of generally accepted accounting principles is subject to the biases and judgment of management.

Financial statements include only the results of past transactions and events. Statements omit other value-relevant information, often because we cannot quantify or objectively measure it. Users must make subjective adjustments to the financial statements to consider such additional relevant information. For example, future changes in interest rates, inflation rates, and other economic trends may have a significant influence on the future performance of the company.

Current generally accepted accounting principles do not value human resources. In a high technology industry, the skills of employees (especially those working in new product research and development) are an extremely valuable, but omitted, asset. Accountants omit human capital because they consider its valuation too subjective. A company's reputation in providing goods and services to customers is also an important asset. This reputation is an intangible asset known as goodwill. Current generally accepted accounting principles include only goodwill which has been purchased in a business combination. Once again, high subjectivity in assigning a value to internally generated goodwill precludes its inclusion on the balance sheet.

Financial accounting numbers are primarily based on historical costs. In periods of inflation, these numbers may be very different from current costs and current values. Current generally accepted accounting principles provide no adjustment for the impact of inflation.

QUESTIONS FOR YOUR REVIEW

1. Which of the following is *true* regarding the usefulness of financial accounting numbers?
   a. Financial accounting numbers help to predict a company's future cash flows.
   b. Financial accounting numbers provide an indication of a company's earning power and solvency position.
   c. Financial accounting numbers help investors and creditors to influence and monitor the business decisions of managers.
   d. Financial accounting numbers are useful in all of the above situations.

2. Which of the following is *not* one of the FASB's financial reporting objectives?
   a. Providing investors and creditors with information to assess future cash flows.
   b. Providing useful information for making investment and credit decisions.
   c. Providing information to assist management decision making.
   d. Providing information about a business's resources and obligations.

3. Which of the following two characteristics can be used to assess the usefulness of accounting information?
   a. Verifiability and timeliness
   b. Relevance and reliability
   c. Comparability and neutrality
   d. Completeness and reliability

4. Which of these is the *least* worrisome reason for departure from an auditor's standard report?
   a. There is a question about whether the company can continue as a going concern in the future.
   b. Major accounting methods have changed.
   c. The auditor's opinion is based in part on the work of another auditor.
   d. The scope of the auditor's examination is affected by conditions that preclude the application of one or more necessary auditing procedures.

5. Which of these is the *most* worrisome reason for departure from an auditor's standard report?
   a. There is a question about whether the company can continue as a going concern in the future.
   b. Major accounting methods have changed.
   c. The auditor's opinion is based in part on the work of another auditor.
   d. The financial statements are affected by uncertainties concerning future events.

6. Which of the following is *not* a limitation of financial accounting information?
   a. Financial statements are significantly influenced by the subjective judgments and incentives of the managers who prepare them.
   b. Financial statements are not adjusted for inflation.
   c. Financial statements do not generally reflect market values.
   d. Financial accounting information suffers from all the above limitations.

7. Consistency refers to consistent use of alternative generally accepted accounting methods:
   a. by several different companies.
   b. by all firms within the same industry.
   c. by a single company across several accounting periods.
   d. by a single company throughout a single accounting period.

8. Where would you look for early signals of a change in a company's profitability?
   a. Interim financial statements
   b. Annual financial statements
   c. Annual reports to stockholders
   d. Annual reports to the SEC

9. Which of the following is *not* a useful employment of financial statement analysis?
   a. Evaluating a company's future performance
   b. Evaluating a company's current financial position
   c. Evaluating a company's past performance
   d. Evaluating a company's past risk

10. Financial accounting numbers which can be reproduced by another system and result in similar measures are called:
    a. relevant.
    b. comparable.
    c. verifiable.
    d. consistent.

11. A general rule in evaluating alternative investments is the greater the risk, the:
    a. lower the expected return required.
    b. greater the expected return required.
    c. lower the expected price of the investment.
    d. greater the expected price of the investment.

12. Which of the following are legally required to be audited by certified public accountants?
    a. All large, privately owned companies
    b. All companies whose stock is traded on public stock exchanges, regardless of size
    c. Only large, publicly traded companies
    d. All U.S.-based companies

13. Which of the following do *not* use credit ratings to evaluate the earning power and solvency of a company?
    a. Investors
    b. Creditors
    c. Auditors
    d. Managers

14. A company's ability to increase its net assets through operations is known as:
    a. financial flexibility.
    b. operating performance.
    c. solvency.
    d. earning power.

15. A company's ability to produce cash through means other than operations is known as:
    a. financial flexibility.
    b. operating performance.
    c. solvency.
    d. earning power.

16. Which of the following is an inherent limitation of generally accepted accounting principles?
    a. Firms may choose from among alternative acceptable accounting methods.
    b. Management may assist the board of directors in selecting an auditor.
    c. Financial statements are prepared by management, not by the auditors.
    d. Internally generated goodwill is not explicitly recognized on the financial statements.

17. One limitation of current generally accepted accounting principles is the lack of fair market value information. For which accounts is this likely to present the most serious problem?
    a. Accounts Receivable
    b. Cash
    c. Property, Plant, and Equipment
    d. Accounts Payable

18. Where would an investor look to determine whether the financial statements have been prepared in accordance with generally accepted accounting principles?
    a. A credit rating agency, such as Moody's
    b. The auditor's report
    c. The Securities and Exchange Commission
    d. The Financial Accounting Standards Board

19. Which of these should *not* be considered in assessing a company's earning power and solvency?
    a. The audit report
    b. Significant transactions
    c. Financial statement analysis
    d. Letters of recommendation

20. The extent to which management has used discretion in preparing the financial statement dollar amounts is known as:
    a. earnings power.
    b. earnings persistence.
    c. earnings quality.
    d. all of the above.

21. Which of the following is a profitability measure?
    a. Earnings per share
    b. Receivables turnover
    c. Current ratio
    d. Debt/equity ratio

22. Which of the following measures is most similar to return on assets?
    a. Asset turnover
    b. Debt/equity ratio
    c. Earnings per share
    d. Quick ratio

23. Which of these should be used as a denominator in preparing a common-size income statement?
    a. Net income
    b. Cost of goods sold
    c. Gross profit
    d. Net sales

24. Why are common-size financial statements useful?
    a. Users can identify companies of the same size.
    b. Users can identify companies of the same fair market value.
    c. Users can assess the potential of two similar size companies in different industries.
    d. Users can compare two different size companies within the same industry.

25. Which of the following should be considered in conducting a horizontal analysis?
    a. Changes in financial statement format
    b. Changes in dollar amounts only
    c. Changes in percentages only
    d. Changes in both dollar amounts and percentages

26. What type of ratio is the current ratio?
    a. Profitability ratio
    b. Solvency ratio
    c. Activity ratio
    d. Market ratio

27. Which of the following transactions would increase a current ratio that is greater than 1.0?
    a. Company purchases merchandise on credit.
    b. Company converts a current liability to a long-term liability.
    c. Company borrows cash and issues a short-term note payable.
    d. Company pays a ten percent cash dividend on its common stock.

28. Which of the following formulas is used to calculate the inventory turnover ratio?
    a. Average inventory divided by net sales
    b. Average net sales divided by net income
    c. Cost of goods sold divided by average inventory
    d. Cost of goods sold divided by net income

29. Which of these statements is an incorrect interpretation of a high inventory turnover ratio?
    a. A high turnover indicates that the inventory turns over frequently.
    b. A high turnover indicates that there is less invested for each dollar of sales.
    c. A high turnover indicates that the inventory is obsolete.
    d. A high turnover indicates that there is sufficient inventory to meet customer demand.

30. Spartan Corporation's current ratio increased during 2003, while the quick ratio decreased. Which of these could explain this set of ratio changes?
    a. Spartan increased accounts payable.
    b. Spartan increased inventory levels.
    c. Spartan's accounts receivable decreased.
    d. Spartan sold marketable equity securities.

31. The current ratio is unaffected by:
    a. payment of a $3,000 accounts payable.
    b. purchasing inventory for $15,000.
    c. a customer's payment of an account receivable by giving land.
    d. payment of wage expense for the month.

32. The current ratio is unaffected by:
    a. sales of goods for cash.
    b. the purchase of inventory for cash.
    c. the purchase of inventory on account.
    d. the payment of wages accumulated during the month.

33. The Beasley Company's 2003 current ratio is 2:1 (current assets = $100,000). In 2004, the current ratio is 3:1 (current assets = $75,000). Current liabilities at the end of 2004 and 2003 are, respectively:
    a. $50,000 [2004] and $25,000 [2003].
    b. $33,333 [2004] and $18,750 [2003].
    c. $200,000 [2004] and $225,000 [2003].
    d. They cannot be determined from the given information.

34. Referring to question 33, which of the following transactions could have resulted in the change in the current ratio from 2003 to 2004?
    a. Beasley collected $25,000 on an account receivable.
    b. Beasley purchased $25,000 of inventory on credit.
    c. Beasley sold inventory which cost $10,000 for $35,000 cash.
    d. Land which cost $25,000 is given to a creditor for payment of a $25,000 account payable.

Questions 35 and 36 refer to the following information.

The following is an excerpt from Buckman Safari Country's 2003 annual report:

Selected information for 2001:

Accounts Receivable, 12/31/01	$ 290,000
Inventory, 12/31/01	70,000
Total Assets, 12/31/01	450,000
Stockholders' Equity, 12/31/01	130,000

Buckman's balance sheet and income statement follow.

Buckman Safari Company
Balance Sheet
December 31, 2003 and 2002

Assets	2003	2002
Cash	$ 70,000	$ 20,000
Accounts receivable	300,000	280,000
Inventory	100,000	60,000
Prepaid rent	10,000	5,000
Total current assets	$480,000	$365,000
Land held for future development	50,000	
Furniture and fixtures	30,000	35,000
Total assets	$560,000	$400,000
Liabilities and stockholders' equity		
Accounts payable	$250,000	$225,000
Wages payable	50,000	60,000
Total current liabilities	$300,000	$285,000
Bonds Payable	100,000	
Total liabilities	$400,000	$285,000
Stockholders' equity		
Common stock, $2 par value	$ 50,000	$ 50,000
Paid in capital in excess of par value	10,000	10,000
Total contributed capital	$ 60,000	$ 60,000
Retained earnings	100,000	55,000
Total stockholders' equity	$160,000	$115,000
Total liabilities and stockholders' equity	$560,000	$400,000

Buckman Safari Company
Income Statement
For the Years Ending December 31, 2003 and 2002

	2003	2002
Revenues	$600,000	$560,000
Cost of goods sold	445,000	409,400
Gross profit	$155,000	$150,600
Operating expenses		
Wage expense	$100,000	$110,000
Rent expense	10,000	9,000
Depreciation expense	5,000	5,000
Total operating expenses	$115,000	$124,000
Operating income	$ 40,000	$ 26,600
Interest expense	10,000	0
Income before tax	$ 30,000	$ 26,600
Income tax	12,000	10,640
Net income	$ 18,000	$ 15,960

35. Compute the ratios in the following table for Buckman Safari Company.

Ratio	Formula	2003	2002
Quick Ratio	(Cash + Accounts Receivable + Marketable Securities) / Current Liabilities		
Current Ratio	Current Assets / Current Liabilities		
Debt/Equity	Average Total Liabilities / Average Total Stockholders' Equity		
Receivables Turnover	Net Credit Sales / Average Accounts Receivable		
Average Days Sales in Accounts Receivable	365 days / Receivables Turnover		
Inventory Turnover	Cost of Goods Sold / Average Inventory		
Average Days Sales in Inventory	365 days / Inventory Turnover		
Interest Coverage Ratio	Net Income Before Interest and Taxes / Interest Expense		
Return on Sales	Net Income + After-tax Interest Expense / Revenues		

Return on Assets	Net Income + After-tax Interest Expense/ Average Total Assets		
Return on Equity	Net Income / Average Stockholders' Equity		
Common Stock Shares Outstanding	Common Stock Total Par Value / Par Value per Share		
Earnings per Share	Net Income / Average Common Shares Outstanding		
Gross Profit	Gross Profit / Revenues		

36. From your calculations in question 35, answer the following. Show how you arrived at your answers.

    a. What is the approximate length of Buckman's operating cycle in 2003 and 2002, respectively?

    b. From your analysis, has the debt-paying ability of Buckman changed during the year? Explain.

    c. From your analysis, is Buckman more or less profitable to the stockholders in 2003 compared to 2002?

37. The balance sheet of the Hoosier Company appears as follows.

Assets

Cash and marketable securities	$ 40,000
Other current assets	40,000
Property, plant, and equipment	60,000
Total assets	$140,000

Liabilities and Stockholders' Equity

Accounts payable	$ 24,000
Long-term debt	76,000
Stockholders' equity	40,000
Total liabilities and stockholders' equity	$140,000

Hoosier entered into the following transactions during 2003:

1. Purchased $4,000 of inventory on account.
2. Sold inventory originally costing $10,000 to customers on account, at a profit of $1,000.
3. Recorded $6,000 of depreciation expense on the property, plant, and equipment.
4. Paid $3,600 in cash for three months rent in advance on December 1, 2003. The rent covers December, January, and February.
5. Purchased a piece of equipment for $16,000 in cash.

Required: Complete the following table, indicating the impact of each of the above transactions on the indicated ratios. Assume that each transaction is independent. Also assume that the above balance sheet is correct prior to each transaction.

Transaction	Quick Ratio	Current Ratio	Debt/Equity Ratio
1			
2			
3			
4			
5			

INC = Increase
DEC = Decrease
NE = No effect

38. The December 31, 2003, balance sheet of Spartan Corporation is as follows.

    Assets

Current assets	$20,000
Long-lived assets	50,000
Total assets	$70,000

    Liabilities and Stockholders' Equity

Current liabilities	$15,000
Long-term liabilities	30,000
Stockholders' equity	25,000
Total liabilities and stockholders' equity	$70,000

    On March 1, 2004, Spartan borrowed $30,000 from the bank on a long-term note payable. Spartan plans to use the cash to purchase various long-lived assets. The debt covenant specifies that Spartan must maintain a minimum current ratio of 2:1 over the term of the note.

    Required:

    a. How much of the $30,000 can Spartan invest in long-lived assets without violating the debt covenant?

    b. Assume that Spartan invested the maximum amount in the long-lived assets. Also assume that Spartan has made no transactions other than the loan and the investment. What is the new current ratio? What is the new debt/equity ratio?

    c. Assume that Spartan invested the maximum amount in the long-lived assets. Also assume that Spartan has made no transactions other than the loan and the investment and operating transactions, which earned a net income of $56,400, all in cash. How large a dividend can Spartan declare and pay at December 31, 2004, without violating the debt covenant?

39. *Comprehensive Review Problem*

Presented on the following pages is a set of financial statements and some additional information for the Hawkeye Corporation for the years ended December 31, 2003 and 2004. Use this information to complete the following exercises.

1. Prepare common-size balance sheets for 2003 and 2004. Also compute the percentage changes in the common-size numbers of each account from 2003 to 2004.

2. Prepare common size-income statements for 2003 and 2004. Also compute the percentage changes in the common-size numbers of each account from 2003 to 2004.

3. Compute the dollar change in each balance sheet account from 2003 to 2004. Also compute the percentage changes in each account from 2003 to 2004.

4. Compute the dollar change in each income statement account from 2003 to 2004. Also compute the percentage changes in each account from 2003 to 2004.

5. Complete the table of key ratios which follows. Make ratio calculations for the year ended December 31, 2004, unless otherwise indicated.

Hawkeye Corporation
Balance Sheets
December 31, 2004 and 2003

	2004	2003
Assets		
Current assets		
Cash	$ 159	$ 148
Marketable equity securities	8	17
Accounts receivable	632	585
Inventory	970	954
Other current assets	36	50
Total current assets	$1,805	$1,754
Land	500	450
Plant and equipment (net)	981	950
Intangible assets	409	375
Total assets	$3,695	$3,529
Liabilities and stockholders' equity		
Current liabilities		
Accounts payable	$ 28	$ 43
Notes payable	110	158
Other accrued liabilities	43	37
Total current liabilities	$ 181	$ 238
Long-term debt	665	685
Deferred income taxes	242	215
Other long-term liabilities	216	161
Total liabilities	$1,304	$1,299
Stockholders' equity		
Common stock	$ 98	$ 98
Retained earnings	2,293	2,132
Total stockholders' equity	$2,391	$2,230
Total liabilities and stockholders' equity	$3,695	$3,529

Hawkeye Corporation
Income Statements
For the Years Ended December 31, 2004 and 2003

	2004	2003
Net sales	$11,097	$10,613
Cost of sales	5,462	5,227
Selling expenses	2,809	2,735
Administrative expenses	2,328	2,194
Interest expense	71	68
Interest income	(19)	(17)
	$10,651	$10,207
Income before taxes	$ 446	$ 406
Income tax expense	134	125
Net income	$ 312	$ 281

Other Information

1. All financial statement amounts above are in thousands of dollars.

2. Average common shares outstanding (thousands):
    2004: 108   2003: 105

3. Dividends per share:
    2004: $.75   2003: $.70

4. Market prices (per share):
    2004:   High $38   Low $18   Close $35
    2003:   High $35   Low $21   Close $30

YOU MAY WISH TO REMOVE THE INFORMATION PAGES TO FACILITATE COMPLETION OF THE COMPREHENSIVE PROBLEM.

Common-Size Balance Sheets

	2004	2003	Percent Change
Assets			
Cash			
Marketable equity securities			
Accounts receivable			
Inventory			
Other current assets			
Land			
Plant and equipment (net)			
Intangible assets			
Total assets			
Liabilities and Stockholders' Equity			
Accounts payable			
Notes payable			
Other accrued liabilities			
Long-term debt			
Deferred income taxes			
Other long-term liabilities			
Common stock			
Retained earnings			
Total liabilities and stockholders' equity			

Common-Size Income Statements

	2004	2003	Percent Change
Net sales			
Cost of sales			
Selling expenses			
Administrative expenses			
Interest expense			
Interest income			
Income before taxes			
Income tax expense			
Net income			

Comparative Income Statements

	2004	2003	Dollar Change	Percent Change
Net sales				
Cost of sales				
Selling expenses				
Administrative expenses				
Interest expense				
Interest income				
Income before taxes				
Income tax expense				
Net income				

Comparative Balance Sheets

	2004	2003	Dollar Change	Percent Change
Assets				
Cash				
Marketable equity securities				
Accounts receivable				
Inventory				
Other current assets				
Land				
Plant and equipment (net)				
Intangible assets				
Total assets				
Liabilities and Stockholders' Equity				
Accounts payable				
Notes payable				
Other accrued liabilities				
Long-term debt				
Deferred income taxes				
Other long-term liabilities				
Common stock				
Retained earnings				
Total liabilities and stockholders' equity				

Ratio	Formula	Calculations	Answer
Return on Equity			
Return on Assets			
Return on Sales			
Interest Coverage Ratio			
Current Ratio			
Quick Ratio			
Receivables Turnover			
Inventory Turnover			
Financial Leverage			
Debt/Equity Ratio			
Earnings per Share			
Price/Earnings Ratio			
Dividend Yield Ratio			
Return on Investment			

SOLUTIONS - CHAPTER 5

1.	d	10.	c	19.	d	28.	c
2.	c	11.	b	20.	c	29.	c
3.	b	12.	b	21.	a	30.	b
4.	c	13.	d	22.	c	31.	b
5.	a	14.	b	23.	d	32.	b
6.	d	15.	a	24.	d	33.	a
7.	c	16.	d	25.	d	34.	b
8.	a	17.	c	26.	b		
9.	a	18.	b	27.	b		

35.

Buckman Safari Company
Selected Ratios

Ratio	Formula	2003	2002
Quick Ratio	(Cash + Accounts Receivable + Marketable Securities) / Current Liabilities	(70 + 300) / 300 = 1.23 : 1	(20 + 280) / 285 = 1.05 : 1
Current Ratio	Current Assets / Current Liabilities	480 / 300 = 1.60 : 1	365 / 285 = 1.28 : 1
Debt / Equity Ratio	Average Liabilities / Average Stockholders' Equity	400 / 160 = 2.50	285 / 115 = 2.48
Receivables Turnover	Net Credit Sales / Avg. Accounts Receivable	600/ [(300 + 280) / 2] = 2.07 times	560 / [(280 + 290)/2] = 1.96 times
Days Sales in Receivables	365 days / Receivables Turnover	365 / 2.07 = 176 days	365 / 1.96 = 186 days
Inventory Turnover	Cost of Goods Sold / Average Inventory	445 / [(100 + 60) / 2] = 5.56 times	409.4 / [(60 + 70)/2] = 6.30 times
Days Sales in Inventory	365 Days / Inventory Turnover	365 / 5.56 = 66 days	365 / 6.30 = 58 days
Interest Coverage Ratio	Net Income Before Interest and Taxes / Interest Expense	40 / 10 = 4.0 times	N/A
Return on Sales	Net Income + After-tax Interest / Revenues	18 / 600 = .0300 or 3.0%	15.96 / 560 = .0285 or 2.85%
Return on Assets	(Net Income + After-tax Interest) / Average Total Assets	(18 + 10) / [(560 + 400) / 2] = .058	(15.96 + 0) / [(400 + 450) / 2] = .038
Return on Equity	Net Income / Average Stockholders' Equity	18 / [(160 + 115) / 2] = .1309	15.96 / [(115 + 130)/2] = .1303
Common Shares Outstanding	Common Stock Total Par Value / Par Value per Share	$50,000 / $2 per share = 25,000	$50,000 / $2 per share = 25,000
Earnings per Share	Net Income / Avg. Common Shares Outstanding	18/[(25 + 25) / 2] = $.72	15.96/[(25 + 25)/2] = $.64
Gross Profit Percentage	Gross Profit / Revenues	155 / 600 = 25.8%	150.6/560 = 26.9%

36. a. Buckman's operating cycle length is estimated by adding together the days' sales in accounts receivable and days' sales in inventory. The operating cycle is 242 (176 + 66) days in 2003 and 244 (186 + 58) in 2002.

    During 2003, Buckman's customers pay in about six months (176 / 30 days per month), and it takes about two months (66 / 30 days per month) for Buckman to sell its inventory. Clearly, these areas are ripe for improvement. Buckman may adopt a policy of charging interest to customers who do not pay in full after a month to encourage payment. Buckman may need to study operations research to develop a system for inventory management to reduce the Inventory on hand and increase inventory turnover. Both strategies could reduce the operating cycle length so that more cash is available for additional investments in operating assets such as plant or equipment, or to pay liabilities and dividends.

    Of course Buckman must be careful in interpreting these results. Buckman should compare its performance to other firms in its industry. In a competitive industry, Buckman may not be able to change its credit policies.

    b. Analysts assess debt-paying ability using the quick ratio, current ratio, accounts receivable turnover, and inventory turnover for debt due in a short time period. They can also use the debt to equity ratio and times interest earned to assess ability to meet long-term obligations.

    As mentioned in part (a), Buckman's operating cycle length (using information derived from the receivables turnover and inventory turnover ratios) is quite long, which could impede payment of debt. Even though Buckman has sufficient current assets to pay current liabilities, it needs cash to pay those liabilities. If customers are not paying on a timely basis and if inventory is not selling on a timely basis, Buckman may not have enough cash to pay its bills as they come due.

    Creditors claim more of Buckman's total resources according to the debt/ equity ratio, 250%. Buckman is leveraged. Buckman's income is four times as large as interest expense during 2004. Buckman's business is bringing in more resources than it costs to produce and sell those resources, which is a good sign. The net increase in resources is more than adequate to cover interest charges. Buckman must pay interest with cash. Thus, the low receivables turnover ratio may be of concern since Buckman is not converting revenues into cash on a rapid basis.

    c. Earnings per share increased by 12.5% [(.72 - .64)/.64] from 2002 to 2003. The profit margin increased by 5.26%. Buckman's return on investment increased by .5%. Buckman's stockholders' investment was slightly more profitable in 2003 compared to 2002.

    Summary: Aside from cash-generating ability, Buckman seems to be in good shape.

37. If you have difficulty determining the effects of transactions on ratios, you may wish to first record the journal entries (using only the available accounts). If you still have difficulty convincing yourself of the effects, then recompute the ratios, after posting each of the transactions to the balance sheet. The journal entries are as follows.

1. Other Current Assets (+A)   4,000
        Accounts Payable (+L)   4,000
   Purchased inventory on credit.

2. Cash (+A)   11,000
        Stockholders' Equity (R,+SE)   11,000
   Stockholders' Equity (E,-SE)   10,000
        Other Current Assets (-A)   10,000
   Sold inventory on credit at a profit.

3. Stockholders' Equity (E,-SE)   6,000
        Property, Plant, and Equipment (-A)   6,000
   Recognized depreciation.

4. Other Current Assets (+A)   3,600
        Cash (-A)   3,600
   Paid three months rent in advance.

5. Property, Plant, and Equipment (+A)   16,000
        Cash (-A)   16,000
   Purchased equipment.

Transaction	Quick Ratio	Current Ratio	Debt/Equity Ratio
1	DEC	DEC	INC
2	INC	INC	DEC
3	NE	NE	INC
4	DEC	NE	NE
5	DEC	DEC	NE

38. A useful way to approach this problem is to prepare a balance sheet under each of the conditions. It is then relatively simple to make the ratio calculations and determine the required minimums to meet the debt covenant.

	12/31/03	After Borrowing	After Investing	After Net Income
Assets				
Current assets	20,000	50,000	30,000	86,400
Long-lived assets	50,000	50,000	70,000	70,000
Total assets	70,000	100,000	100,000	156,400
Liabilities and Equity				
Current liabilities	15,000	15,000	15,000	15,000
Long-term liabilities	30,000	60,000	60,000	60,000
Stockholders' equity	25,000	25,000	25,000	81,400
Total liabilities and equity	70,000	100,000	100,000	156,400

a. In order to maintain the 2:1 current ratio, look at the After Borrowing column. Spartan could invest a maximum of $20,000. This would change the balance sheet to the results in the After Investing column. This gives a current ratio of 2:1.

b. Use the After Investing column and make the calculations.
    Current Ratio   = Current Assets / Current Liabilities
                    = 30,000 / 15,000
                    = 2.0

    Debt/Equity Ratio = Total Liabilities / Stockholders' Equity
                      = 75,000 / 25,000
                      = 3.0

c. Use the After Net Income column. The maximum dividend to maintain the 2:1 current ratio is $56,400.

39. Comprehensive Review Problem

Hawkeye Corporation
Common-Size Income Statements
For the Years Ended December 31, 2004 and 2003

	2004	2003	Percent Change
Net sales	100.0%	100.0%	0.0%
Cost of sales	(49.2)	(49.3)	(0.1)
Selling expenses	(25.3)	(25.8)	(0.5)
Administrative expenses	(21.0)	(20.7)	0.3
Interest expense	(0.6)	(0.6)	0.0
Interest income	0.2	0.2	0.0
Income before taxes	4.0	3.8	0.2
Income tax expense	1.2	1.2	0.0
Net income	2.9%	2.6%	0.3%

Hawkeye Corporation
Common-Size Balance Sheets
December 31, 2004 and 2003

	2004	2003	Percent Change
Assets			
Cash	4.3%	4.2%	0.1%
Marketable equity securities	.2	.5	(0.3)
Accounts receivable	17.1	16.6	0.5
Inventory	26.3	27.0	(0.7)
Other current assets	1.0	1.4	(0.4)
Land	13.5	12.8	0.7
Plant and equipment (net)	26.5	26.9	(0.4)
Intangible assets	11.1	10.6	0.5
Total assets	100.0%	100.0%	0.0%
Liabilities and Stockholders' Equity			
Accounts payable	0.8%	1.2%	(0.4)%
Notes payable	3.0	4.5	(1.5)
Other accrued liabilities	1.2	1.0	0.2
Long-term debt	18.0	19.4	(1.4)
Deferred income taxes	6.5	6.1	0.4
Other long-term liabilities	5.8	4.6	1.2
Common stock	2.7	2.8	(0.1)
Retained earnings	62.1	60.4	1.7
Total liabilities and stockholders' equity	100.0%	100.0%	0.0%

Hawkeye Corporation
Comparative Balance Sheets
December 31, 2004 and 2003

	2004	2003	Dollar Change	Percent Change
Assets				
Cash	$ 159	$ 148	$ 11	7.4%
Marketable equity securities	8	17	(9)	(52.9)
Accounts receivable	632	585	47	8.0
Inventory	970	954	16	1.7
Other current assets	36	50	(14)	(28.0)
Land	500	450	50	11.1
Plant and equipment (net)	981	950	31	3.3
Intangible assets	409	375	34	9.1
Total assets	$3,695	$3,529	$166	4.7%
Liabilities and Stockholders' Equity				
Accounts payable	$ 28	$ 43	$(15)	(34.9)%
Notes payable	110	158	(48)	(30.4)
Other accrued liabilities	43	37	6	16.2
Long-term debt	665	685	(20)	(2.9)
Deferred income taxes	242	215	27	12.6
Other long-term liabilities	216	161	55	34.2
Common stock	98	98	0	0.0
Retained earnings	2,293	2,132	161	7.6
Total liabilities and stockholders' equity	$3,695	$3,529	$166	4.7%

Hawkeye Corporation
Comparative Income Statements
For the Years Ended December 31,

	2004	2003	Dollar Change	Percent Change
Net sales	$11,097	$10,613	$484	4.6%
Cost of sales	5,462	5,227	235	4.5
Selling expenses	2,809	2,735	74	2.7
Administrative expenses	2,328	2,194	134	6.1
Interest expense	71	68	3	4.4
Interest income	(19)	(17)	(2)	(11.8)
Income before taxes	$ 446	$ 406	$ 40	9.9
Income tax expense	134	125	9	7.2
Net income	$ 312	$ 281	$ 31	11.0%

Chapter 5

Ratio	Formula	Calculations	Answer
Return on Equity	Net Income / Average Stockholders' Equity	312 / [(2,391 + 2,230) / 2]	.135 or 13.5%
Return on Assets	(Net Income + Interest Expense) / Average Total Assets	(312 + 71) /[(3,695 + 3,529) / 2]	.106 or 10.6%
Return on Sales	Net Income / Net Sales	312 / 11,097	.028 or 2.8%
Interest Coverage Ratio	Net Income Before Interest & Taxes / Interest Expense	446 + 71 / 71	7.282 times
Current Ratio	Current Assets / Current Liabilities	1,805 / 181	9.972 : 1
Quick Ratio	(Cash + Accounts Receivable + Marketable Securities) / Current Liabilities	(159 + * + 632) / 181	4.414 : 1
Receivables Turnover	Net Credit Sales / Average Accounts Receivable	11,097 / [(632 + 585) / 2]	18.237 times
Inventory Turnover	Cost of Goods Sold / Average Inventory	5,462 / [(970 + 954) / 2]	5.678 times
Financial Leverage	Return on Equity - Return on Assets	.135 - .106	.029 or 2.9%
Debt / Equity	Total Liabilities / Total Stockholders' Equity	1,304 / 2,391	.545 or 54.5%
Earnings per Share	Net Income / Average Number of Common Shares Outstanding	312 / 108	$ 2.89
Price / Earnings	Average Market Price per Share / Earnings per Share	[(38 + 18) / 2] / 2.89	9.689 times
Dividend Yield	Dividends per Share / Average Market Price per Share	.75 / [(38 + 18) / 2]	.027 or 2.7%
Annual Return on Investment	(Ending Market Price - Beginning Market Price + Dividends) / Beginning Market Price	(35 - 30 + .75) / 30	.192 or 19.2%

Notes on Table of Key Ratios and Solutions

1. All answers in the ratio table are in decimal form, not in percentages.

2. Some ratios require an average amount. For example, return on assets uses average total assets as the denominator. These averages are calculated by adding the beginning and end-of-year balances and then dividing by two. The only exception to this rule is for average shares outstanding, which is simply given in the additional information.

3. Percentages may not total to 100% in the comparative and common-size financial statements due to slight rounding differences.

4. You can compute common-size balance sheet amounts by dividing each individual balance sheet account balance by total assets. For example, the 2004 common-size amount for accounts receivable divides December 31, 2004, accounts receivable by total assets. Multiply by 100 to convert to a percentage.

$$[(\$632 / \$3,695) \times 100 = 17.1 \%]$$

5. You can common-size income statement amounts by dividing each individual income statement account balance by net sales. For example, the 2004 common-size amount for Cost of Sales divides 2004 Cost of Sales by net sales. Multiply by 100 to convert to a percentage.

$$[(\$5,462 / \$11,097) \times 100 = 49.2 \%]$$

6. The "percent changes" in the common size balance sheet and income statement are simply the 2004 percentages less the 2003 percentages.

7. The "dollar changes" in the comparative financial statements are the 2004 balances less the 2003 amounts for each account. The "percentage changes" are the "dollar changes" divided by the 2003 balances. Multiply by 100 to convert to a percentage. Refer to net sales in the comparative income statement as an example. Calculate the dollar change as:

$$[\$11,097 - \$10,613 = \$484]$$

Calculate the percentage change as:

$$[(\$484 / \$10,613) \times 100 = 4.6 \%]$$

CHAPTER 6

The Current Asset Classification, Cash, and Accounts Receivable

REVIEW OF KEY CONCEPTS

The Basics of Accounting for an Asset

The next several chapters provide a more detailed study of accounting for various types of assets. There are three accounting questions you should consider in accounting for all assets.

1. How should you record an asset at acquisition?
2. How should you account for the asset and any related revenue or expense during the period the asset is held (the holding period)?
3. How should you account for an asset at disposition?

You can answer questions 1 and 3 with very general rules. Looking first at **acquisitions**, accounting originally record all assets at their **historical cost**. The historical cost of an asset includes the initial purchase price plus any additional costs required to bring the asset to the location and condition for its intended use in the business.

A general rule can also be applied to asset **dispositions**. When disposing of an asset, compare the selling price to the **book value** (or carrying value) of the asset. Record the difference between selling price and book value as a gain or loss on disposition of the asset. The book value is the asset's historical cost. For some assets, accountants may consider this cost from time to time during the holding period. We will consider these cases in the discussion of individual assets over the next few chapters.

The rules for asset accounting during the **holding period** vary across different types of assets. We will discuss holding period accounting for individual assets. Included in holding period accounting is the issue of how to report assets are (classify assets) in the company's financial statements.

The Current Asset Classification

Current assets are those assets which are intended to be converted into cash within one year, or a company's **operating cycle**, whichever is longer. The current asset classification includes cash, short-term notes and accounts receivable, inventory, short-term investments in marketable securities, and prepaid expenses. A company's operating cycle is the normal time taken to complete a cycling of cash. Cash originally received from investors is used to purchase Inventory, which is then sold to customers, and cash is eventually collected from the customers. This chapter discusses accounting for cash and receivables; we discuss problems unique to accounting for inventories and marketable securities in later chapters.

Current assets provide a measure of the company's short-term **solvency** (liquidity). Since these assets are intended to be converted to cash, they indicate the availability of cash to meet short-term obligations and liabilities as these become due.

Cash

Cash is the most liquid of all assets. Liquidity is a measure of how quickly an asset can be converted into cash. Due to its liquidity, cash requires considerable safeguarding and control.

Adequate amounts of cash on hand are essential to permit companies to pay obligations as they become due.

Accounts Receivable

Accounts Receivable arise from credit sales to customers. In the normal course of business, customers will settle the accounts in cash. Accounts receivable represent an asset, because the company will derive a future benefit from the receipt of cash. Typical journal entries to record credit sales and subsequent collections are as follows:

Accounts Receivable (+A)	385	
Sales (R,+SE)		385

Recognize a credit sale.

Cash (+A)	385	
Accounts Receivable (-A)		385

Collected cash on account.

Uncollectible Accounts Receivable

Unfortunately, not all customers pay their accounts. If some customers fail to pay, then the asset balance for Accounts Receivable will be overstated (a portion of the future benefit will not be realized). A company cannot determine in advance which customers will fail to pay. (If they could, they would never have sold to these customers on a credit basis!) The cost of **uncollectible accounts receivable** is a **selling expense**. It arises from the decision to sell on credit. Selling on credit is a tool to generate additional sales. A proper matching of expenses (Uncollectible Accounts Expense) with the related revenue generated (Sales) is required under accrual accounting. The Uncollectible Accounts Expense should be recorded in the same period that the related revenue appears. We accomplish this through the use of the **allowance method**, and an adjusting entry.

Allowance for Uncollectible Accounts

Under the allowance method, a company estimates the amount of uncollectible accounts and makes an adjusting entry to ensure the proper matching of expenses with revenues. At a later date, when it is finally realized that the customer is unable to pay, the account receivable balance will be written off. Accounting facilitates this approach by setting up the **Allowance for Uncollectible Accounts**) which is a contra asset account. This account is also known as the Allowance for Doubtful Accounts or the Allowance for Bad Debts. Assume that on December 31, 2003, a company estimates that $500 of outstanding Accounts Receivable will become uncollectible, and on March 18, 2004, John Jones' account in the amount of $115 is written off. The basic entries are as follows:

12/31/03	Uncollectible Accounts Expense (E,-SE)	500	
	Allowance for Uncollectible Accounts (-A)		500

Estimated uncollectible accounts.

3/18/04	Allowance for Uncollectible Accounts (+A)	115	
	Accounts Receivable (-A)		115

Wrote off John Jones' account as uncollectible.

The Allowance for Uncollectible Accounts appears as a deduction from Accounts Receivable on the balance sheet. After deducting the allowance, the net amount of Accounts Receivable is the amount expected to be received in the future, or the **net realizable value**. Note that the adjusting entry matches the estimated expense from uncollectible accounts with the related revenues recognized in the year the sale was made. The actual write-off of an account in a subsequent year does not change the total net realizable value of accounts receivable. Further, the entry to write off an account does not affect net income in the year the account becomes uncollectible. The expense was estimated and recorded in the year of the sale.

Recoveries of Accounts Previously Written Off

In some cases a customer repays an account at a later date, after the account has been written off. Accountants record these recoveries by essentially reversing the entry from the write-off date. For example, suppose that John Jones has recovered from his financial difficulties and wishes to pay the balance of his account on February 1, 2005. You would record the collection as follows:

2/1/05	Accounts Receivable (+A)	115	
	Allowance for Uncollectible Accounts (-A)		115
	Reinstated John Jones' account.		
	Cash (+A)	115	
	Accounts Receivable (-A)		115
	Received cash on reinstated account.		

Estimating Uncollectible Accounts Receivable

A company estimates uncollectible accounts based on past experience, either with its own customers or from a more general information source. For example, a company may choose to look at collection experiences of other companies in the same industry. Accountants use two basic approaches to make the estimate and the resultant adjusting entries.

The first estimate is made based on a **percentage of credit sales** made during the period. Note that Credit Sales is an **income statement** account. The amount estimated under this approach is the correct balance for another income statement account, Uncollectible Accounts Expense. Assume that a retail appliance company has recorded $500,000 in Credit Sales during 2003. Based on the industry average over the past five years, appliance retailers typically experience losses of 1 percent on total credit sales. The company estimates its Uncollectible Accounts Expense as $5,000 (1% x $500,000), ignoring any existing balance in the Allowance for Uncollectible Accounts. The adjusting entry to record the estimated uncollectibles is simply:

Uncollectible Accounts Expense (E,-SE)	5,000	
Allowance for Uncollectible Accounts (-A)		5,000

An alternative method is to make the estimate based on the outstanding balance of **Accounts Receivable**. Note that Accounts Receivable is a **balance sheet** account. The amount estimated under this approach is the correct balance for another balance sheet account, Allowance for Uncollectible Accounts. Assume that our retail appliance company has recorded $500,000 in Credit Sales during 2003. Of this amount, $24,000 in Accounts Receivable have not yet been collected on December 31. The company's Allowance for Uncollectible Accounts has a credit balance of $150 on December 31. Based on the industry average over the past five years, appliance retailers typically experience losses of 5 percent on outstanding Accounts Receivable. The company would estimate its required Allowance for Uncollectible Accounts as $1,200 (5% x $24,000). The company must consider any existing balance in the Allowance for Uncollectible Accounts under this method. The adjusting entry to record the estimated uncollectibles in this example is:

Uncollectible Accounts Expense (E,-SE)	1,050	
Allowance for Uncollectible Accounts (-A)		1,050

There is a variation of the balance sheet approach known as an **aging of accounts receivable**. Aging takes into account that a better estimate can be made by looking at how long an account has been outstanding, not just the total accounts receivable outstanding. For example, if we sold to one customer on December 30, but payment is not due until January 30, we would not be concerned that the balance had not been paid on December 31. We would be much more uncertain about collecting from a customer whose balance was six months past due on December 31. The aging approach takes this uncertainty into account by assigning different percentages, depending on the length of time that an account is overdue. Once again, the percentages used in making the estimate would be based on past experience. The aging approach is likely to provide a more accurate estimate than the other approaches described above. Assume that our appliance retailer provides a more detailed breakdown of the $24,000 in outstanding accounts receivable at December 31, as follows:

Age	Receivable Amount	Percent Uncollectible	Estimated Uncollectible
Current	$14,000	1%	$ 140
1-30 days past due	4,000	5%	200
31-60 days past due	2,000	10%	200
61-90 days past due	2,500	20%	500
Over 90 days past due	1,500	50%	750
Totals	$24,000		$1,790

Recall that the allowance has a credit balance of $150 prior to adjustment. The required adjusting entry based on the aging of accounts receivable is:

Uncollectible Accounts Expense (E,-SE)	1,640	
Allowance for Uncollectible Accounts (-A)		1,640

QUESTIONS FOR YOUR REVIEW

1. Companies often offer their customers a purchase discount. Under what circumstances should the customer take advantage of the discount?
    a. When their borrowing rate exceeds the annual rate provided by the discount.
    b. When their borrowing rate is less than the annual rate provided by the discount.
    c. Whenever they can pay in cash without borrowing.
    d. Purchase discounts should never be taken.

2. Robin's Pet Shelter, Inc. purchased feed and supplies from Karl's Kat Foods on June 15, 2003. The total cost was $2,400 and Karl offered terms of 2/10, n/30. If Robin uses the gross method to record purchases, and pays on July 14, what is the correct journal entry?

    a. | Accounts Payable (-L) | 2,400 | |
        |---|---|---|
        | Cash (-A) | | 2,400 |

    b. | Accounts Payable (-L) | 2,352 | |
        |---|---|---|
        | Cash (-A) | | 2,352 |

    c. | Accounts Payable (-L) | 2,400 | |
        |---|---|---|
        | Purchase Discounts Lost (E,-SE) | 48 | |
        | Cash (-A) | | 2,352 |

    d. | Accounts Payable (-L) | 2,400 | |
        |---|---|---|
        | Purchase Discounts (R,+SE) | | 48 |
        | Cash (-A) | | 2,352 |

3. Karl's Kat Foods sold $1,300 of supplies to Robin's Pet Shelter on October 11, under Karl's normal terms of 2/10, n/30. Karl received Robin's payment on October 20. The correct entry for Karl to record this receipt, under the gross method, is:

    a. Cash (+A)   1,300
            Accounts Receivable (-A)   1,300

    b. Cash (+A)   1,300
            Accounts Receivable (-A)   1,274
            Sales Discounts (R,+SE)   26

    c. Cash (+A)   1,274
            Accounts Receivable (-A)   1,274

    d. Cash (+A)   1,274
        Sales Discounts (-R,-SE)   26
            Accounts Receivable (-A)   1,300

4. Which of the following items would be excluded in calculating a company's quick ratio?
    a. Cash
    b. Marketable securities
    c. Accounts payable
    d. Inventory

5. Which of the following items would be excluded in calculating a company's current ratio?
    a. Cash
    b. Marketable securities
    c. Land
    d. Inventory

6. Choose the best definition of a company's operating cycle from the following list.
    a. The twelve-month period that a firm uses as its fiscal year
    b. The average time required to sell a firm's inventory
    c. The average time required to collect accounts receivable from a firm's customers
    d. Total time between date inventory is originally purchased and date cash is eventually collected from customers

7. Short-term accounts receivable from customers should be included on a company's balance sheet based on:
    a. the total price of credit sales.
    b. net realizable value.
    c. present value of the expected future cash flows.
    d. present value of the expected future cash flows, adjusted for expected inflation up to the maturity date of the receivables.

8. Larry's Lawn Service accepted a $6,000 note receivable from a customer on June 1. The note includes interest at 6% annually, and matures on September 30. How much interest revenue will Larry earn on this note?
    a. $120
    b. $180
    c. $360
    d. $540

9. Which of the following should be excluded in determining a company's working capital?
   a. Accounts payable
   b. Accounts receivable
   c. Allowance for doubtful accounts
   d. Prepaid premiums on a three-year insurance policy

10. Which of these is most useful in measuring a company's short-term liquidity?
   a. Current ratio and quick ratio
   b. Current ratio and return on total assets
   c. Current ratio and dividend payout ratio
   d. Quick ratio and dividend payout ratio

11. Venus Candy Company reported Accounts Receivable balances of $130,000 and $115,500 on January 1 and December 31, 2003, respectively. Credit sales in 2003 totaled $658,000. What is the average collection period for accounts receivable?
   a. 72 days
   b. 64 days
   c. 57 days
   d. 68 days

12. John's Deli uses the allowance method to account for uncollectible accounts. Which of the following describes the impact of writing off a customer's account under this approach?
   a. The carrying value of accounts receivable will increase during the year in which the account is written off.
   b. The carrying value of accounts receivable will decrease during the year in which the account is written off.
   c. The carrying value of accounts receivable is unaffected during the year in which the account is written off.
   d. John's net income will decrease during the year in which the account is written off.

13. Which of the following statements describes the reason for the preference for the allowance methods over the direct write-off method?
   a. The allowance method results in the lowest cost.
   b. This method provides the best matching of Uncollectible Accounts Expense and Credit Sales Revenue.
   c. The allowance method is easier to use.
   d. The allowance method has been shown to minimize the number of accounts which must be written off.

14. University Advertising Company reports a credit balance of $21,000 in the Allowance for Doubtful Accounts on January 1, 2003. Based on prior experience, University estimates that 2% of receivables eventually become uncollectible. During 2003, customer accounts totaling $14,500 were written off. The balance in Accounts Receivable was $683,000 on December 31, 2003. What is University' Uncollectible Accounts Expense for 2003?
   a. $14,500
   b. $13,660
   c. $ 7,160
   d. $ 6,500

15. Which of the following methods produces the most reliable estimate for an Allowance for Doubtful Accounts?
   a. Percentage of cash sales
   b. Percentage of credit sales
   c. Percentage of outstanding accounts receivable
   d. Aging of accounts receivable

16. Pete's Pottery uses an aging method to estimate uncollectible accounts. Pete assembled the following information as of December 31, 2003.

Age of Accounts	Percent Balance	Collectible
Current	$400,000	97
1-30 days overdue	150,000	92
31-60 days overdue	100,000	90
61-90 days overdue	50,000	80
Over 90 days overdue	30,000	75

On January 1, Pete's books indicated a debit balance of $625,000 in Accounts Receivable and a credit balance of $22,000 in the Allowance for Doubtful Accounts. During the year, Pete wrote off customer accounts totalling $1,650 as uncollectible.

Required:

a. Calculate the total Accounts Receivable balance on December 31, 2003.

b. Prepare the entry to record Uncollectible Accounts Expense for 2003.

c. What is the correct balance in the Allowance for Doubtful Accounts on December 31, 2003?

17. John's Original Vermont Maple Syrup Company purchased 200,000 gallons of "raw materials" from a Canadian supplier on November 1, 2003. John agreed to pay the supplier in equal amounts over the coming three months, with payments due on December 1, January 1, and February 1. John is not required to pay any interest charges. The total payments under the

contract amount to 450,000 Canadian dollars. Exchange rates are provided below. John's fiscal year ends on December 31.

Date	**U.S. Dollars per Canadian Dollar**
11/1	$.85
12/1	.80
12/31	.84
1/1	.84
2/1	.82

Required: Prepare all journal entries on John's books related to the purchase and eventual cash payment.

18. Doug's Appliance Company reports a balance in Accounts Receivable of $56,350 on January 1, 2003. The Allowance for Uncollectible Accounts has a credit balance of $1,165 on the same date. Prepare summary journal entries to reflect the following activities during 2003.

    a. Accounts receivable from customers in the amount of $2,050 were written off during the year.

    b. Sales in 2003 totaled $361,500, of which $350,000 was on credit.

    c. A customer account in the amount of $700, which had been written off during 2001, was finally collected.

18. d.   Collections on accounts receivable, in addition to the above $700, totaled $326,500.

    e.   Based on an aging of accounts receivable on December 31, Doug estimates that $2,610 of customer accounts will be written off in future periods.

19. Spartan Electric Products enters into the following transactions during the year ended December 31, 2003. Prepare all required journal entries and adjusting journal entries related to these transactions. Spartan does not recognize any discounts on its note transactions.

    a.   On March 15, Spartan sold merchandise for $75,000, accepting a two-year, 10% note from the customer.

    b.   On July 31, Spartan accepted a $10,000, six-month note from a customer on an open account receivable. The stated interest rate was 12%.

    c.   On August 15, Spartan accepted a one-year, $12,000 note from a customer on an open account receivable. The stated interest rate was 12%.

19. d. On November 30, Spartan sold merchandise for $60,000, accepting a one-year, 10% note
        from the customer.

    e. On December 15, the customer paid the balance due on the note signed on August 15.

    f. Prepare any required adjusting entries on December 31.

CHAPTER 6 - SOLUTIONS

1.	b	5.	c	9.	d	13.	b
2.	a	6.	d	10.	a	14.	c
3.	d	7.	b	11.	d	15.	d
4.	d	8.	a	12.	c		

16. a.

Gordon's Pottery
Accounts Receivable Aging Schedule

Accounts Receivable	Percent Uncollectible	Uncollectible Amount
$400,000	.03	$12,000
150,000	.08	12,000
100,000	.10	10,000
50,000	.20	10,000
30,000	.25	7,500
$730,000		$51,500

b. Uncollectible Accounts Expense (E,-SE)   31,150
       Allowance for Doubtful Accounts (-A)   31,150

16.   c.   Correct balance is a credit of $51,500.

17. Nov. 1   Purchases (E,-SE)(or Inventory)   382,500
               Accounts Payable (+L)   382,500

    Dec. 1   Accounts Payable (-L)   120,000
               Cash (-A)   120,000

    Dec. 31   Accounts Payable (-L)   10,500
               Exchange Gain (Ga,+SE)   10,500

    Jan. 1   Accounts Payable (-L)   126,000
               Cash (-A)   126,000

    Feb. 1   Accounts Payable (-L)   126,000
               Cash (-A)   123,000
               Exchange Gain (Ga,+SE)   3,000

18. a.   Allowance for Doubtful Accounts (+A)   2,050
               Accounts Receivable (-A)   2,050

    b.   Accounts Receivable (+A)   350,000
          Cash (+A)   11,500
               Sales Revenue (R,+SE)   361,500

    c.   Accounts Receivable (+A)   700
               Allowance for Doubtful Accounts (-A)   700

         Cash (+A)   700
               Accounts Receivable (-A)   700

    d.   Cash (+A)   326,500
               Accounts Receivable (-A)   326,500

    e.   Uncollectible Accounts Expense (E,-SE)   2,795
               Allowance for Doubtful Accounts (-A)   2,795

The December 31 balance in the Allowance is a *debit* balance of $185. The initial balance was a credit of $1,165. Entries made to the Allowance account to reflect transactions during the year included (a) a debit of $2,050, and (c) a credit of $700. A credit of $2,795 is required to bring the Allowance account to its desired ending credit balance of $2,610.

19. a.   Notes Receivable (+A)   75,000
               Sales (R,+SE)   75,000

    b.   Notes Receivable (+A)   10,000
               Accounts Receivable (-A)   10,000

    c.   Notes Receivable (+A)   12,000
               Accounts Receivable (-A)   12,000

    d.   Notes Receivable (+A)   60,000
               Sales (R,+SE)   60,000

19. e.   Cash (+A)   12,480
                   Notes Receivable (-A)   12,000
                   Interest Revenue (R,+SE)   480

     f.   Interest Receivable (+A)   6,937.50
                   Interest Revenue (R,+SE)   6,937.50

Adjusting entry for interest earned, but not yet received on December 31, 2003.

Calculation:

$75,000 X 10% X 9.5/12 =	$ 5,937.50
$10,000 X 12% X 5/12 =	500.00
$60,000 X 10% X 1/12 =	500.00
	$ 6,937.50

CHAPTER 7

Inventory

REVIEW OF KEY CONCEPTS

Inventory is an important asset for manufacturers, wholesalers, and retailers since its what they eventually sell, generating revenues. The focus here is inventory accounting by retailers and wholesalers. You will cover specific issues related to inventory accounting by manufacturers in management accounting courses.

Inventory accounting affects the balance sheet, income statement and statement of cash flows. Inventory is initially recorded as an asset when purchased (it is **capitalized**). Later on, when benefits are provided to the company through sales, a portion of the inventory becomes an expense, **Cost of Goods Sold**. Eventually, inventory sales and purchases are settled in cash which is reflected on a company's statement of cash flows.

Like any other asset, the company must account for acquisitions, holding period activity, and disposal of inventory. Unique to inventory, a company decides to adopt either a **periodic** or a **perpetual** inventory system. Most companies also choose a **cost flow assumption**. Finally, if the value of inventory declines significantly (below its historical cost) over time, the asset balance will be overstated. This potential problem is handled by making a **lower of cost or market** adjustment if needed.

Recording Inventory Acquisitions

The cost to record any asset is the acquisition price plus all costs incurred to bring the asset to the location and condition for its intended use. In the case of inventory, the recorded cost of the asset normally includes the purchase price, plus any shipping charges (**transportation-in**), less any **cash discounts** offered by the supplier.

Recording Inventory Sales and Dispositions

The asset Inventory provides **future benefits** to the company in the form of **sales revenues** when the inventory is sold to customers. Proper **matching** requires that we associate an expense (**Cost of Goods Sold**) with the earned revenue. The expense is the cost of the item sold.

Matching can be easily understood conceptually by using the **specific identification method**. Under this method, the company keeps track of all individual items in inventory and their historical cost. The cost of goods sold is the historical cost of each item actually sold. As a practical matter, this method is cumbersome (and costly) when there are large numbers of inventory items being sold. This method is used only when individual inventory items have large dollar values and can be easily identified (e.g., by a serial number stamped on the item).

To alleviate record keeping problems (and costs), most companies adopt a cost flow assumption. The cost flow assumption is a simplification. Actual physical flow of goods need not (and generally does not) match the cost flow assumption adopted. The three cost flow assumptions are: (1) first in, first out (**FIFO**), (2) last in, first out (**LIFO**), and (3) **average cost**.

A Comprehensive Example. The following example, while a very simple one, highlights the financial statement impact of the choice of an inventory method (i.e., periodic versus perpetual) and a cost flow assumption (i.e., FIFO, LIFO, average cost). The choices impact the balance sheet in the valuation of the reported amount for the ending Inventory. The reported net income is affected because the choices may produce different amounts for Cost of Goods Sold. Remember that total inventory-related costs will be the same under all choices. The choices determine how cost is allocated between the balance sheet (ending inventory) and the income statement (cost of goods sold).

The following information is available for the month of June:

Date	Transaction	Units	Unit Cost	Total Cost
6/ 1	Beginning inventory	20	$10	$200
6/10	Purchase	10	16	160
6/20	Sale	9		

Periodic Inventory System

Assume that the company adopts a periodic inventory system. The following calculations illustrate the computation of ending inventory and cost of goods sold under the various cost flow assumptions. Consider the physical flow of units during June. There were a total of 30 units which could have been sold (goods available for sale), having a total cost of $360. Nine units were sold and twenty-one remain in the ending inventory. The objective is to allocate the total cost between an asset which will benefit future periods (ending inventory) and an expense of the current period (cost of goods sold).

First-In, First-Out - FIFO. Under this assumption, the units sold were those purchased FIRST, costing $10 each. Total Cost of Goods Sold is, therefore, $90. The remaining units in ending Inventory include 11 units costing $10 each and 10 units costing $16 each, for a total of $270.

Last-In, First-Out - LIFO. Under this assumption, the units sold were those purchased LAST, costing $16 each. Total cost of goods sold is, therefore, $144. The remaining units in ending inventory include 20 units costing $10 each and 1 unit costing $16, for a total of $216.

Average Cost. Under this assumption, all units have the same cost, i.e., the average cost [$360 / 30 units]. The units sold cost $12 each. Total cost of goods sold is, therefore, $108. The remaining units in ending inventory include 21 units costing $12 each, for a total of $252.

Specific Identification. Recall that specific identification is not a cost flow assumption. Under this method, cost allocation must match the actual physical flow of goods. We include this method here for completeness. Under specific identification, there are any number of possible combinations. For example, the company may have sold seven of the units from beginning inventory and two of the units from the June 10 purchase. This would produce a cost of goods sold of $102 [7 units @ $10 plus 2 units @ $16] and an ending inventory valuation of $258 [13 units @ $10 plus 8 units @ $16]. Alternatively, the company might have sold five of the units from beginning inventory and four of the units from the June 10 purchase. This would produce a cost of goods sold of $114 [5 units @ $10 plus 4 units @ $16] and an ending inventory of $246 [15 units @ $10 plus 6 units @ $16].

Perpetual Inventory System

Assume that the company adopts a perpetual inventory system instead of periodic. The physical flow of units in and out of the company during June is unaffected. There are still a total of 30 units which could have been sold, having a total cost of $360. Nine units are sold, and twenty-one remain in the ending inventory. You'll notice that all of the purchases occur before any sales, this problem's unique timing of purchases and sales will result in the same values for Cost of Goods Sold and Ending Inventory under LIFO and Average Cost methods using perpetual and periodic methods.

First-In, First-Out - FIFO. Under this assumption, the units sold were those purchased FIRST, costing $10 each. Total cost of goods sold is, therefore, $90. The remaining units in ending inventory include 11 units costing $10 each and 10 units costing $16 each, for a total of $270. These amounts are identical to those calculated under the periodic system. This will always be the case with the FIFO cost flow assumption.

Last-In, First-Out - LIFO. Under this assumption, the units sold are those purchased LAST, costing $16 each. Total cost of goods sold is, therefore, $144. The remaining units in ending inventory include 20 units costing $10 each and 1 unit costing $16, for a total of $216. Once again, these amounts are identical to those calculated under the periodic system. This will NOT always be the case with the LIFO cost flow assumption. These calculations depend on the timing of purchases and sales within the accounting period.

Average Cost. Under this assumption, all units on hand at the time of the sale will have the same unit cost, i.e., the average cost [$360 / 30 units]. The units sold cost $12 each. Total cost of goods sold is, therefore, $108. The remaining units in ending inventory include 21 units costing $12 each, for a total of $252. Once again, these amounts are identical to those calculated under the periodic system. This will NOT always be the case with the average cost flow assumption. These calculations are also dependent on the timing of purchases and sales within the accounting period.

The Impact of the Timing of Purchases and Sales within the Period

As noted above, the timing of purchases and sales within the period has an affect on the calculation of the dollar amount of ending inventory and cost of goods sold. Let's modify the original example, and assume that two sales occurred totaling 9 units.

Date	Transaction	Units	Unit Cost	Total Cost
6/ 1	Beginning inventory	20	$10	$200
6/10	Sale	4		
6/20	Purchase	10	16	160
6/23	Sale	5		

LIFO Perpetual Inventory System

Under this assumption, the units sold were those purchased LAST as of the date of the sale. For the June 10th sale, 4 units were sold and cost $10 each. For the June 25th sale, 5 units were sold and cost $16 each. Total cost of goods sold is, therefore, $40 + $80 or $120. The remaining units in ending inventory include 16 units costing $10 each and 5 units costing $16 each, for a total of $240. The changing the timing of purchases and sales has changed the amounts for ending inventory and cost of goods sold.

Moving Weighted (Perpetual) Average Cost

Under this assumption, all units have the same cost, i.e., the average cost. When the sale takes place on June 10, the only units available for sale are those from the beginning inventory. The units sold cost $10 each [$200 / 20 units]. The June 10th cost of goods sold is $40. The average cost of the inventory on hand just before the June 25th sale is $12.31[16 units @ $10 and 10 units @ $16]. Cost of goods sold for the June 25th sale is $61.55. Total cost of goods sold is $101.55. The remaining units in ending inventory include 21 units costing an average of $12.31 each for a total of $258.45. Different timing of purchases and sales has changed the amounts for ending inventory and cost of goods sold.

As noted above, the calculations under the periodic system will not be affected by the timing of transactions within the accounting period. This is also true of the perpetual system / FIFO combination. You may wish to check these.

Accounting for Inventory During the Holding Period

The Lower-of-Cost-or-Market Adjustment

Over time, the value of the inventory may decline due to physical obsolescence, changing technology, or changing styles and tastes of customers. Recall that inventory is carried on the balance sheet at its historical cost. Should the market value of the inventory decline below its cost, then the asset balance will be overstated and requires an adjustment. The adjusting entry is an easy one:

Loss on Inventory Write-Down (Lo,-SE)	xxx	
Inventory (-A)		xxx

There are four basic steps to determine the amount of the adjustment, if any: (1) determine the cost of the ending Inventory, by applying the company's chosen cost flow assumption, (2) determine the market value of the ending inventory, (3) compare the cost and market values and (4) adjust *only* if market is *less* than cost. When market is greater than cost, no adjustment is required.

QUESTIONS FOR YOUR REVIEW

1. Which of the following items would be excluded in determining Spectra Company's December 31 ending inventory?
    a. Goods in transit sold FOB destination that have been shipped, but not yet received by the customer.
    b. Goods in transit purchased FOB shipping point that were shipped by the supplier on December 28, but not yet received by Spectra.
    c. Goods that Spectra holds for sale on consignment, received from Goudeaux Corporation.
    d. Goods that Goudeaux Corporation sells on consignment for Spectra that remain unsold at December 31.

2. Which costs should not be included in determination of ending inventory?
    a. Transportation-in
    b. Transportation out
    c. Import duties paid on purchased goods
    d. Wages paid to workers in the receiving department

3. Which of the following is not a benefit of a perpetual inventory costing system?
    a. Provides more timely and useful information for management
    b. Provides more timely and useful information for financial statement users
    c. Provides greater control over inventory ordering and storage costs
    d. Provides reduced bookkeeping costs

4. Identify the type of firm for which specific identification would be an appropriate inventory method.
    a. Hardware store
    b. Retail grocery
    c. Fine arts gallery
    d. Paper manufacturer

5. Which inventory cost flow assumption reports the most current inventory values on a company's balance sheet?
    a. FIFO
    b. LIFO
    c. Weighted average cost
    d. Moving average cost

6. Which inventory cost flow assumption reports the most current inventory values in cost of goods sold on a company's income statement?
    a. FIFO
    b. LIFO
    c. Weighted average cost
    d. Moving average cost

7. Which inventory cost flow assumption best approximates current replacement cost for the ending inventory?
   a. FIFO
   b. LIFO
   c. Weighted average cost
   d. Moving average cost

8. Handy Andy uses a periodic inventory system. What is the financial statement impact of an understatement of ending inventory in the current year?
   a. Current year's net income will be overstated.
   b. Next year's net income will overstated.
   c. Next year's ending inventory will be understated.
   d. Next year's ending inventory will be overstated.

9. Choose the true statement about calculation of net purchases from the following list.
   a. Gross purchases less returns and allowances less purchase discounts
   b. Gross purchases plus returns and allowances plus purchase discounts
   c. Gross purchases plus returns and allowances less purchase discounts
   d. Gross purchases less returns and allowances less purchase discounts plus transporation-in

10. Jay's Hardware recorded net purchases of $12,000 during June. Jay's beginning inventory was $9,000, which was $1,000 higher than the ending inventory. Jay's cost of goods sold for June was:
    a. $21,000
    b. $20,000
    c. $13,000
    d. $ 3,000

    Answer questions 11 through 16 using the following information.

Date	Transaction	Units	Unit Cost	Total
7/ 1	Beg. inv.	400	$ 12	$ 4,800
7/ 6	Purchase	600	13	7,800
7/10	Sale	500	?	?
7/14	Purchase	200	14	2,800
7/16	Sale	500	?	?
7/21	Purchase	200	14	2,800
7/26	Purchase	400	15	6,000
7/28	Sale	400	?	?

11. Assume that the company uses a periodic inventory system and a FIFO cost flow assumption. What is the cost of goods sold for July?
    a. $24,200
    b. $19,400
    c. $18,822
    d. $18,200

12. Assume that the company uses a periodic inventory system and a LIFO cost flow assumption. What is the cost of goods sold for July?
    a. $24,200
    b. $19,400
    c. $18,822
    d. $18,200

13. Assume that the company uses a periodic inventory system and an average cost flow assumption. What is the cost of goods sold for July?
    a. $24,200
    b. $19,400
    c. $18,822
    d. $18,200

14. Assume that the company uses a periodic inventory system and a LIFO cost flow assumption. What is the cost of ending inventory on July 31?
    a. $6,000
    b. $5,200
    c. $4,800
    d. $3,000

15. Assume that the company uses a perpetual inventory system and a FIFO cost flow assumption. What is the cost of goods sold for July?
    a. $24,200
    b. $19,400
    c. $18,822
    d. $18,200

16. Assume that the company uses a perpetual inventory system and a LIFO cost flow assumption. What is the cost of ending inventory on July 31?
    a. $6,000
    b. $5,200
    c. $4,800
    d. $3,000

17. Millie's Catering reported sales of $55,800 and cost of sales of $34,200 for 2003. Millie's beginning inventory was $15,000, and ending inventory totaled $21,000. Purchases were $40,200 during 2003. What was Millie's inventory turnover ratio in 2003?
    a.   1.90
    b.   2.28
    c.   1.63
    d.   3.10

18. Lizzy's Kitchens is a leading specialty cookie maker. In preparing for the Valentine's Day rush, Lizzy purchases flour on January 20, 2002 to be used in production in early February. On January 20, Lizzy receives an invoice for a gross amount of $100,000 and terms 2/10, net 30. Lizzy pays ½ of the invoice amount within the discount period, the remainder of the invoice will be paid in February. What amounts will appear on Lizzy's balance sheet on January 31, 2002 related to inventory and accounts payable?

 a. $99,000; $50,000
 b. $98,000; $50,000
 c. $50,000; $49,000
 d. $100,000; $50,000

19. Margie's Munchies shipped goods f.o.b. destination point to a customer on December 31, 2003. The customer received the goods on January 5, 2004. Margie recorded a sale for $5,000 on January 5, 2004. The goods originally cost Margie $3,000. Margie did not include the goods in its inventory on December 31, 2003. What is the impact of this transaction on Margie's 2003 financial statements?
 a. Margie properly accounted for the transaction.
 b. Inventory is okay, Sales are understated by $5,000.
 c. Inventory is understated by $3,000, Sales are okay.
 d. Inventory is understated by $3,000, Sales are understated by $3,000.

20. An accounting clerk errs in calculating the cost of ending inventory for 2003, overstating the amount by $36,000. What is the impact on 2003 and 2004 Net Income?

	2003 Net Income	**2004 Net Income**
a.	$36,000 overstated	$36,000 overstated
b.	$36,000 overstated	$36,000 understated
c.	$36,000 understated	$36,000 overstated
d.	$36,000 understated	$36,000 understated

21. Jake's Gym, selling home exercise and fitness equipment, opened for business on May 1. Record the following transactions for Jake's Gym, assuming that Jake uses a periodic inventory system.

 May 2.   Purchases 3 stationary bicycles for $150 each, 4 rowing machines for $200 each, and 5 stair steppers for $175 each, agreeing to pay the supplier within 60 days.

 May 9.   Sells 1 rowing machine for $400 cash.

21. May 14.   Purchases 20 copies of Slim Jim's latest exercise video tape for $10 each, agreeing to pay the supplier within 30 days.

May 19.   Sells 1 stationary bicycle for $420. The purchaser agrees to pay in 30 days.

May 24.   Sells 4 video tapes for $20 cash each.

May 26.   Purchases 5 Miracle Machines for $1,750 each, agreeing to pay the supplier within 60 days. The Miracle Machine enables the user to sit at home, watch sports on television, eat lots of snacks, and maintain peak physical condition.

May 28.   Customers flock to the Gym. Jake sells all 5 Miracle Machines for $4,000 cash each. Thousands of other customers express an interest in buying the new machines when they become available. Two of the Miracle Machine purchasers feel that more is always better, and each purchases a copy of the video tape for $22 in cash to view while enjoying the Miracle Machine.

May 30.   Jake finishes cleaning up the debris left by customers on the 28th and counts up the remaining inventory. His count finds: 0 Miracle Machines, 3 rowing machines, 2 stationary bicycles, 5 stair steppers, and 12 video tapes.

22. Repeat question 21, but now assume that Jake's Gym uses the perpetual inventory system.

    May 2.   Purchases 3 stationary bicycles for $150 each, 4 rowing machines for $200 each, and 5 stair steppers for $175 each, agreeing to pay the supplier within 60 days.

    May 9.   Sells 1 rowing machine for $400 cash.

    May 14.   Purchases 20 copies of Slim Jim's latest exercise video tape for $10 each, agreeing to pay the supplier within 30 days.

    May 19.   Sells 1 stationary bicycle for $420. The purchaser agrees to pay in 30 days.

    May 24.   Sells 4 video tapes for $20 cash each.

    May 26.   Purchases 5 Miracle Machines for $1,750 each, agreeing to pay the supplier within 60 days. The Miracle Machine enables the user to sit at home, watch sports on television, eat lots of snacks, and maintain peak physical condition.

May 28. Customers flock to the Gym. Jake sells all 5 Miracle Machines for $4,000 cash each. Thousands of other customers express an interest in buying the new machines when they become available. Two of the Miracle Machine purchasers feel that more is always better, and each purchases a copy of the video tape for $22 in cash to view while enjoying the Miracle Machine.

May 30. Jake finishes cleaning up the debris left by customers on the 28th and counts up the remaining inventory. His count finds: 0 Miracle Machines, 3 rowing machines, 2 stationary bicycles, 5 stair steppers, and 12 video tapes.

23. Presented below are inventory transactions for Carpet City for the month of June. Calculate both ending inventory and cost of goods sold for June under the various cost flow assumptions.

June 1. Beginning inventory of 30 carpets costing $60 each.
June 3. Sold 10 carpets for $100 each.
June 8. Purchased 15 carpets for $50 each.
June 12. Sold 12 carpets for $120 each.
June 19. Purchased 10 carpets for $70 each.
June 24. Sold 15 carpets for $120 each.
June 29. Purchased 10 carpets for $75 each.

a. Carpet City uses a periodic, FIFO system.

b. Carpet City uses a periodic, LIFO system.

c.   Carpet City uses a perpetual, FIFO system.

d.   Carpet City uses a perpetual, LIFO system.

e.   Carpet City uses a periodic, average cost system.

24.   The following partial information has been taken from the accounting records of Dave's Discount Store.

	12/31/03	12/31/04	12/31/05
Beginning inventory	$ 50,000	$ 62,500	$ (e)
Purchases	25,000	30,000	37,500
Purchase discounts	(a)	(d)	(f)
Cost of goods sold	5,000	22,500	40,000
Cost of goods available for sale	67,500	(c)	90,000
Ending inventory	(b)	67,500	(g)
Sales	26,300	61,240	104,600

Required:

a.   Compute the missing amounts.

b. Assume that Dave uses a periodic inventory system. Prepare the closing entry to recognize ending inventory and cost of goods sold for each year.

25. The Toy Store reported the following amounts on December 31, 2003: ending inventory (based on a physical count), $275,000 and accounts payable, $81,000. The Toy Store uses a periodic inventory system. A review of the records revealed the additional information presented below.

Required:
a. Prepare the required adjusting entry, if any, for each of the items below.

(1) The Toy Store ordered $12,000 of merchandise from a supplier on December 28, with terms FOB shipping point. The merchandise was shipped on December 29 and received on January 4.

(2) The Toy Store had ordered $7,000 of merchandise from a supplier on December 29, with terms FOB destination. The merchandise was shipped on December 29 and received on January 2.

(3) The Toy Store had shipped $17,000 of merchandise to a customer on December 29, with terms FOB destination. The merchandise originally cost $9,000. The merchandise was received on January 2.

(4) The physical inventory count included $14,500 of merchandise that was held on consignment for Marx Brothers Manufacturing.

(5) The physical inventory count included $4,300 of merchandise that was received late on December 31, but not recorded in Accounts Payable until January 2.

(6) The Toy Store ordered $28,000 of merchandise from a supplier on December 22, with terms FOB destination. The merchandise was shipped on December 24 and received on December 28.

b. Calculate ending balances for Inventory and Accounts Payable on December 31.

CHAPTER 7 - SOLUTIONS

1.	c	6.	b	11.	d	16.	b
2.	b	7.	a	12.	b	17.	a
3.	d	8.	b	13.	c	18.	a
4.	c	9.	d	14.	c	19.	c
5.	a	10.	c	15.	d	20.	b

21.

May 2	Purchases (E,-SE)		2,125	
	Accounts Payable (+L)			2,125
May 9	Cash (+A)		400	
	Sales (R,+SE)			400
May 14	Purchases (E,-SE)		200	
	Accounts Payable (+L)			200
May 19	Accounts Receivable (+A)		420	
	Sales (R,+SE)			420
May 24	Cash (+A)		80	
	Sales (R,+SE)			80
May 26	Purchases (E,-SE)		8,750	
	Accounts Payable (+L)			8,750
May 28	Cash (+A)		20,044	
	Sales (R,+SE)			20,044
May 30	Inventory (+A)		1,895	
	Cost of Goods Sold (E,-SE)		9,180	
	Purchases (E,-SE)			11,075

Purchases: $2,125 + $200 + $8,750 = $11,075$

Ending Inventory: (3 @ $200) + (2 @ $150) + (5 @ $175) + (12 @ $10) = $1,895

	Beginning inventory	$ 0
+	Purchases	11,075
	Cost of goods available for sale	$11,075
-	Ending inventory	(1,895)
	Cost of goods sold	$ 9,180

22. May 2   Inventory (+A)   2,125
                    Accounts Payable (+L)   2,125

     May 9   Cash (+A)   400
                    Sales (R,+SE)   400

              Cost of Goods Sold (E,-SE)   200
                    Inventory (-A)   200

     May 14   Inventory (+A)   200
                    Accounts Payable (+L)   200

     May 19   Accounts Receivable (+A)   420
                    Sales (R,+SE)   420

              Cost of Goods Sold (E,-SE)   150
                    Inventory (-A)   150

     May 24   Cash (+A)   80
                    Sales (R,+SE)   80

              Cost of Goods Sold (E,-SE)   40
                    Inventory (-A)   40

     May 26   Inventory (+A)   8,750
                    Accounts Payable (+L)   8,750

     May 28   Cash (+A)   20,044
                    Sales (R,+SE)   20,044

              Cost of Goods Sold (E,-SE)   8,770
                    Inventory (-A)   8,770

If all of the above entries are posted to the T-accounts for Inventory and Cost of Goods Sold, the ending balances will be $1,915 and $9,160, respectively. However, if Cost of Goods Sold is calculated (see below), the amount should be $9,180. The difference is due to an inventory shortage (theft, damages, etc.). Jake purchased 20 video tapes, 6 were sold, but only 12 remain in inventory. Two tapes ($20 total cost) were lost. Note that this amount was simply included in Cost of Goods Sold under the periodic system. The required adjusting entry is:

     May 30   Inventory Shortage (E,-SE)   20
                    Inventory (-A)   20
Purchases: $2,125 + $200 + $8,750 = $11,075

Ending inventory: (3 @ $200) + (2 @ $150) + (5 @ $175) + (12 @ $10) = $1,895

22.

	Beginning inventory	$ 0
+	Purchases	11,075
	Cost of goods available for sale	$11,075
-	Ending inventory	(1,895)
	Cost of goods sold	$ 9,180

23. Begin this problem by accounting for the physical units of inventory and determining cost of goods available for sale.

The beginning inventory was 30 units and purchases totaled 35 units. A total of 37 units were sold, leaving an ending inventory of 28 units. Note that the accounting for the physical units is unaffected by the choice of inventory system or cost flow assumption.

Cost of Goods Available for Sale

		Units	Unit Cost	Total Cost
6/1	Beginning inventory	30	60	$1,800
6/8	Purchase	15	50	750
6/19	Purchase	10	70	700
6/29	Purchase	10	75	750
	Goods available for sale	65		$4,000

a. FIFO, periodic (ending inventory is 28 units)

		Units	Unit Cost	Total Cost
6/8	Purchase	8	50	$ 400
6/19	Purchase	10	70	700
6/29	Purchase	10	75	750
	Ending inventory	28		$1,850

$$
\begin{aligned}
\text{CGS} &= \text{CGAS} - \text{EI} \\
&= \$4,000 - \$1,850 \\
&= \$2,150
\end{aligned}
$$

b. LIFO, periodic (ending inventory is 28 units)

		Units	Unit Cost	Total Cost
6/1	Beginning inventory	28	60	$1,680
	Ending inventory	28		$1,680

$$
\begin{aligned}
\text{CGS} &= \text{CGAS} - \text{EI} \\
&= \$4,000 - \$1,680 \\
&= \$2,320
\end{aligned}
$$

c. FIFO, perpetual (ending inventory is 28 units). You may wish to work this out, but it is easier to simply recall that FIFO yields identical amounts under the periodic and perpetual systems. The answers are therefore the same as in part (a).

d. The perpetual inventory records must be maintained to determine LIFO inventory and cost of goods sold. Units are in parentheses.

		Inventory		**Cost of Goods Sold**		
6/1	Beg. inventory (30)	30	@ $60		-	
6/3	Sale (10)	20	@ $60	10	@	$60
6/8	Purchase (15)	20	@ $60		-	
		15	@ 50			
6/12	Sale (12)	20	@ $60	12	@	$50
		3	@ 50			
6/19	Purchase (10)	20	@ $60		-	
		3	@ 50			
		10	@ 70			
6/24	Sale (15)	18	@ $60	10	@	$70
				3	@	50
				2	@	60
6/29	Purchase (10)	18	@ $60		-	
		10	@ 75			

The ending inventory is the units remaining on June 29. The total cost is $1,830 (18 @ $60 and 10 @ $75). Cost of goods sold is obtained by either adding up the total entries made to the account, or subtracting the ending inventory from cost of goods available for sale. Cost of goods sold is $2,170.

e. Average cost, periodic (ending inventory is 28 units). The average cost amounts can be computed using the initial calculation made for cost of goods available for sale. There were 65 units available at a total cost of $4,000. This gives an average cost of $61.54 (rounded). Using the average cost:

Ending inventory = 28 units @ $61.54 = $1,723.12

Cost of goods sold = 37 units @ $61.54 = $2,276.88

24. a. It is easiest to solve for the missing amounts by recalling the basic conceptual relations among these variables, and then applying simple algebraic techniques.

(a) BI   +   P   -   PD   =   CGAS
     $50,000 + $25,000   -   PD   = $67,500
     PD   = $7,500

(b) CGAS   -   EI   =   CGS
     $67,500 -   EI   = $5,000
     EI   = $62,500

(c) CGAS   -   EI   =   CGS
     CGAS   - $67,500   = $22,500
     CGAS   = $90,000

(d) BI   +   P   -   PD   =   CGAS
     $62,500 + $30,000   -   PD   = $90,000
     PD   = $2,500

(e) BI(2004) =   EI (2003)
     BI(2004) = $67,500

(f) BI   +   P   -   PD   =   CGAS
     $67,500 + $37,500   -   PD   = $90,000
     PD   = $15,000

(g) CGAS   -   EI   =   CGS
     $90,000 -   EI   = $40,000
     EI   = $50,000

b. Closing entries

Account	2003 Debit (Credit)	2004 Debit (Credit)	2005 Debit (Credit)
Cost of Goods Sold (E,-SE)	5,000	22,500	40,000
Inventory (ending) (+A)	62,500	67,500	50,000
Purchase Discounts (E,-SE)	7,500	2,500	15,000
Inventory (beginning) (-A)	(50,000)	(62,500)	(67,500)
Purchases (-E,+SE)	(25,000)	(30,000)	(37,500)

25.a.   (1) Inventory (+A)   12,000
               Accounts Payable (+L)   12,000

        (2) No adjustment required.

        (3) Inventory (+A)   9,000
               Cost of Goods Sold (-E,+SE)   9,000

        (4) Cost of Goods Sold (E,-SE)   14,500
               Inventory (-A)   14,500

        (5) Cost of Goods Sold (E,-SE)   4,300
               Accounts Payable (+L)   4,300

        (6) No adjustment required.

b.   The correct ending balances for Inventory and Accounts Payable are easily computed by
        preparing T-accounts and posting the adjusting entries.

Inventory			Accounts Payable	
275,000	14,500			81,000
12,000				12,000
9,000				4,300
281,500				97,300

CHAPTER 8

Investments in Equity Securities

REVIEW OF KEY CONCEPTS

An **equity security** investment represents an ownership interest in another firm. Equity securities include common and preferred stocks, as well as rights or options to obtain or sell such securities. As in the text, our discussion emphasizes investments in common stocks.

Investments in equity securities are assets to the investor. The same basic rules introduced in earlier chapters apply here in accounting for investments in equity securities at acquisition, disposal, and during the holding period. You should focus on the unique aspects of accounting for this type of asset compared to other assets.

Companies make investments in equity securities issued by other companies for two primary reasons. First, cash may be invested to earn a return [in the form of dividends and/or price appreciation (capital gains)]. Management will convert these investments back into cash whenever the need arises to pay current liabilities as they come due. Such investments are appropriately classified as current assets on the balance sheet. An investment is classified as a **trading security** if the investment is primarily held in order to sell it in the near future to profit from short-term price fluctuations. Other marketable security investments are classified as **available-for-sale securities**. Trading securities are always classified as current assets. Depending upon management's intent regarding their holding period, available-for-sale securities may be classified as current or long-term assets.

Second, management may invest in another firm to establish an ability to *significantly influence* or *control* the financial and operating decisions of the investee firm. For example, management may invest in a major supplier in order to guarantee a steady source of needed raw materials. Such investments are classified as noncurrent (long-term) assets on the balance sheet. The balance sheet classification (current or noncurrent) of an equity investment is thus dependent on the intentions of management. Accounting for investments during the holding period is affected by the balance sheet classification of the investment.

Recording Acquisitions

The cost to record any asset is the acquisition price plus all costs incurred to bring the asset to the location and condition for its intended use. Typical additional costs encountered in purchasing equity securities include brokerage commissions, exchange fees, and transfer taxes. These costs are added to the purchase price when recording investment acquisitions. For example, assume that Spartan Corporation purchases 200 shares of the common stock of Small Company for $25 per share. Additional commissions and fees total $132. Assuming the investment is recorded as a trading security, the purchase is recorded as follows:

Trading Securities (+A)   5,132
    Cash (-A)   5,132

Lump Sum Purchase

A company may purchase several equity securities in a single transaction. The total cost of a lump sum (or basket) purchase is allocated among the assets acquired, based on their relative fair market values. Assume that Spartan Corporation acquires 5,000 shares of the common stock and 2,000 shares of the preferred stock of Johnson, Inc., a new corporation, for $200,000. The estimated value of the shares is $30 per share for common and $50 per share for preferred.

To compute the amount assigned to each security, the relative value of each is computed. The estimated total market value of the common stock is $150,000 [5,000*$30] and the preferred is $100,000 [2,000 * $30] for a total estimated market value for the basket purchase of $250,000. The common stock is weighted 60% ($150,000/$250,000) and the preferred stock is weighted 40% ($100,000/$250,000). The historical cost of the basket is $200,000 so $120,000 (.6 * $200,000) is assigned to the common stock and $80,000 (.4*$200,000) is assigned to the preferred stock.

Assuming the investments are both trading securities, the journal entry to record the purchase is:

Trading Securities - Common (+A)   120,000
Trading Securities - Preferred (+A)   80,000
    Cash (-A)   200,000

Accounting for Investments at Disposition

The company may choose to sell its investments. The company will record the receipt of cash or other assets received from the sale. The equity securities sold must be removed from the accounting records. A gain or loss on sale is recorded, based on any difference between the selling price and the book value (carrying value) of the investment.

Assume that Spartan sells the preferred stock of Johnson acquired in the last example stock is for $92,000. The journal entry to record the sale is:

Cash (+A)   92,000
    Trading Securities - Preferred (-A)   80,000
    Realized Gain on Sale of Trad.Sec. (Ga,+SE)   12,000

The book value (carrying value) of an investment will *not* always be equal to its original cost because of accounting procedures applied during the **holding period** which are discussed below.

Accounting for Investments in Equity Securities During the Holding Period

Accounting for equity securities during the holding period is dependent on their balance sheet classification (trading, available-for-sale or other long-term) and the accounting method employed.

All trading and available-for-sale (whether considered current or long-term) investments are accounted for using the **cost method**. When an investment is accounted for under the cost method, firms are generally also required to make an adjustment to reflect the market value at the balance sheet date. In addition to applying the cost method to available-for-sale securities classified as long-term investments, the **equity method** and the preparation of **consolidated financial statements** may be appropriate to account for long-term equity investments under certain circumstances which are discussed later in the chapter. All of the alternative accounting methods record acquisitions and dispositions in the same manner, as described previously. The choice among the alternative accounting methods directly affects only accounting during the holding period. The choice will indirectly affect accounting for dispositions due to changes in the carrying value of investments during the holding period.

Recognition and Realization

Two accounting concepts are important to understanding the differences among the alternative accounting methods for investments. The first, **recognition**, means that an item is formally recorded in the accounting records. The amount of such item affects the amounts reported in the company's financial statements. **Realization** indicates that an amount has been confirmed in an exchange transaction. For example, suppose that you purchase an asset for $500. At a later date, you sell that asset for $600. You have realized a gain as a result of the price appreciation and sale of the asset. Alternatively, suppose that you do not sell the asset, but simply observe that it has increased in market value to $600. Although you may be economically better off, the gain due to price appreciation has not been realized in an exchange transaction.

As a general rule, all realized gains and losses are recognized. In the following sections, we will review situations where **unrealized gains** or **losses** are sometimes recognized as well.

Current Investments in Marketable Equity Securities

Investments classified as current assets are properly accounted for using the cost method, with an adjustment to mark them to their market value (i.e., **mark-to-market**). Under the cost method, the investor will recognize income earned on the investment as it is received in the form of *dividends*. Assume that Gabby Company owns 1,000 shares of Max, Inc. and receives a dividend of $1.20 per share on December 15. The receipt would be recorded with the following journal entry:

Cash (+A)	1,200	
Dividend Income (R,+SE)		1,200

The above entry recognizes the increase in cash and the revenue earned on the investment under the cost method. Notice that the entry has no impact on the book value of the investment. This is the only type of entry normally made during the holding period for investments carried under the cost method. However, an additional entry is needed when the cost method is modified to include the mark-to-market (MTM) adjustment.

Mark-to-Market Method

The MTM adjustment is made when preparing financial statements. *SFAS No. 115* requires a mark-to-market adjustment for all securities (debt and equity) carried under the cost method, for which a fair value can be determined. Nonmarketable securities are carried at historical cost, with no market adjustment. SFAS No.115 provides for separate and different treatments of investments classified as trading versus available-for-sale.

The general approach is to compare the cost and market value of each security investment at each balance sheet date. If the security is classified as a trading security and market is *more* than cost, the investment account is increased or debited so that the balance sheet date market value is reflected in the asset account. The corresponding credit is to *Unrealized Gain on Trading Securities*. If the market value is less than cost, the trading security account is decreased (or credited) and *Unrealized Loss on Trading Securities* is debited. The unrealized gain or loss is included in the income statement under the *Other Revenue and Expense* classification.

Example: American Company, which began operations in 2003, had the following investments appropriately classified as trading securities at the end of 2003 and 2004.

December 31, 2003

Company	Cost	Market Value	Unrealized Gain (Loss)
Bluejay Corporation	$ 20,000	$ 16,000	$(4,000)
Sparrow Corporation	60,000	52,000	(8,000)
Robin Company	40,000	46,000	6,000
Totals	$120,000	$114,000	$(6,000)

December 31, 2004

Company	Book Value	Market Value	Unrealized Gain (Loss)
Bluejay Corporation	$ 16,000	$ 20,000	$4,000
Sparrow Corporation	34,667	30,000	(4,667)
Robin Company	46,000	54,000	8,000
Finch Corporation	28,000	24,000	(4,000)
Totals	$124,667	$128,000	$3,333

Since cost exceeds market, the required 2003 year-end adjusting entry is:

Trading Securities (Robin) (+A)	6,000	
Unrealized Loss on Trading Securities (Lo,-SE)	12,000	
Unrealized Gain on Trading Securities (Ga,+SE)		6,000
Trading Securities (Bluejay) (-A)		4,000
Trading Securities (Sparrow) (-A)		8,000

The unrealized gain and loss will appear on American's 2003 income statement.

During 2004, American sold a third of its shares of Sparrow for $26,000. American has classified the investments as current.

The entry to record the sale of Sparrow Corp. investment is:

Cash (+A)	26,000	
Trading Securities (Sparrow) (-A)		17,333
Realized Gain on Sale of Trading Sec. (Ga,+SE)		8,667

Since the Sparrow investment was written down to $52,000 at the end of 2004, the book value of the investment sold was $52,000/3 = $17,333.

The adjusting entry for 2004 is:

Trading Securities (Bluejay) (+A)	4,000	
Trading Securities (Robin) (+A)	8,000	
Unrealized Loss on Trading Securities (Lo,-SE)	8,667	
Unrealized Gain on Trading Securities (Ga,-SE)		12,000
Trading Securities (Sparrow) (-A)		4,667
Trading Securities (Finch) (-A)		4,000

Available-for-Sale Security Investments

If the security is classified as available-for-sale, the investment may be classified as current or long-term depending upon management's intention. The investment is accounted for under the cost method. An adjustment is made at the balance sheet date to mark the investment to market. Like the trading security mark-to-market result, the carrying value of the asset becomes its market value after the adjustment. Unlike trading securities, the unrealized gains and losses resulting from applying mark-to-market are recorded in Unrealized Price Increases (Decreases) accounts which are shown directly in the stockholders' equity section of the balance sheet. When securities are sold, the realized gain (loss) on the investment sale is the difference between the securities original cost and its sale price.

Example: Using the American Company example, the 2003 adjusting entry would be:

Available-for-Sale Securities (Robin) (+A)	6,000	
Unrealized Price Dec. on AFS Securities (-SE)	12,000	
Unrealized Price Inc. on AFS Sec. (+SE)		6,000
AFS Securities (Bluejay) (-A)		4,000
AFS Securities (Sparrow) (-A)		8,000

The Unrealized Price Increase (Dec.) appears as an addition to (reduction of) stockholders' equity.

The entry to record the sale of Sparrow Corp. investment is:

Cash (+A)	26,000	
AFS Securities (Sparrow) (-A)		17,333
Unrealized Price Dec. on AFS Securities (+SE)		2,667
Realized Gain on Sale of AFS Sec. (Ga,+SE)		6,000

Since the Sparrow investment was written down to $52,000 at the end of 2003, the book value of the investment sold was $52,000/3 = $17,333. The Unrealized Price Dec. account contains the 8,000 Sparrow write down. $2,667 of this relates to the one-third sold. As a result, the total amount credited is $17,333 + $2,667 = $20,000, the original cost. As a result, the realized gain amounts to $6,000, the difference between the sales price and the original cost.

The adjusting entry for 2004 is:

AFS Securities (Bluejay) (+A)	4,000	
AFS Securities (Robin) (+A)	8,000	
Unrealized Price Dec. on AFS Sec. (-SE)	8,667	
Unrealized Price Dec. on AFS (-SE)		12,000
AFS Securities (Sparrow) (-A)		4,667
AFS Securities (Finch) (-A)		4,000

Other Long-Term Equity Investments

There are three different methods available: (1) the *cost method*, (2) the *equity method* and (3) *consolidation*. The choice of method depends on the degree of control exercised by the investor. The cost method is used when the investor exercises no control or significant influence over the investee. These securities are classified as available-for-sale. A rule of thumb is to use the cost method whenever an investor holds less than 20% of the investee's outstanding shares. The equity method is used to account for long-term investments in common stock in which the investor exercises significant influence over the investee. This method is normally used when an investor owns between 20% and 50% of the investee's outstanding shares. Consolidation is used when the investor owns a **controlling interest** in the investor. This method will normally be used when the investor owns more than 50% of the investee's outstanding shares.

The Equity Method

Under the equity method, the investor recognizes a proportionate share of the investee's earned net income as investment revenue and as an increase in the book value of the investment. Additionally, the investment account balance is reduced for any dividends received.

Example: On January 2, 2003, Fox Company purchased 30,000 shares of the common stock of Brown Corporation, a closely held company, for $450,000. During 2003 and 2004, Brown had 200,000 common shares outstanding. Brown reported net income of $400,000 and $300,000 in 2003 and 2004, respectively. Dividends paid by Brown were $160,000 in 2003 and $120,000 in 2004. Since Fox owns 15% of Brown's outstanding shares, Fox will recognize 15% of dividends and income each year.

Assuming that the investment allows Fox to exert significant influence over the operating and financing policies of Brown, prepare journal entries for Fox related to the investment in Brown for 2003 and 2004.

Equity Method Entries

1/ 2/03	Investment in Equity Securities (+A)	450,000	
	Cash (-A)		450,000
	Purchased 30,000 shares of Brown stock at $15.		
12/31/03	Investment in Equity Securities (+A)	60,000	
	Income from Equity Investments (R,+SE)		60,000
	Recognized 15% of Brown's 2003 net income.		
12/31/03	Cash (+A)	24,000	
	Investment in Equity Securities (-A)		24,000
	Received dividends from Brown.		
12/31/04	Investment in Equity Securities (+A)	45,000	
	Income from Equity Investments (R,+SE)		45,000
	Recognized 15% of Brown's 2004 net income.		
12/31/04	Cash (+A)	18,000	
	Investment in Equity Securities (-A)		18,000
	Received dividends from Brown.		

If Brown had incurred a net loss during the year, Fox must adjust its equity method entry accordingly. For example, assume that Brown incurred a net loss of $100,000 in 2003. The entry becomes:

12/31/03	Income from Equity Investments (Lo,-SE)	15,000	
	Investment in Equity Securities (-A)		15,000
	Recognized 15% of Brown's 2003 net loss.		

Consolidated Financial Statements

If an investor purchases a controlling interest in another company's equity securities (i.e., more than 50% of the outstanding shares), then we prepare financial statements as if the combined companies were a single reporting entity. This process is known as the preparation of consolidated financial statements. Your text (including the appendix) provides some examples on consolidated reporting. This topic is covered in considerably more detail in advanced financial accounting courses.

QUESTIONS FOR YOUR REVIEW

1. Which of the following accounting methods is not used for short-term investments in equity securities?
   a. Equity method
   b. Cost method
   c. Mark-to-market
   d. Any of these methods might be used.

2. Which of the following accounting methods is used for long-term investments in equity securities?
   a. Equity method
   b. Consolidation method
   c. Mark-to-market
   d. Any of these methods might be used.

3. A company received dividend payments of $500 from an investment appropriately carried under the equity method of accounting. Which of the following statements is true?
   a. Dividend Income is debited for $500.
   b. Dividend Income is credited for $500.
   c. The Investment account is debited for $500.
   d. The Investment account is credited for $500.

4. A company received dividend payments of $500 from an investment appropriately carried under the cost method of accounting. Which of the following statements is true?
   a. Dividend Income is debited for $500.
   b. Dividend Income is credited for $500.
   c. The Investment account is debited for $500.
   d. The Investment account is credited for $500.

5. The cost method should be used to account for an investment in equity securities when:
   a. the investor lacks any ability to control or significantly influence the operating activities of the investee.
   b. the investor can control the operating activities of the investee.
   c. the investor lacks the ability to control but can significantly influence the operating activities of the investee.
   d. the investor owns a majority interest in the investee's common stock.

6. The equity method should be used to account for an investment in equity securities when:
   a. the investor lacks any ability to control or significantly influence the operating activities of the investee.
   b. the investor can control the operating activities of the investee.
   c. the investor lacks the ability to control but can significantly influence the operating activities of the investee.
   d. the investor owns a majority interest in the investee's common stock.

7. Which of the following is not an equity security?
   a. Common stock
   b. Stock warrant
   c. Convertible bond
   d. Stock option

8. Which of the following is used to determine whether an equity security should be classified as a current or a noncurrent asset?
   a. The maturity date.
   b. Any investments held over six months must be classified as noncurrent assets.
   c. Any investments costing over $10,000 must be classified as noncurrent assets.
   d. The classification is based on the intentions of management.

9. Investments in available-for-sale equity securities, carried under the cost method, require a mark-to-market adjustment. Which of the following statements is true regarding unrealized price changes?
   a. Only unrealized price changes not deemed to be permanent will affect reported net income.
   b. Only unrealized price changes on trading securities investments affect reported net income.
   c. Only unrealized losses reduce reported net income.
   d. Only unrealized price changes on available-for-sale investments affect reported net income.

10. Which of the following investments would most likely be reported using the equity method of accounting?
    a. The investor owns 35% of the investee's preferred stock.
    b. The investor owns 35% of the investee's common stock.
    c. The investor owns 65% of the investee's preferred stock.
    d. The investor owns 65% of the investee's common stock.

11. Shaq's Basketballs, Inc. purchased 20% of the outstanding common shares of the Jordan Company on January 1, 2003, for $120,000 in cash. During 2003, Jordan reported net income of $80,000 and paid dividends of $20,000. Assuming that this investment is appropriately carried under the cost method, what is the amount of investment income which would appear on Shaq's 2003 income statement?
    a. $4,000
    b. $16,000
    c. $20,000
    d. $80,000

12. Shaq's Basketballs, Inc. purchased 20% of the outstanding common shares of the Jordan Company on January 1, 2003, for $120,000 in cash. During 2003, Jordan reported net income of $80,000 and paid dividends of $20,000. Assuming that this investment is appropriately carried under the equity method, what is the amount of investment income which would appear on Shaq's 2003 income statement?
    a. $4,000
    b. $16,000
    c. $20,000
    d. $80,000

13. Shaq's Basketballs, Inc. purchased 20% of the outstanding common shares of the Jordan Company on January 1, 2003, for $120,000 in cash. During 2003, Jordan reported net income of $80,000 and paid dividends of $20,000. Assuming that this investment is appropriately carried under the equity method, what is the correct ending balance of the Investment account which would appear on Shaq's 2003 balance sheet?
    a. $120,000
    b. $132,000
    c. $136,000
    d. $140,000

14. Which of the following uses the mark-to-market rule?
    a.   Equity method
    b.   Long-term nonmarketable equity securities
    c.   The cost method for available-for-sale investments
    d.   Consolidation method

Use the following information to answer questions 15 through 17.
Carolina Corporation holds the following securities in its current portfolio of trading securities.

		Market Value at December 31,	
Company	Cost	2003	2004
Wolf, Inc.	$5,000	$5,200	$4,800
Blitzen, Inc.	2,500	2,200	2,200

Assume Wolf is properly classified as a trading security and Blitzen as an available-for-sale security.

15. The required adjustment at December 31, 2003 for the investment in Wolf is:
    a. Trading Securities (+A) 200
       Unrealized Gain on Trading Sec. (Ga, +SE) 200
    b. Trading Securities (+A) 200
       Unrealized Price Inc. on Trading Sec. (+SE) 200
    c. Trading Securities (+A) 200
       Realized Gain on Trading Sec. (Ga,+SE) 200
    d. Trading Securities (+A) 200
       Realized Price Inc. on Trading Sec. (+SE) 200

16. Which of the following adjusting entries is required at December 31, 2003 for the Blitzen investment?
    a. Unrealized Loss on AFS Securities (Lo,-SE) 300
       Available-for-Sale Sec. (-A) 300
    b. Unrealized Price Dec. on AFS Securities (-SE) 300
       Available-for-Sale Sec. (-A) 300
    c. Realized Loss on AFS Securities (Lo,-SE) 300
       Available-for-Sale Sec. (-A) 300
    d. Realized Price Dec. on AFS Securities (-SE) 300
       Available-for-Sale Sec. (-A) 300

17. Assume that during 2004, Carolina sells its investment in Blitzen for $2,100. The entry to record the sale is:

    a. Unrealized Loss on AFS Sale (Lo,-SE) 400
       Cash(+A) 2,100
          Available-for-Sale Sec. (-A) 2,200
          Unrealized Price Decrease (+SE) 300
    b. Realized Loss on AFS Sale (Lo,-SE) 400
       Cash(+A) 2,100
          Available-for-Sale Sec. (-A) 2,200
          Unrealized Price Decrease (+SE) 300
    c. Realized Loss on AFS Sale (Lo,-SE) 100
       Cash(+A) 2,100
          Available-for-Sale Sec. (-A) 2,200
    d. Unrealized Price Decrease on AFS (Lo,-SE) 100
       Cash(+A) 2,100
          Available-for-Sale Sec. (-A) 2,200

Use the following information to answer questions 18 through 19.

On January 1, 2003, Tiger Corporation made long-term investments in Razorbacks and Wave Companies. Information on those investments and their 2003 income and dividends follows:

Company	Razorbacks	Wave
Total price	$800,000	$500,000
Ownership percent	15%	30%
Net income	$200,000	$ 90,000
Dividends	$ 60,000	$ 25,000

18. Assuming that Tiger had no other investments, what amount of dividend income will it report for 2003?
   a. $85,000
   b. $60,000
   c. $16,500
   d. $ 9,000

19. On January 1, 2004, what is the total book value of Tiger's portfolio (assuming that there were no changes in the market value of the investments)?
   a. $1,302,000
   b. $1,319,500
   c. $1,400,000
   d. $1,439,000

20. On July 1, 2003, the Nittany Corporation made the following trading security investment:

   200 shares of Wolverine Company for $4,000

   On December 31, 2003, the market price for Wolverine Company was $30 per share. What entry, if any, is necessary when Nittany adjusts their books on December 31, 2003?
   a. Trading Securities (+A)   2,000
          Unrealized Gain on Trad. Sec. (Ga,+SE)   2,000
   b. Trading Securities (+A)   2,000
          Unrealized Price Inc. on Trad. Sec. (+SE)   2,000
   c. Trading Securities (+A)   2,000
          Realized Gain on Trad. Sec. (Ga,+SE)   2,000
   d. No entry is necessary.

21. Saints Corporation had the following transactions related to its investments in available-for-sale equity securities during 2003. Saints had no securities investments prior to 2003. All securities are correctly classified as current assets, and none of the investments are large enough to allow significant operating influence. Prepare all required journal entries and adjusting entries.

   1/5   Purchased 5,000 shares of Patriots Company for $15 each.

3/13   Purchased 1,000 shares of Rams, Inc. for $20 each.

4/25   Sold 500 shares of Patriots Company for $18 each.

6/30   Received dividends from Rams, Inc. in the amount of $1,200.

9/2   Purchased 500 shares of Hawkeye Corporation for $30 per share.

12/15   Received notice that Rams, Inc. had declared a dividend of $1.50 per share, to be paid
        on January 6, 2004.

12/31   Noted the following market values per share:
       Patriots Company $21
       Rams, Inc.   10
       Hawkeye Corporation   32

22.   During 2003, Buffalo Corporation made the following trading security investments in stock:

    10 shares of Wings Company common at $30/share
    25 shares of Legs Company common at $20/share

At the end of the fiscal year, Wings Company stock was selling for $40/share and Legs Company for $15/share.

During 2004, Buffalo sold 10 shares of Legs Company for $23/share. Buffalo also purchased 20 shares of Blizzard Company for $14/share.

At the end of 2004, Buffalo's stock had the following market values:

    Wings Company $35/share
    Legs Company $25/share
    Blizzard Company $10/share

Required: Record all transactions related to Buffalo's investments during 2003 and 2004. Also prepare any required year-end adjusting entries.

23. Anthony Industries, Inc. made the following available-for-sale investments during 2003:

     100 shares of Clement Corporation for $62/share
     325 shares of Lion Corporation for $27/share

     At the end of 2003, market prices for the stock were:

     Clement $70/share
     Lion $22/share

     During 2004 Anthony made no other investments. The end of the year market prices for the stock were:

     Clement $71/share
     Lion $25/share

     Required: Record all transactions related to Anthony's investments during 2003 and 2004. Also prepare any required year-end adjusting entries.

24. Hawkeye Corporation purchased the following long-term investments in 2003:

    200 shares, or 45% of Badger Company for $100/share
    600 shares, or 30% of Illini Industrials for $20/share

Year-end information on the investments is:

Company	Badger	Illini
Market price per share	$ 145.00	$ 37.00
Net income	$42,392.00	$56,436.00
Dividends per share	$ 0.27	$ 1.21

Required: Record all of the journal entries Hawkeye will make regarding its long-term investments.

CHAPTER 8 - SOLUTIONS

1.	a	6.	c	11.	a	16.	b
2.	d	7.	c	12.	b	17.	b
3.	d	8.	d	13.	b	18.	d
4.	b	9.	b	14.	c	19.	b
5.	a	10.	b	15.	a	20.	a

21.

1/5	AFS Securities (+A)		75,000	
	Cash (-A)			75,000
	Purchased 5,000 shares of Patriots			
	Company for $15 each.			

3/13	AFS Securities (+A)		20,000	
	Cash (-A)			20,000
	Purchased 1,000 shares of Rams,			
	Inc. for $20 each.			

4/25	Cash (+A)		9,000	
	AFS Securities (-A)			7,500
	Realized Gain on Sale of AFS. Sec. (Ga,+SE)			1,500
	Sold 500 shares of Patriots			
	Company for $18 each.			

6/30	Cash (+A)		1,200	
	Dividend Income (R,+SE)			1,200
	Received dividends from Rams,			
	Inc. in the amount of $1,200.			

9/2	AFS Securities (+A)		15,000	
	Cash (-A)			15,000
	Purchased 500 shares of Hawkeye			
	Corporation for $30 per share.			

12/15	Dividends Receivable (+A)		1,500	
	Dividend Income (R,+SE)			1,500
	Received notice that Rams, Inc.			
	had declared a dividend of $1.50			
	per share, to be paid on January 6, 2004.			

12/31	AFS Securities (Patriots) (+A)		27,000	
	Unrealized Price Increase on AFS Sec. (+SE)			27,000

12/31   Unrealized Price Decrease on AFS Sec. (-SE)   10,000
      AFS Securities (Rams) (-A)   10,000

    AFS Securities (Hawkeye) (+A)   1,000
      Unrealized Price Increase on AFS Sec (+SE)   1,000
    Mark-to-market adjustment.

22.   Trading Securities (+A)   300
      Cash (-A)   300
    Purchased 10 shares of Wings
    Company common at $30/share.

    Trading Securities (+A)   500
      Cash (-A)   500
    Purchased 25 shares of Legs
    Company common at $20/share.

<u>December 31, 2003</u>

Company	Cost	Market
Wings Company	$300	$400
Legs Company	500	375
Totals	$800	$775

Trading Securities (Wings) (+A)   100
Unrealized Loss on Trad. Sec. (Lo,-SE)   25
    Trading Securities (Legs) (-A)   125

<u>2004</u>

Cash (+A)   230
    Trading Securities (-A)   150
    Realized Gain on Sale of Mark. Sec. (R,+SE)   80
Sold 10 shares of Legs Company
common at $23/share.

Trading Securities (+A)   280
    Cash (-A)   280
Purchased 20 shares of Blizzard Company
common at $14/share.

December 31, 2004

Company	Cost	Market
Wings Company	$400	$350
Legs Company	225	375
Blizzard Company	280	200
Totals	$905	$925

Trading Securities (Legs) (+A)	150	
Unrealized Gain on Trad. Sec. (Ga,+SE)		20
Trading Securities (Wings) (-A)		50
Trading Securities (Blizzard) (-A)		80

23.

AFS Securities (Clement) (+A)	6,200	
Cash (-A)		6,200

Purchased 100 shares of Clement Corporation for $62/share.

AFS Securities (Lion) (+A)	8,775	
Cash (-A)		8,775

Purchased 325 shares of Lion Corporation for $27/share.

Company	Cost	2003	2004
Clement	$ 6,200	$ 7,000	$ 7,100
Lion	8,775	7,150	8,125
Totals	$14,975	$14,150	$15,225

December 31, 2003

AFS Sec. (Clement) (+A)	800	
Unrealized Price Increase on AFS Sec.(+SE)		800

Unrealized Price Decrease on AFS Sec. (-SE)	1,625	
AFS Sec. (Lion) (-A)		1,625

December 31, 2004

AFS Sec. (Clement) (+A)	100	
Unrealized Price Increase on AFS Sec.(+SE)		100

AFS Sec. (Lion) (+A)	975	
Unrealized Price Increase on AFS Sec.(+SE)		975

24.   Investment in Equity Securities (+A)   20,000.00
             Cash (-A)   20,000.00
        Purchased 200 shares of Badger Company
        for $100/share.

        Investment in Equity Securities (+A)   12,000.00
             Cash (-A)   12,000.00
        Purchased 600 shares of Illini
        Industrials for $20/share.

        Investment in Equity Securities (+A)   19,076.40
             Income from Equity Investments (R,+SE)   19,076.40
        Recognized 45% of Badger net income.

        Investment in Equity Securities (+A)   16,930.80
             Income from Equity Investment (R,+SE)   16,930.80
        Recognized 30% of Illini net income.

        Cash (+A)   54.00
             Investment in Equity Securities (-A)   54.00
        Received dividends from Badger.

        Cash (+A)   726.00
             Investment in Equity Securities (-A)   726.00
        Received dividends from Illini.

CHAPTER 9

Long-Lived Assets

REVIEW OF KEY CONCEPTS

This chapter discusses accounting for a group of productive assets. Basic principles discussed in previous chapters still apply. The long-lived assets discussed here differ from other assets in that they are used to produce goods and services provided by the business over multiple future time periods. These are *operating assets*. Management does not intend to sell these assets in the normal course of business but intends to use them in producing goods or services which will be sold. We discuss accounting for asset acquisition and disposal, as well as accounting during the holding period. Due to the economic nature and long life of these assets, holding period accounting is critically important.

Land is often owned as a location for the company's operating activities. **Fixed assets** include buildings, machinery, furniture, and equipment used in the daily operations of the company. **Intangible assets** are long-lived assets that have value in the rights conveyed to the company, rather than in their physical substance. Examples in this category include patents, copyrights, trademarks, and goodwill. Observe that the physical value of the paper on which a patent is printed is of little value. However, the 20-year exclusive right to produce a product protected by the government's patent may produce significant future revenues for the company. **Natural resources** such as rights to extract coal, petroleum, timber, or other minerals are a significant source of revenues in many industries. The final category of long-lived assets is **deferred costs**. Deferred costs are a miscellaneous type of long-lived assets and could include long-term prepaid expenses, organization costs, and similar items. Accounting for these groups of long-lived assets is virtually identical to other long-lived assets. There are only minor differences in details of calculations and identification of these categories on the balance sheet.

Recording Long-Lived Asset Acquisitions

Recall the basic rule in accounting for acquisition of assets. *Assets are recorded based on their historical cost, which includes the purchase price plus all costs to get the asset into the condition and location for its intended use.* The only differences in accounting for the acquisition of long-lived assets from other assets we have studied are in the types of additional costs included in the recorded amounts for these assets.

For example, a company acquires land on which it intends to construct a new retail store. Land should be recorded at its cost plus all costs to get the asset into the condition and location for its intended use. These additional costs for a land purchase include legal fees, title search costs, surveying costs, and other closing costs. If the land has an existing structure which must be removed, then demolition costs are added to the Land account increasing the cost of the land. If the company can salvage the old building materials, then any proceeds from sales of salvage material should be netted (credited) against the balance in the Land account. If a company purchases machinery for use in a factory, it may face significant additional costs for delivery and installation. These costs are considered a part of the total cost of the machinery and should be *capitalized*. Recall that to capitalize a cost means to add it to the balance in an asset account and amortize the cost over future time periods benefitted by use of the asset.

Lump-sum purchases are common for fixed assets. Often a company will purchase land and an existing building. Allocation of the lump-sum purchase price is important, since land has an indefinite life and its assigned cost is not amortized. It is important to assign a reasonable amount to the Building account, as amortization of this asset will affect net income in future periods.

Example: Barnes Corporation purchases an existing bookstore operation. Barnes pays $300,000 for the land, building, store fixtures and equipment, and existing inventory of the bookstore. Barnes must use estimated fair market values for these assets in order to make the proper allocation to the balance sheet accounts. Barnes estimates the fair market values of the purchased assets as follows:

Land	$100,000
Building	200,000
Inventory	50,000
Fixtures and equipment	50,000
	$400,000

The allocation of the cost is based on the assets' relative fair market values.

Asset	Allocation Formula	Allocated Cost
Land	($100,000/$400,000) x $300,000	$ 75,000
Building	($200,000/$400,000) x $300,000	150,000
Inventory	($50,000/$400,000) x $300,000	37,500
Fixtures	($50,000/$400,000) x $300,000	37,500
		$300,000

Accounting During the Holding Period

Operating assets are used to produce revenues for the company over the asset's estimated useful life. Proper application of the matching principle requires that the cost of these assets be allocated to expense over the time periods to be benefitted. The cost allocation process produces annual amortization expense, which is the cost allocated to a specific time period due to the use of long-lived assets. Accountants use special terms to identify the amortization of various types of assets.

Buildings, equipment, and other physical assets used in the business are often referred to as either fixed assets or property, plant, and equipment. Amortization arising from the use of these assets is known as depreciation expense. There is no external transaction which creates depreciation expense. Depreciation expense is recorded using an adjusting journal entry, as follows:

Depreciation Expense (E,-SE)	XXX	
Accumulated Depreciation (-A)		XXX

Estimates Required in Accounting for Long-Lived Assets

Long-lived assets provide benefits for many future time periods. For example, a factory building may be used for twenty years or more. One can never be certain of the physical or economic life of such an asset. For accounting purposes, it is necessary to estimate the useful economic life, which may differ from the asset's physical life. It may take over 100 years for a modern concrete and steel building to physically collapse. However, that building may only be useful as an efficient production facility for say, twenty years. It is this productive life that constitutes the building's *economic useful life*. Proper application of the matching principle would allocate the cost of this building to the twenty years over which it is expected to provide revenues from the manufacture of the company's products. Since technology is constantly changing, often rapidly, management can do no better than to estimate the building's economic life.

It is also necessary to estimate the **salvage value** or **residual value** of productive assets. This is the amount at which the asset can be sold, once it has outlived its usefulness to the company. A company should not allocate the total cost of an asset purchased for $500,000 as an expense if the company can sell it at a later date (the end of its estimated economic useful life) for $300,000. Only the difference, $200,000, should be expensed over the asset's life.

Depreciation Methods and Computations

Chapter 9 of your text provides a good description of alternative depreciation methods. The focus in the study guide is on the basic concepts and limits examples to the straight-line method. There are several exercises to allow you to practice computations from the alternative methods which you have learned from the text. It is worthwhile to take some time to explore the conceptual basis for the various **accelerated depreciation** methods.

Straight-Line Method

The simplest method to calculate depreciation expense is the straight-line method. Under the straight-line method, the annual expense is calculated by dividing the **depreciation base** by the estimated useful life of the asset. The depreciation base is simply the amount to be depreciated and is calculated by subtracting the salvage value from the asset's historical cost.

Example. Volunteer Construction purchases a piece of heavy equipment for $370,000. In addition, Volunteer pays delivery costs of $6,000 and installation costs of $11,000. The equipment is estimated to have a useful life, under normal operating conditions, of ten years. At the end of its normal life, Volunteer estimates it can sell the used equipment for $40,000.

The historical cost for the equipment is $387,000, the total cost to purchase the asset and get it into the condition and location for its intended use. The depreciation base for the equipment is $347,000, the historical cost less the estimated salvage value. Under the straight-line method, the annual depreciation expense is $34,700. The adjusting entry to record the depreciation is:

Depreciation Expense (E,-SE)   34,700

    Accumulated Depreciation (-A)   34,700

Accelerated Depreciation Methods

Accelerated depreciation methods are illustrated in the text. Accelerated depreciation methods charge a greater depreciation expense in early years of an asset's life than that obtained using the straight-line method. However, in later years, these methods will result in a lower expense than the straight-line method. All depreciation methods will result in the same total depreciation expense over the life of the asset. The asset's depreciation base cost is allocated over its total life. The alternative methods affect only the amounts charged in individual years.

Accelerated depreciation methods attempt to provide a smoothing of total operating expense over the life of an asset. If you purchase a new automobile, you are likely to experience very low maintenance and repair costs in the first few years of its life (perhaps even zero if you have a good warranty). As the vehicle ages, repair costs increase. If you depreciate the vehicle using the straight-line method, you would record a higher total operating expense (depreciation expense plus repair and maintenance expense) in the later years. If you use accelerated depreciation the lower depreciation expense of later years is combined with the higher repair costs to yield approximately equal total operating expense over each year of the asset's life.

Amortization of Other Long-Lived Assets

If you have carefully followed your text, you should realize that amortization of long-lived assets other than fixed assets is accomplished in an almost identical manner to fixed asset depreciation. Accountants employ different terms for the expense. For example, amortization of an intangible asset is referred to as amortization expense and amortization of a natural resource is referred to as depletion expense. The methods used to calculate amortization also differ to reflect underlying economic differences in the way in which these assets generate future revenues. Accelerated amortization methods are rarely used for intangible assets. Depletion expense is normally calculated using the production method. These are only minor differences in terminology and details. The basic amortization or cost allocation concept is identical for all long-lived assets.

Betterments Versus Maintenance Expense

Long-lived assets differ from assets discussed in previous chapters in that often a company will make additional expenditures related to the asset over its extended useful life. These expenditures fall into two categories: betterments and maintenance. Maintenance costs are routine costs to maintain the assets in proper working order. For example, changing the engine oil and other minor repairs would be considered maintenance for a personal automobile. Maintenance costs are expensed in the period in which they are incurred.

Betterments are expenditures to improve the asset's performance. Betterments are capitalized costs. The cost of a betterment is added to the asset balance and depreciated over the remaining life of the asset. Expenditure resulting in one or more of the following characterizes a betterment:

- increased useful life of the asset.
- increased quality of the asset's output.
- increased quantity of the asset's output.
- reduced operating costs of the asset.

Example. Return to the last example, and assume that Volunteer made the following expenditures during the third year of the asset's life. Volunteer paid $20,000 for a new computerized control panel. The new part will allow the machine to operate more smoothly and will increase its output by 20%. The smoother operating control will also increase the life of the equipment by two years. Volunteer also paid $1,200 to lubricate the machine. Lubrication is required approximately every year. Volunteer makes the following entries during the year.

Maintenance Expense (E,-SE)	1,200	
Cash (-A)		1,200
Recognized ordinary lubrication costs.		
Equipment (+A)	20,000	
Cash (-A)		20,000
Recognized betterment control panel.		
Depreciation Expense (E,-SE)	29,760	
Accumulated Depreciation (-A)		29,760
Recognized depreciation based on the betterment.		

Depreciation is calculated as follows. The betterment cost is added to the historical cost of the asset, bringing total cost up to $407,000. The salvage value is deducted to arrive at the revised depreciation base of $367,000. However, only $297,600 of the depreciation base remains to be depreciated, since depreciation expense in the first two years of operations totalled $69,400. The estimated useful life is extended two years by the betterment. The equipment has a remaining life of ten years. The depreciation calculation is made by taking the remaining depreciation base and dividing it by the revised remaining estimated life ($297,600 / 10 years = $29,760 per year).

This provides a general rule for changes in accounting estimates. Accounting estimate changes are only accounted for in current and future periods. Prior periods' revenues and expenses are unaffected. In the case of changes related to the depreciation expense estimate, current and future depreciation will be calculated by expensing the *revised remaining depreciation base* over the *revised remaining useful life* of the asset.

Disposal of Long-Lived Assets

The basic accounting entry to record disposal of a long-lived asset is no different from that of any other asset. The selling company will record the asset received in the exchange and eliminate the existing asset from its accounts. Any difference between selling price and book value (or carrying value) is recorded as gain or loss on sale.

For example, Wave Corporation purchased land on which it intended to build a storage facility. Wave paid $250,000 for the land. Wave's plans have now changed, and it sells the land for $270,000. The journal entry to record the sale is:

Cash (+A)	270,000	
Land (-A)		250,000
Gain on Sale (Ga,+SE)		20,000
Sold land for gain.		

If the asset has been depreciated, then the company must also remove the related accumulated depreciation balance when the asset is sold. For example, assume Wave Corporation sold equipment which originally cost $150,000 for $80,000. Up to the date of the sale, Wave has recorded total depreciation expense of $50,000. The journal entry to record the sale is:

Cash (+A)	80,000	
Loss on Sale (Lo,-SE)	20,000	
Equipment (-A)		150,000
Accumulated Depreciation (+A)	50,000	
Sold equipment for loss.		

The loss on sale (or gain on sale) of long-lived assets is included as a component of operating expense on the company's income statement.

QUESTIONS FOR YOUR REVIEW

1. Which of the following long-lived assets is not subject to amortization?
   a. A copyright on a science fiction novel
   b. A patent for an underwater camera
   c. A trademark
   d. goodwill

2. Falcons Corporation purchased a delivery truck on October 30, 2003. The following costs were incurred with the purchase of the truck.

Purchase price	$80,000
Sales tax on purchase price	1,600
Interest on the loan to buy	4,000
Spare parts inventory	1,600
Freight charges on delivery	1,000

   How much should Falcon debit to the Truck account?
   a. $81,600
   b. $82,600
   c. $85,600
   d. $88,200

3. The book value of an asset reported on the balance sheet is a measure of:
   a. estimated fair market value.
   b. estimated replacement cost.
   c. realizable value.
   d. historical cost less depreciation expense taken to date.

4. Which of the following costs should be excluded from the asset account for the purchase of factory production equipment?
   a. Utility costs to operate the equipment during its first year in service
   b. Freight charges
   c. Installation charges
   d. Sales tax paid on the equipment

5. The primary purpose of depreciation expense is to:
   a. provide a cash reserve for replacement when the asset becomes obsolete.
   b. match costs with revenues.
   c. inform investors of asset replacement cost.
   d. reflect changes in the fair market value of an asset.

6. The allocation of the cost of natural resources is termed:
   a. amortization expense.
   b. depreciation expense.
   c. depletion expense.
   d. production expense.

7. Which of the following costs is excluded from the Land account for land purchased for use in a manufacturing process?
   a. Demolition of an existing building
   b. Real estate broker's commissions and fees
   c. Interest on a mortgage loan made to purchase the land
   d. Appraisal fees, survey fees, and other real estate closing costs

8. The portion of a lump-sum purchase of $600,000 allocated to Land when the land is appraised at $180,000 and the building on the land is appraised at $540,000 is:
   a. $ 60,000.
   b. $150,000.
   c. $180,000.
   d. $200,000.

9. Land and a building are purchased for $450,000. The appraised values of the land and building are $67,500 and $270,000, respectively. The building should be recorded at:
   a. $ 90,000.
   b. $270,000.
   c. $337,500.
   d. $360,000.

10. A gain on sale of a long-lived asset is recorded when:
    a. selling price exceeds the book value of the asset sold.
    b. selling price exceeds the historical cost of the asset sold.
    c. book value exceeds the selling price of the asset sold.
    d. selling price exceeds the fair market value of the asset sold.

11. Which method produces the highest depreciation expense for the first year of an asset's life?
    a. Straight-line
    b. Activity base method
    c. Double-declining-balance
    d. It's impossible to tell without more information.

12. Nittany Company acquired a new machine at a cost of $76,000, with an expected salvage value of $4,000 and estimated life of 8 years or 36,000 units of output. Nittany produced 5,000 units in the machine's first year of use and 2,000 in the second year of use. Using the units of production method, depreciation expense for the *second year* of the asset's life is:
    a. $ 4,000.
    b. $ 4,222.
    c. $14,000.
    d. $14,788.

13. Nittany Company acquired a new machine at a cost of $76,000, with an expected salvage value of $4,000 and estimated life of 8 years or 20,000 units. What is depreciation expense for the *second year*, using the double-declining balance method?
    a. $14,400
    b. $14,250
    c. $18,000
    d. $19,000

14. Nittany Company acquired a new machine at a cost of $76,000, with an expected salvage value of $4,000 and estimated life of 8 years. Assuming Nittany depreciated this new machine using the straight-line method, what would be the accumulated depreciation after the third year?
    a. $18,000
    b. $19,000
    c. $27,000
    d. $28,500

15. Panthers, Inc. bought a building which cost $75,000 on January 1, 2003. At that time of purchase, the building's estimated useful life was ten years with a salvage value of $15,000. Panthers sold the building on January 1, 2006, for $54,000. If the straight-line depreciation method was used, what is the gain or loss on disposal?
    a. $12,000 gain
    b. $12,000 loss
    c. $3,000 loss
    d. $3,000 gain

16. On January 1, 2003, the Holland Brewing Corporation purchased new equipment costing $270,000 and estimated to have a useful life of 5 years. Salvage value was estimated to be $30,000. Using the double-declining balance depreciation method, what would be depreciation expense for the year ending December 31, 2003?
    a. $48,000
    b. $54,000
    c. $96,000
    d. $108,000

17. On January 1, 1999, Seminoles, Inc. purchased a new boiler for $1,000,000. The boiler had an expected life of 9 years and its expected salvage value is $100,000. On January 1, 2003, Seminoles spent $240,000 for a renovation to the boiler, which extended the useful life by 5 years (14 years total). Salvage value is unchanged. If Seminoles uses the straight-line method of depreciation, what is the depreciation expense for 2003?
    a. $84,000
    b. $74,000
    c. $60,000
    d. $50,000

Use the following information to answer questions 18 through 20.

On January 1, 2003, Seahawks Corporation purchased new equipment at a total cost of $88,000. Seahawks expects to use the equipment for 5 years with a salvage value of $8,000 after the fifth year.

18. What is depreciation expense for the fourth year using the double-declining balance method of depreciation?
    a. $6,912
    b. $7,603
    c. $16,000
    d. $17,600

19. What is the book value after two years using the straight-line method of depreciation?
    a. $40,000
    b. $48,000
    c. $52,000
    d. $56,000

20. After 2 years, Seahawks revised the useful life from 5 to 6 years. Salvage value is unchanged. What is depreciation expense for year 3 using the straight-line method? (Assume straight-line had been used in the previous two years and round answers to nearest whole dollar).
    a. $ 9,600
    b. $12,000
    c. $13,332
    d. $14,668

21. On January 1, 2003, Colts Construction purchased new equipment costing $920,000. The equipment was expected to be in service for 10 years after which it would be worth $40,000. Colt's fiscal year ends on December 31.

    Colt is considering two alternative depreciation methods for the new equipment. Colt's management would like to choose the method which will provide the maximum total depreciation expense over the first three years of the life of the new equipment. Calculate depreciation expense for years 1 through 3, using the following methods.

    a. Straight-line method

    b. Double-declining balance method

22. Juban Corporation purchased a retail outlet for $600,000 on January 1, 2003. The price included land, building, and equipment. A professional appraiser estimates the land is worth $225,000, the building $360,000, and the equipment $315,000. Juban depreciates all assets using the straight-line method. Salvage value is estimated as 10% of an asset's historical cost. Juban estimates that a building will normally last 20 years and equipment must be replaced every 10 years.

Required: Prepare all required journal entries and adjusting entries related to the purchased assets for the year ended December 31, 2003.

23. A piece of equipment that cost $16,200 and on which $9,000 of accumulated depreciation had been recorded was disposed of an January 2, the first day of business of the current year.

    a.   What is the correct journal entry if the equipment was scrapped?

    b.   What is the correct journal entry if the equipment was sold for $3,000 cash?

23. c. What is the correct journal entry if the equipment was sold for $9,000 cash?

d. What is the correct journal entry if the equipment is traded in on other dissimilar equipment having a list price of $28,000? A $7,800 trade-in is allowed, and the balance is paid in cash. If the company had paid all cash for the new equipment, it would have paid $24,000.

e. What is the correct journal entry if the equipment is traded in on other dissimilar equipment having a list price of $28,000? A $3,600 trade-in is allowed, and the balance is paid in cash. If the old equipment had been sold separately, it would have sold for $3,000.

24. Showtime Publishing Company purchased the copyright to a basic accounting textbook for $50,000. The usual life of a textbook is about five years. However, the copyright will remain in effect for another 75 years. Prepare the journal entry to record the annual amortization expense on the copyright?

25. Michigan Mining Corporation purchased land containing an estimated 10 million tons of iron ore for a cost of $4,400,000. The land without the iron ore is estimated to be worth $1,800,000. The company expects that all the usable iron can be mined in ten years. Buildings costing $600,000 with an estimated useful life of twenty years were erected on the site. Equipment costing $700,000 with an estimated useful life of ten years was installed. Because of the remote location, neither the buildings nor the equipment has an estimated residual value. During its first year of operations, Michigan Mining mined and sold one million tons of iron ore.

    a. Prepare the journal entry to record the depletion expense for the first year of operations?

    b. What is the amount of annual depreciation expense for the buildings, if Michigan Mining wishes to make it *proportional* to the depletion expense?

CHAPTER 9 - SOLUTIONS

1.	d	6.	c	11.	d	16.	d
2.	b	7.	c	12.	a	17.	b
3.	d	8.	b	13.	b	18.	b
4.	a	9.	d	14.	c	19.	d
5.	b	10.	a	15.	c	20.	b

21. a. Straight-line method.
Depreciation Base = Cost - Salvage Value
= $920,000 - $40,000
= $880,000

Depreciation Expense = Depreciation Base / Estimated Life
= $880,000 / 10 years
= $88,000 per year

Total Depreciation Expense - Years 1 through 3 = $264,000

b. Double-declining-balance method.
The estimated useful life is ten years. This gives a straight-line rate of 10% per year for Depreciation Expense. Double-declining balance Depreciation Expense is calculated by multiplying the book value of an asset times the declining balance rate. The book value, or carrying value, of an asset is its cost less any accumulated depreciation taken to date. Since the straight-line rate is 10%, the double-declining balance rate will be 20%.

Year 1: $920,000 x .20 = $184,000
Year 2: ($920,000 - $184,000) x .20 =   147,200
Year 3: ($920,000 - $184,000 - $147,200) x .20 =   117,760
Total Depreciation Expense = $448,960

22. Land (+A)   150,000
Building (+A)   240,000
Equipment (+A)   210,000
  Cash (-A)   600,000
Purchased fixed assets.

Asset	Allocation Formula	Allocated Cost
Land	($225,000/$900,000) x $600,000	$150,000
Building	($360,000/$900,000) x $600,000	240,000
Equipment	($315,000/$900,000) x $600,000	210,000
		$600,000

Depreciation Expense (E,-SE)   10,800
    Accumulated Depreciation (-A)   10,800
Recognized annual depreciation on building.
[($240,000 - $24,000) x 1/20]

Depreciation Expense (E,-SE)   18,900
    Accumulated Depreciation (-A)   18,900
Recognized annual depreciation on equipment.
[($210,000 - $21,000) x 1/10]

23. a. Accumulated Depreciation (+A)   9,000
    Loss on Retirement (E,-SE)   7,200
        Equipment (-A)   16,200
    Disposed of asset with no salvage value.

    b. Cash (+A)   3,000
      Accumulated Depreciation (+A)   9,000
      Loss on Retirement (E,-SE)   4,200
        Equipment (-A)   16,200
    Disposed of asset with $3,000 salvage value.

    c. Cash (+A)   9,000
      Accumulated Depreciation (+A)   9,000
        Equipment (-A)   16,200
        Gain on Retirement (R,+SE)   1,800
    Disposed of asset with $9,000 salvage value.

    d. Equipment (+A)   24,000
      Accumulated Depreciation (+A)   9,000
        Equipment (-A)   16,200
        Cash (-A)   16,200
        Gain on Retirement (R,+SE)   600
    The fair value of the new equipment is $24,000. The cash given up is $16,200 and book value of the asset given up is $7,200 or a total of $23,400, so a gain of $600 is recorded on the transaction.

    e. Equipment (+A)   27,400
      Accumulated Depreciation (+A)   9,000
      Loss on Retirement (E,-SE)   4,200
        Equipment (-A)   16,200
        Cash (-A)   24,400
    The new equipment's market value is equal to cash paid, $24,400 ($28,000 - $3,600) and the market value of the asset given up, $3,000. The resulting loss is the book value given up, $7,200 - $3,000 = $4,200.

24. Amortization Expense (E,-SE)   10,000
         Copyright (-A)   10,000
     Amortized intangible asset.

     Amortization should be based on the estimated useful life of the copyright, not its legal life. Amortization is therefore based on the five-year life.

25. a. Depletion Expense (E,-SE)   260,000
             Accumulated Depletion (-A)   260,000
         Recognize depletion based on first-year production.
         Total cost of property $4,400,000
         Less: Residual value   (1,800,000)
         Depletion base $2,600,000

     Depletion rate: $2,600,0000 / 10,000,000 tons = $.26 / ton

     1,000,000 tons x $.26/ton = $260,000

     b. Cost of Buildings $600,000
         Base   10,000,000 tons

     Depreciation rate = $600,000 / 10,000,000 tons = $.06 per ton

     Depreciation expense = 1,000,000 tons x $.06 per ton = $60,000

CHAPTER 10

Introduction to Liabilities:
Economic Consequences, Current Liabilities, and
Contingencies

REVIEW OF KEY CONCEPTS

The last few chapters have emphasized accounting for various categories of assets. In Chapters 10 and 11, the focus shifts to the other side of the balance sheet to discuss accounting for liabilities. Liabilities are divided into two general categories: *current liabilities* and *long-term liabilities*. This chapter discusses the accounting for liabilities in general as well as focusing on current liabilities and contingent liabilities. Long-term liabilities are discussed in Chapter 11.

Liabilities are defined as "probable future sacrifices of economic benefits arising from present obligations of a particular entity, to transfer assets or provide services to other entities in the future as a result of past transactions or events." In other words, liabilities are amounts that are owed by the company and must be settled in some future time period.

Accounting for Liabilities

As was the case with assets, there are three basic accounting problems to be addressed for liabilities. Liabilities must be originally recorded, ultimately settled or discharged, and accounted for in the interim period.

A simple accounts payable example illustrates the initial accounting and discharge of a liability. A company purchases merchandise on credit for $450, and pays the supplier within thirty days. The following journal entries are required:

Merchandise Inventory (+A)	450	
Accounts Payable (+L)		450
Recorded liability from a credit purchase.		

Accounts Payable (-L)	450	
Cash (-A)		450
Paid supplier for credit purchase.		

Although the example is a simple one, it represents the basic concepts of recording and settling liabilities.

Current Liabilities

Current liabilities are liabilities that are expected to require the use of current assets or incur other current liabilities in settlement of the initial current liability.

The ratio of current assets divided by current liabilities, the **current ratio**, is an important indicator of a company's short-term solvency or liquidity. Even if a company is highly profitable, if it does not have sufficient current assets on hand to pay its liabilities when they become due, the company will not survive.

Current liabilities can be divided into two broad categories: *determinable current liabilities* and *contingent liabilities*.

Determinable Liabilities

Determinable liabilities have terms of payment which are contractually fixed and therefore easily measured both in amount and as to their due date. Included in this category are Accounts and Notes payable (or short-term debts), dividends payable, unearned revenues, third-party collections, and accrued liabilities. Most of these liabilities have already been introduced earlier in the text. In this chapter, we will discuss liabilities which you have not encountered before.

Short-term debts or notes payable are liabilities arising out of a formal borrowing agreement, normally with a bank. A common type of notes payable is where the borrower repays the face value of the note and accumulated interest at a specified future date. For example, Brewcrew, Inc. borrows $10,000 from Third National Bank on January 1, 2003. The note is due in six months and the interest rate is 8%. Normally, the quoted interest rate is an annual rate. So Brewcrew is actually paying 4% for the six months of loan term. At the end of six months, Brewcrew pays $10,400 to the bank; the initial amount borrowed, $10,000, and $400 ($10,000 X .08 X 6/12) interest expense.

The journal entries to account for the note are:

1/1/03	Cash (+A)	10,000	
	Notes payable (+L)		10,000
6/30/03	Notes payable (-L)	10,000	
	Interest expense (E, -SE)	400	
	Cash (-A)		10,400

Another type of note payable is a note issued at a discount. In this case, the borrower initially receives less than the face value of the note, but must repay the higher face value. The difference between the amount borrowed and the amount repaid is the cost of borrowing or the interest expense.

Example. Tech Corporation borrows $15,000 from the Hoosier National Bank on June 1. Tech signs a three-month note with a face value of $15,225. The $225 difference between the amount borrowed and the face value is a discount on notes payable. The discount is originally recorded as a contra-liability (an account which has a debit balance and is subtracted from the amount of the note payable on the balance sheet). Each month a portion of the discount will be amortized, i.e., converted to interest expense through an adjusting journal entry. The journal entries over the term of the note are as follows:

Cash (+A)	15,000	
Discount on Notes payable (-L)	225	
Notes Payable (+L)		15,225

Issued short-term note payable for cash.

Interest Expense (E,-SE)	75	
Discount on Notes Payable (+L)		75

Recognized accrual of interest on
the note ($225 / 3 months).

The above entry is repeated at the end of each of the three months.

Notes Payable (-L)	15,225	
Cash (-A)		15,225

Paid face value on the note.

Note that initially, the net note payable is $15,000, $15,225 [Note payable, a credit balance account] - $225 [Discount on notes payable, a debit balance account]. Observe that just prior to the repayment of $15,225, the discount on notes payable has been reduced to a zero balance by the three adjusting entries so that the net note payable is $15,225 (the total amount owed). Over the term of the note, Tech has recognized interest expense in the amount of $225. The payment of $15,225 includes the repayment of the $15,000 borrowed plus the $225 of interest expense.

Alternatively, the note could be recorded net of the discount. The entries that would be made under this alternative are:

Cash (+A)	15,000	
Notes Payable-net (+L)		15,000

Issued short-term note payable for cash.

Interest Expense (E,-SE)	75	
Notes Payable-net (+L)		75

Recognized accrual of interest on
the note ($225 / 3 months)

The above entry is repeated at the end of each of the three months.

Notes Payable (-L)	15,225	
Cash (-A)		15,225

Paid face value on the note.

Third-Party Collections

Companies often serve as collecting agents for the government, and sometimes for other companies as well. A common example is sales tax. If a firm sells a product for $100, and the state levies a 5% sales tax, then the company must collect $105 from the customer. Of this amount, $5 will be held (normally until month's end) and then remitted to the state government. Payroll tax withholding is another third-party collection for a governmental unit. Third-party collections for other companies might include union dues and employee health or life insurance premiums. Accounting for these types of collections is illustrated using the sales tax example.

Cash (+A)	105	
Sales (R,+SE)		100
Sales Tax Payable (+L)		5

Sold merchandise and collected 5% sales tax.

Sales Tax Payable (-L)	5	
Cash (-A)		5

Paid sales tax to the state government.

Accrued Liabilities

Accrued liabilities are obligations created when an expense is incurred prior to a cash payment. *Normal accrued liabilities* arise from common transactions such as wages payable, interest payable, and rent payable, and are recorded through adjusting entries. These accruals were discussed in Chapter 4. *Contingent accrued liabilities* are dependent on a future event, and therefore cannot be as precisely measured. Contingent accrued liabilities require estimation by management. For example, businesses (and some individuals) are required to make income tax payments to the federal government during the year, usually every 3 months or quarterly. Such income taxes payments can only be calculated by using estimates of taxable income. The final tax settlement for the year is based on actual net taxable income.

Contingencies and Contingent Liabilities

A *contingency* is an existing condition which may (or may not) give rise to a future gain or loss to the company. Lawsuits are a frequently encountered example. Depending on the final settlement, a company may incur a loss in a suit filed against them, or realize a gain if a suit filed against another party is successful.

Gain contingencies usually do not appear in either the financial statements or the footnotes until the gain is actually realized (i.e. when the lawsuit is settled). This practice is justified by the concept of conservatism.

The same concept of conservatism requires that **loss contingencies** be disclosed or accrued under certain circumstances before it is realized. Two criteria are applied to determine whether a loss contingency should be accrued. The contingency must be *highly probable* and *estimable*. When both conditions are met, then the loss contingency is accrued; i.e., the contingent liability appears on the balance sheet and a loss appears on the income statement. Significant loss contingencies which meet one, but not both, criteria must be disclosed in the financial statement footnotes. As a rule, companies will normally disclose all significant loss contingencies in the footnotes, even when neither criteria is met. The criteria are highly subjective, require management discretion, and typically require the assistance of outside legal counsel.

The required entries to record a contingent liability are straightforward, once management has determined that both criteria have been met. The contingency is initially recorded using management's best estimate of the likely outcome. An adjustment may be required when the issue is finally resolved. For example, assume that Shady Company has been sued by a customer for $2 million. At December 31, 2003, I.M. Sharp, attorney at law, estimates that the suit will probably be settled for $500,000. The suit is finally settled on June 30, 2004, for $600,000. The following journal entries are required.

12/31/03	Contingent Loss (Lo,-SE)	500,000	
	Contingent Liability (+L)		500,000
	Recorded contingent loss due to lawsuit.		

6/30/04	Contingent Loss (Lo,-SE)	100,000	
	Contingent Liability (-L)	500,000	
	Cash (-A)		600,000
	Record final settlement of lawsuit.		

Other Loss Contingencies

Lawsuits are not the only type of loss contingencies recorded by companies. Companies often offer a warranty or a guarantee to their customers for products or services sold. The precise terms of such warranties vary widely, but all represent a contingency which should be accrued. Although companies strive to maintain high quality control standards over production, manufacturing processes are not perfect. Some products will be defective and require repair or replacement under the customer's warranty. Managers can look at past performance and develop reliable estimates of future costs under warranty and guarantee obligations. Since, warranties are offered to customers to promote sale of the company's products, proper matching requires that the estimated future warranty costs be recorded as an expense in the same period that the company records the sales revenues which may be earlier than when the actual return or repair occurs.

Example. Tiger Manufacturing Company was formed on January 1, 2003. Tiger sells a line of golf balls which are guaranteed to fly straight up the middle of the fairway. If the balls fail to meet expectations, customers may return them for a full cash refund. During 2003, Tiger sold 500,000 balls for $10 each. Also during 2003, customers returned 10,000 balls and received their promised refunds. Tiger estimates that approximately 10 percent of the balls will be returned by the customers. Tiger would make the following journal entries during 2003.

Cash or Accounts Receivable (+A)	5,000,000	
Sales (R,+SE)		5,000,000
Sold 500,000 golf balls for $10 each.		

Warranty Expense (E,-SE)	500,000	
Contingent Warranty Liability (+L)		500,000
Recognized contingent liability (ten percent of sales).		

Contingent Warranty Liability (-L)	100,000	
Cash (-A)		100,000

Paid warranty liability on balls
returned by customers.

The above entries will leave an ending balance of $400,000 in the Contingent Warranty Liability account. This will cover future estimated returns of golf balls sold during 2003.

The **Conservatism Ratio** is a metric which can roughly assess how "conservative" a company's management is in choosing reporting methods. It is the ratio of reported income before taxes divided by taxable income. The underlying logic of the ratio is that since companies generally desire lower taxable income and resulting lower taxes currently due, they will select relatively conservative (income-reducing) methods for taxes. The ratio of reported income to this taxable amount provides a gauge of how conservative reported income is. This measure can aid in assessing how comparable reported income is among companies.

For example, assume that Noble Industries has reported income before taxes of $500,000 and reports income tax expense of $200,000. In addition, Noble's deferred tax liability account increased by $50,000. Noble's tax payable is income tax expense ($200,000) - increase in deferred tax liability ($50,000) = $150,000.

Noble's effective tax rate is income tax expense / reported income before taxes = $200,000/ $500,000 = .40. Since Noble's tax payable is equal to the effective tax rate multiplied by taxable income, Noble's taxable income is $150,000 / .40 = $375,000.

Noble's conservatism ratio is $500,000 / $375,000 = 1.333. If, for example, the industry average is 1.10, then Noble appears to be less conservative in its reporting method choice than its rivals. An analyst would need to examine the footnotes carefully to determine where Noble is more liberal relative to its rivals and adjust its income for differences. This would improve the comparability of the income numbers and presumably improve the decisions made.

QUESTIONS FOR YOUR REVIEW

1. Which of the following is *not* a contingent accrued liability?
   a. Dividends Payable
   b. Bonus Liability
   c. Vacation Pay Liability
   d. Income Taxes Payable

2. Which of the following is an accrued loss contingency?
   a. Sales Tax Payable
   b. Warranty Liability
   c. Accounts Payable
   d. All of the above are accrued loss contingencies.

3. Which of the following would most likely *not* be recorded as a contingent liability?
    a. Warranty Liability
    b. Lawsuit Liability
    c. Vacation Pay Liability
    d. Accounts Payable to Attorneys

4. Tiger Corporation is the issuer of a $10,000, 6-month, 10% note. Which of the following is *true* regarding the recording of the transaction?
    a. Note Payable should be credited for $10,500.
    b. Note Payable should be credited for $11,000.
    c. Note Payable should be credited for $10,000.
    d. Cash should be credited for $10,500.

Questions 5 and 6 refer to the following information.

On November 1, 2003, Wildcat Corporation signed an 8-month, 6%, $50,000 note payable with principal and interest due at maturity.

5. If the fiscal year ends on December 31, which of the following is *true* at year-end?
    a. Interest Expense is $500.
    b. Interest Expense is $750.
    c. Note Payable is $50,500.
    d. Note Payable is $53,000.

6. What is Wildcat's total liability on the note as of July 1, 2004?
    a. $50,000
    b. $53,000
    c. $52,000
    d. $51,500

Questions 7 through 10 refer to the following information.

On October 1, 2003, D.A. Bulls, Inc. borrowed $20,000 from the bank. As part of the deal, Bulls signed a note agreeing to pay the bank $21,800 on June 30, 2004.

7. What is the annual interest rate on this note?
    a. 9%
    b. 12%
    c. 10%
    d. 110%

8. Which of the following is *true* regarding the journal entry required on the day Bulls signed the note?
    a. Discount on Notes Payable should be debited for $1,000.
    b. Discount on Notes Payable should be credited for $1,800.
    c. Notes Payable should be credited for $21,800.
    d. Notes Payable should be debited for $20,000.

9. Which of the following is *true* regarding Bulls' balance sheet on December 31, 2003?
    a. Discount on Notes Payable is $1,200.
    b. Carrying value of Notes Payable is $20,000.
    c. Discount on Notes Payable is $600.
    d. Carrying value of Notes Payable is $21,200.

10. Which of the following is *true* regarding Bulls' income statement for 2003?
    a. Interest Payable is $600.
    b. Interest Expense is $600.
    c. Interest Payable is $1,800.
    d. Interest Expense is $1,800.

11. On January 1, 2003, Gator, Inc. signed a five-year, 10%, $50,000 note. As part of the agreement, Gator promised to make annual interest payments on January 1 of each year. Which of the following is correct regarding the effect of the note on Gator's financial statements on December 31, 2003?
    a. Gator should report $55,000 of long-term debt.
    b. Interest expense will be $0.
    c. Gator should report a current liability of Notes Payable of $50,000.
    d. Gator should report current liabilities of $5,000.

12. David's Pro Shop has a 100% satisfaction guaranteed policy for all golf clubs sold. If a customer isn't completely satisfied, he can return the clubs for a full refund. David's currently has a credit balance in the Contingent Warranty Liability account of $1,000. What is the effect on David's Warranty Expense when a customer returns a golf club?
    a. Decrease
    b. Increase
    c. No effect
    d. We need more information.

Questions 13 and 14 refer to the following.

Lions, Inc. sells football helmets. Each helmet costs Lions $10, sells for $25, and includes a money-back guarantee. Sales history indicates that 2% of the helmets sold are returned. During 2003, Lions had $100,000 of net sales.

13. What is the Guarantee Expense for the year?
    a. $800
    b. $2,000
    c. $80
    d. $50,000

14. Assume that the Guarantee Expense for 2003 was $1,000. Lions had a $1,200 credit balance in the Contingent Guarantee Liability account on January 1, 2003. During 2003, customers returned 90 helmets. What is the balance in Contingent Guarantee Liability at the end of 2003?
    a. $50 debit balance
    b. $200 credit balance
    c. $2,200 credit balance
    d. $1,300 credit balance

Questions 15 and 16 refer to the following.

Patriot Company sells stopwatches. Each watch costs Patriot $10, sells for $25, and is guaranteed for life. If a watch ever fails, Patriot will replace it at no cost to the customer. Sales history indicates that 2% of stopwatches sold are returned. During 2003, Patriot sold 100,000 stopwatches.

15. What is the Warranty Expense for the year?
    a. $100,000
    b. $2,000
    c. $50,000
    d. $20,000

16. Assume that the Warranty Expense for 2003 was $10,000. Patriot had a $12,000 credit balance in the Contingent Warranty Liability account on January 1, 2003. During 2003, customers returned 1,500 stopwatches. What is the balance in Contingent Warranty Liability at the beginning of 2003?
    a. $18,000 credit balance
    b. $22,000 credit balance
    c. $3,000 debit balance
    d. $7,000 credit balance

17. Under which of the following conditions should a loss contingency be accrued?
    a. When it is estimable
    b. When it is highly probable
    c. When it is either estimable or highly probable
    d. When it is both estimable and highly probable

18. Which of the following plans requires no actuarial assumptions?
    a. A post retirement health care plan
    b. A post retirement life insurance plan
    c. A defined-benefit pension plan
    d. A defined-contribution pension plan

Questions 19 and 20 refer to the following.

Campus Bus Services began operations on January 1, 2003. Campus Bus Service sells monthly passes good for thirty days of unlimited travel. During 2003, Campus sold monthly passes for a total of

$126,000. On December 31, 2003, Campus estimates that unexpired passes are outstanding with a value of $3,700.

19. What is the Unearned Revenue and Monthly Pass Revenue for 2003?

	Unearned Revenue	Monthly Pass Revenue
a.	$0	$126,000
b.	$3,700	$126,000
c.	$3,700	$122,300
d.	$126,000	$126,000

20. If instead, campus had a beginning balance in Unearned Revenue of $5,000, what would be the Monthly Pass Revenue for 2003?
    a. $122,300
    b. $126,000
    c. $132,300
    d. $136,000

21. Lass Stereo and Electronics recognizes most expenses when the cash payments are made. Lass began doing business in June, 2003. Lass made the following payments during December 2003:

    12/1/03   Prepaid insurance premium of $600 for a policy covering the six months ended May 31, 2004. Recorded entire amount as insurance expense.
    12/1/03   Paid $500 interest on an outstanding Note Payable. Under the terms of the note, Lass makes an interest payment on the first of each month, for the prior month's expense.
    12/10/03   Paid $400 in rent for the month ended November 30.

    12/16/03   Paid employee wages of $5,000. Employees are paid on the first and sixteenth of each month for the half month just ended. The next payday is January 1, 2004.

    On December 31, 2003, Lass reported total current assets of $30,000 and total current liabilities of $20,000. Lass's income statement showed a net income (cash basis) of $12,000 for the partial year ended December 31, 2003.

    a. What is Lass's current ratio, before any accrual adjustments?

b.   Prepare all required adjusting journal entries to convert from Lass's cash basis to the accrual basis of accounting for the above listed expenses.

c.   What is Lass's net income on the accrual basis?

d.   What is Lass's current ratio on the accrual basis?

22. The following relates to Bass, Inc.:

Income before taxes	$100,000
Income tax expense	35,000
Reported net income	$ 65,000
Decrease in deferred tax liability balance	$ 5,000

a. Compute estimated taxes payable for the year.

b. Compute the estimated effective tax rate.

c. Compute estimated taxable income.

d. Compute the conservatism ratio.

e. If the industry average conservatism ratio is 1.00, is Bass more or less conservative in choosing its financial reporting methods than its rivals? Explain.

23. Bates Motel Construction instituted a defined-benefit pension plan for its employees on December 31, 2001. Bates makes annual contributions in the amount of $25,000 to the Last National Bank which manages the pension plan. The first deposit was made on December 31, 2001. The bank invests the funds for the plan and earns a 10% annual return. The annual return is deposited directly to the fund; it does not go to Bates. On December 31, 2003, prior to making the 2003 contribution, Bates estimates that promised future retirement payments under the plan would require a total fund of $100,000.

   a. Prepare all journal entries that have been made by Bates related to the pension plan.

   b. What amount of Pension Liability should appear on Bates' December 31, 2003, balance sheet?

   c. What would be Bates' December 31, 2003, journal entry if the pension were a defined-contribution plan, rather than the defined-benefit plan?

d.   What would be Bates' December 31, 2003, Pension Liability if the pension were a defined-contribution plan, rather than the defined-benefit plan?

24.   Glacier Company operates a local sporting goods retail store. On a typical Michigan spring day, after a heavy snowfall, a customer, Robert McMillan, slipped and fell on the icy sidewalk as he was leaving the store. Mr. McMillan contends that everyone should realize that snow and ice are common in this area in late April, and Glacier should have cleared and salted the sidewalks. McMillan sued Glacier for $2,000,000 in damages for injuries sustained in the accident. The suit had not been settled on December 31, 2003.

S. Remington, Glacier's attorney, believes that McMillan has a valid claim for at least a part of the damages. Remington estimates that final settlement will be somewhere between $500,000 and $1,200,000. Remington's best guess is that the suit will result in a loss of $800,000.

McMillan and Glacier finally agree to settle out of court for $850,000 on April 15, 2004.

a.   Assume that Glacier agrees that a contingent liability exists on December 31, 2003. What journal entry is required to record this contingency?

b.   What journal entry is required to record the final settlement on April 15, 2004?

25. Cueva Corporation has $40,000 of net income before inclusion of depreciation expense. The only depreciable asset Cueva owns is a new delivery truck. The truck was purchased on January 1, 2003, for $30,000. Cueva plans on using the truck for five years, at which point it will be worthless. Cueva depreciates the truck using the straight-line method for financial reporting purposes. For tax purposes, the IRS will allow depreciation of $12,000, $8,000, $5,000, $3,000, and $2,000 for years one through five, respectively. There are no other differences between financial reporting and tax return income. Cueva's federal income tax rate is 30%.

Prepare Cueva's journal entry to record its 2003 tax liability. Show all supporting calculations.

CHAPTER 10 - SOLUTIONS

1.	a	6.	c	11.	d	16.	d
2.	b	7.	b	12.	c	17.	d
3.	d	8.	c	13.	b	18.	d
4.	c	9.	a	14.	b	19.	c
5.	a	10.	b	15.	d	20.	c

21. a. Current Ratio = Current Assets / Current Liabilities
         $30,000 / $20,000 = <u>1.50</u>

     b. Prepaid Insurance (+A)   500
             Insurance Expense (-E,+SE)   500
         Adjust for the prepaid portion of insurance expense.
         Lass would have recorded the entire $600
         as Insurance Expense under the cash basis.

         Interest Expense (E,-SE)   500
             Accrued Interest Payable (+L)   500
         Record accrued expense for December. Lass
         made an entry on December 1, but that
         represented the November expense.

         Rent Expense (E,-SE)   400
             Accrued Rent Payable (+L)   400
         Record accrued expense for December. Lass
         made an entry on December 10, but that
         represented the November expense.

         Wage Expense (E,-SE)   5,000
             Accrued Wages Payable (+L)   5,000
         Record accrued expense for the last half
         of December. Lass made an entry on
         December 16, but that represented the
         expense for the first half of the month.

     c. Net income as reported (cash basis) $12,000
         Plus: Reduction in insurance expense   500
         Less: Accrued expenses   (5,900)
         Net income on accrual basis   <u>$ 6,600</u>

     d. Current Ratio = Current Assets / Current Liabilities
         $30,500 / $25,900 = <u>1.18</u>

22. a. Estimated taxes paid during the year are:

         Income Tax Expense   35,000
         Deferred Tax Liability   5,000
             Income Tax Payable   40,000

     b. Estimated effective tax rate is:

         Income Tax Expense / Reported Income Before Tax = $35,000 / $100,000 = .35

c. Estimated taxable income is:

Taxable Income x Effective Tax Rate = Income Tax Payable
Taxable Income = Income Tax Payable / Effective Tax Rate
Taxable Income = $40,000 / .35 = $114,286

d. Conservatism Ratio is:

Reported Income Before Taxes / Taxable Income =
$100,000 / $114,286 = .875

e. Compared to its industry, Bass appears to be more conservative than its rivals because its conservatism ratio is lower than the industry average. In order to determine what this difference is due to, the deferred tax liability footnotes of the companies should be examined.

23. 2001 Pension Expense (E,-SE)   25,000
               Pension Liability (+L)   25,000
           Recognized $25,000 pension liability.

           Pension Liability (-L)   25,000
               Cash (-A)   25,000
           Paid $25,000 to pension fund.

     2002 Pension Expense (E,-SE)   25,000
               Pension Liability (+L)   25,000
           Recognized $25,000 pension liability.

           Pension Liability (-L)   25,000
               Cash (-A)   25,000
           Paid $25,000 to pension fund.

12/31/03 Pension Expense (E,-SE)   42,500
               Pension Liability (+L)   42,500
           Recognized $42,500 additional pension
           liability based on revised estimates
           from the actuary. The total fund
           balance should be $100,000. The current
           balance is only $57,500 [$25,000 (2001
           contribution) + $25,000 (2002 contribution)
           + $2,500 (10% interest earned in 2002)
           + $5,000 (10% interest earned in 2003)].

b. The total Pension Liability should be $100,000, based on the estimate.

c. Pension Expense (E,-SE)   25,000
        Cash (-A)   25,000
    Paid defined contribution of $25,000
    to pension fund.

d. Bates' Pension Liability is zero under a defined-contribution plan. Bates records no liability
    unless a required contribution has not been made. The actuarially determined liability does
    not apply to defined-contribution plans.

24. a. Contingent Loss (Lo,-SE)   800,000
            Contingent Liability (+L)   800,000
        Accrued contingent liability due
        to McMillan lawsuit.

    b. Contingent Liability (-L)   800,000
        Contingent Loss (Lo,-SE)   50,000
            Cash (-A)   850,000
        Settled accrued contingent liability
        due to McMillan lawsuit.

25. Cueva's taxable income (per the tax return) is $28,000. This is calculated by taking the $40,000
    operating income, less the tax depreciation expense of $12,000. Cueva's Income Tax Payable
    (the current liability) is $8,400. This is calculated by taking the $28,000 taxable income,
    multiplied by the tax rate of 30%.

    Cueva's tax benefit is due to the difference in depreciation expense between the tax return and
    the income statement.

Tax depreciation	$12,000
Straight-line depreciation	(6,000)
Excess depreciation	$ 6,000
x Tax rate	x 30%
Tax Benefit	$ 1,800

    Cueva's journal entry for 2003 is:

    Income Tax Expense (E,-SE)   10,200
        Income Tax Payable (+L)   8,400
        Deferred Tax Liability (+L)   1,800

    Note that the Income Tax Payable and the Deferred Tax Liability are calculated directly. The
    Income Tax Expense is "plugged" for an amount needed to balance the journal entry.

CHAPTER 11

Long-Term Liabilities: Notes, Bonds, and Leases

REVIEW OF KEY CONCEPTS

This chapter extends the discussion of liabilities from Chapter 10 to include long-term liabilities. There are three primary types of long-term liabilities: notes payable, bonds payable, and lease liabilities. The discussion here will focus on accounting for Bonds Payable, which represent an important source of capital financing for many companies.

Before continuing with this chapter, you should review several important items, if you have not already done so. First, be certain that you understand the **time value of money** concepts presented in Appendix 4B to the text. These concepts are critical to understanding accounting for long-term liabilities. Second, go back and carefully reread the sections titled **EFFECTIVE INTEREST RATE** and **ACCOUNTING FOR LONG-TERM OBLIGATIONS: THE EFFECTIVE INTEREST METHOD** in Chapter 11 of your text. These sections provide an excellent introduction to the concepts being discussed below in accounting for bonds payable.

Before beginning discussion of bonds payable, recall an important definition:

The effective interest rate is the actual interest rate paid by the issuer of the obligation. It is determined by finding the discount rate that sets the present value of the obligation's cash outflows equal to the fair market value of that which is received in the exchange.

As in Chapter 10, our approach here will look at accounting for long-term liabilities (1) when originally recorded, (2) during the holding period, and (3) when discharged.

Your text sets up separate accounts to record discounts and premiums related to bonds. Our experience indicates that many students grasp the concepts more easily using the net method. The net method uses no separate premium or discount accounts. Instead, we net (add premiums and subtract discounts) into the bonds payable account.

Understanding How a Bond Works

A bond payable is a long-term debt security issued by a company to private investors. Under the terms of a standard bond contract (called an indenture), the investors lend money to the company. The company agrees to repay the *principal amount* (the face value or the amount borrowed) at a future *maturity date*. Typically, companies issue bonds for long time periods, often 10 or 20 years.

In addition to the principal repayment, the issuer (borrower) agrees to make periodic cash interest payments to the investors. Most bonds issued by corporations pay interest on a semiannual basis. You can determine the amount of the interest payments from the terms of the indenture. Bonds pay interest based on the face value of the bond and the stated (or coupon) interest rate. For example, assume Nittany Corporation issues a $10,000, eight percent bond which pays interest semiannually on January 1 and July 1. On each interest payment date, Nittany writes investors a check for $400, based on the stated terms ($10,000 x .08 x 1/2 year). Nittany bases cash payments for interest on the stated rate and the face value; changes in the fair market price of the bonds or the effective interest rate do not change the cash payments for interest specified in the bond contract.

Accounting for Issuance of Bonds Payable

The issuer initially records the liability for bonds payable based on the face value of the bond issue. Issuers also record the receipt of cash from the bond issue, which is known as the **proceeds** of the bond issue.

Bonds always sell at *fair market value*. Investors determine the fair market value of a bond by the riskiness of the company's business operations, the time period until maturity, and the general market rate of interest. The market rate of interest for a bond of a given risk level and term to maturity is known as the **effective interest rate**. The effective interest rate changes over time due to changing economic conditions. For example, a company may diversify into several different lines of business, decreasing its overall operating risk. The decrease in risk leads to a decrease in the effective interest rate. However, the stated rate on a bond is fixed by the indenture and does not respond to changing economic conditions. Bond prices adjust for differences between the stated rate and the effective rate, so that the bond always sells for its fair market value.

Bond prices adjust to fair market value as follows. If the stated interest rate equals the effective interest rate, then the bond sells for its face value. If the stated interest rate is less than the effective interest rate, then the bond sells for less than its face value. The bond sells at a **discount**. If the stated interest rate is greater than the effective interest rate, then the bond sells for more than its face value. The bond sells at a **premium**.

Investors seek to earn a fair rate of return on investments. You can calculate rate of return by dividing the interest received by the cost of the investment. Consider the case of a bond selling at a discount. Since the indenture terms fix cash interest payments, the investors earn the fair market rate of return (the effective interest rate) by reducing the price they pay for the bond. The numerator of the rate of return is fixed by the bond indenture. The rate of return can only change by adjusting the denominator (the bond price).

Example. Illini Corporation decides to raise needed funds for a major plant expansion by issuing $800,000 in ten-year, 8% bonds, on January 1, 2003. The bonds pay interest semiannually on June 30 and December 31, and mature on December 31, 2012.

Bonds Issued at Face Value

Assume that the effective interest rate is 8% on January 1, 2003. The bonds have a stated rate equal to the effective rate, and sell for face value of $800,000. You can verify that this is the fair market value of the bonds.

First, identify the future cash flows associated with the bond. There will be an $800,000 outflow at the end of 20 periods (ten years, with semiannual interest payments) for repayment of the face value. There will be semiannual payments of $32,000 each (an annuity) representing the cash payments for interest. Calculate this by multiplying the stated interest rate (8% or 4% per semiannual payment period) times the principal amount of the bond ($800,000).

Next, calculate the present value of these future cash flows using the effective interest rate of 8% (4% per semiannual payment period) for the 20 periods until maturity.

The table factor for the present value of a dollar for 20 periods, discounted at 4%, is .4564. Multiplying by the principal amount gives the present value of the $800,000 principal repayment as $365,120.

The table factor for the present value of an ordinary annuity for 20 periods, discounted at 4%, is 13.5903. Multiplying by the interest payment amount gives the present value of the $32,000 annuity as $434,890.

Adding the present values together gives the total present value of the remaining cash flows as $800,010. This amount equals the face value of $800,000. (There is a $10 difference due to rounding). The present value of the future cash flows is the fair market value of the bond. Illini makes the following journal entry to record the issue of the bond.

Cash (+A)	800,000	
Bonds Payable (+L)		800,000

Bonds Issued at More Than Face Value

Assume that the effective interest rate is 6% on January 1, 2003. The bonds have a stated rate greater than the effective rate, and sell for a premium over the face value of $800,000. You can determine the price of the bonds.

First, identify the future cash flows associated with the bond. There will be an $800,000 outflow at the end of 20 periods (ten years, with semiannual interest payments) for repayment of the face value. There will be semiannual payments of $32,000 each (an annuity) representing the cash payments for interest. You can calculate this by multiplying the stated interest rate (8% or 4% per semiannual payment period) times the principal amount of the bond ($800,000).

Next, calculate the present value of these future cash flows using the effective interest rate of 6% (3% per semiannual payment period) for the 20 periods until maturity.

The table factor for the present value of a dollar for 20 periods, discounted at 3%, is .5537. Multiplying by the principal amount gives the present value of the $800,000 principal repayment as $442,960. The table factor for the present value of an ordinary annuity for 20 periods, discounted at 3% is 14.8775. Multiplying by the interest payment amount gives the present value of the $32,000 annuity as $476,080.

Adding the present values together gives the total present value of the remaining cash flows as

$919,040. This is the fair market value of the bond. The bond sells for $919,040. This price indicates a premium of $119,040 over the face value of the bond. Investors pay more than face value, because the bond offers stated interest higher than the effective rate at the issue date. Using the net method, Illini makes the following journal entry to record the issue of the bond at a premium.

Cash (+A)	919,040	
Bonds Payable (+L)		919,040

Bonds Issued at Less Than Face Value

Assume that the effective interest rate is 10% on January 1, 2003. The bonds have a stated rate less than the effective rate, and sell for a discount. You can determine the price of the bonds, as was done in the above cases. Adding the present values together gives the total present value of the remaining cash flows as $700,310. This is the fair market value of the bond. The bond sells for $700,310. This price indicates a discount of $99,690 from the face value of the bond. Investors pay less than face value, because the bond offers stated interest lower than the effective rate at the issue date. Using the net method, Illini makes the following journal entry to issue the bond at a discount.

Cash (+A)	700,310	
Bonds Payable (+L)		700,310

Accounting for Bonds at Maturity

Under terms of the bond indenture, the issuer repays the **face value** at the **maturity date**. Note that this is independent of the original issue price of the bond. In all three of the above cases, Illini repays the $800,000 face value of the bond when it matures on December 31, 2012. Illini records redemption of the bond with the following journal entry.

Bonds Payable (-L)	800,000	
Cash (-A)		800,000

Accounting for Bonds During the Holding Period

Bonds Issued at Face Value

Illini makes semiannual interest payments beginning June 30, 2003, continuing until the final payment on December 31, 2012. Illini bases the amount of interest paid on the stated rate and the face value. The cash payments are $32,000 each ($800,000 x .08 x ½ year). Illini calculates interest expense using the effective interest method. Under the effective interest method, to calculate the expense, multiply the bond liability amount by the effective interest rate. In this example, interest expense is $32,000 ($800,000 x .08 x ½ year). Illini makes the following journal entries to record interest payments on June 30 and December 31 each year.

Interest Expense (E,-SE)	32,000	
Cash (-A)		32,000

Recognized interest expense
($800,000 x .08 x ½ year).

The balance sheet value of the bond liability always equals the balance in the bonds payable account, when the bond is originally issued at face value. In this case, Illini reports a bond payable balance of $800,000 on its balance sheet every year until maturity. Note that since the bond liability does not change over the life of the bond, the interest expense calculated under the effective interest method is the same each period.

Bonds Issued at a Premium

Illini still makes semiannual interest payments, calculating the amount of the cash interest payment based on the stated rate and the face value. The cash payments are still $32,000 each. In the case of the bond issued at a premium, Illini makes the following journal entry to record the June 30, 2003, interest payment.

Interest Expense (E,-SE)	27,571	
Bonds Payable (-L)	4,429	
Cash (-A)		32,000

[Bonds Payable x .06 x ½ year]
[919,040 x .06 x ½ = 27,571]

By now, you have noted that the interest expense is not equal to the interest payment amount. You calculate interest expense using the effective interest method. Under the effective interest method, calculate the expense multiplying the bond liability amount by the effective interest rate. The total bond liability is $919,040 (which includes the bond payable of $800,000 plus the premium on bonds of $119,040). In this example, the interest expense for the six months ended June 30, 2003, is $27,571. The reduction of bonds payable represents amortization of the premium and is a plug figure to balance the journal entry for the difference between the interest expense amount and the cash interest payment amount.

The balance sheet value of the bond liability equals the balance in the bonds payable account, when the bond is originally issued at a premium, and Illini uses the net method. The total bond liability equals the principal amount plus the remaining unamortized premium. You must recalculate the interest expense at each interest payment date, using the effective interest method. The entry to record the December 31, 2003, payment is as follows.

Interest Expense (E,-SE)	27,438	
Bonds Payable (-L)	4,562	
Cash (-A)		32,000

[Bonds Payable x .06 x ½ year]
[(919,040 - 4,429)) x .06 x ½]

The bond liability at a balance sheet date equals the bonds payable principal plus the unamortized premium. The balance sheet values for the bond liability in 2003 are as follows:

	6/30/03	12/31/03
Bonds Payable - principal	$800,000	$800,000
Plus: Premium on Bonds *	114,611	110,049
Balance sheet value	$914,611	$910,049

*   The original premium was $119,040. The remaining balance after the two amortization entries ($4,429 and $4,562) is $110,049.

Bonds Issued at a Discount

Illini makes semiannual interest payments and calculates the cash interest payments based on the stated rate and the face value. The cash payments are still $32,000 each. In the case of the bond issued at a discount, Illini makes the following journal entry to record the June 30, 2003, payment.

Interest Expense (E,-SE)	35,016	
Bonds Payable (+L)		3,016
Cash (-A)		32,000

[Bonds Payable x .10 x ½ year]
[700,310 x .10 x ½ = 35,016]

As for a bond sold at a premium, interest expense does not equal the interest payment amount. Illini calculates interest expense using the effective interest method. Under this method, multiplying the bond liability amount by the effective interest rate gives the interest expense. The total bond liability is $700,310 (which includes the bond principal of $800,000 less the discount on bonds of $99,690). In this example, interest expense for the six months ended June 30, 2003, is $35,016. The difference between interest expense and cash interest payments is a plug figure to balance the journal entry and amortize the discount .

The balance sheet value of the bond liability equals to the bonds principal amount less any remaining unamortized discount when the bond is originally issued at a discount. The entry to record the interest payment increases the Bonds Payable balance. Illini must recalculate interest expense at each payment date, using the effective interest method. The entry to record the December 31, 2003, payment is as follows.

Interest Expense (E,-SE)	35,166	
Bonds Payable (+L)		3,166
Cash (-A)		32,000

[Bonds Payable x .10 x ½ year]
[703,326 x .10 x ½]

The balance sheet values for the bond liability in 2003 are as follows:

	6/30/03	12/31/03
Bonds Payable - principal	$800,000	$800,000
Less: Discount on Bonds *	(96,674)	(93,508)
Balance sheet value	$703,326	$706,492

* The original discount was $99,690. The remaining balance after the two amortization entries ($3,016 and $3,166) is $93,508.

You can verify the balance sheet value for the bond liability by applying the concepts of the effective interest rate method. The calculations below illustrate this verification in the case of the Illini bond issued at a discount for December 31, 2003. Once you have reviewed these calculations, you should make a similar verification of the December 31, 2003, balance sheet value for the case of the bond issued at a premium.

First, identify the remaining future cash flows associated with the bond. There will be an $800,000 outflow at the end of 18 periods (nine years, with semiannual interest payments) for repayment of the face value. Note that you use 18 periods, not 20, since one year (2 periods) has elapsed as of December 31, 1999. There will be 18 semiannual payments of $32,000 each (an annuity) representing the cash payments for interest. Calculate this by multiplying the stated interest rate (8% or 4% per semiannual payment period) times the principal amount of the bond ($800,000).

Next, calculate the present value of the future cash flows using the effective interest rate of 10% (5% per semiannual payment period) for the 18 periods until maturity. The table factor for the present value of a dollar for 18 periods, discounted at 5% is .4155. Multiplying by the principal amount gives the present value of the $800,000 principal repayment as $332,400.

The table factor for the present value of an ordinary annuity for 18 periods, discounted at 5%, is 11.6896. Multiplying by the interest payment amount gives the present value of the $32,000 annuity as $374,067.

Adding the present values together gives the total present value of the remaining cash flows as $706,467. This amount equals the balance sheet value of $706,492 calculated above. (There is a $25 difference due to rounding.) The present value of the future cash flows is the fair value of the bond.

QUESTIONS FOR YOUR REVIEW

1. Which of the following bond types may be retired before maturity, at the option of the bond issuer?
   a. Callable bonds
   b. Serial bonds
   c. Debenture bonds
   d. Coupon bonds

2.   Which of the following describes the impact of issuing a bond at a discount?
      a.   The issuer records interest expense at a higher rate of interest than is stated on the bond.
      b.   The issuer records a loss on issuance.
      c.   The interest payment is greater than the interest expense.
      d.   The purchaser pays less than fair market value for the bond.

3.   Which of the following describes the impact of issuing a bond at a premium?
      a.   The issuer pays a higher rate of interest than is stated on the bond.
      b.   The issuer records a gain on issuance.
      c.   The interest payment is greater than the interest expense.
      d.   The purchaser pays more than fair market value for the bond.

4.   When a bond is issued at a discount, the balance sheet value of the bond you calculated it by:
      a.   adding the unamortized discount on bonds to the bonds principal.
      b.   adding the amortized discount on bonds between the issue date and the balance sheet date to the bond principal.
      c.   deducting the unamortized discount on bonds from the bond principal.
      d.   deducting the amortized discount on bonds between the issue date and the balance sheet date from the bond principal.

5.   When a bond is issued at a premium, the balance sheet value of the bond you calculate it by:
      a.   adding the unamortized premium on bonds payable to the bond principal.
      b.   adding the amortized premium on bonds payable between the issue date and the balance sheet date to the bond principal.
      c.   deducting the unamortized premium on bonds payable from the bond principal.
      d.   deducting the amortized premium on bonds payable between the issue date and the balance sheet date from the bond principal.

6.   Which of the following describes the behavior of interest expense and the amortization of discount on bonds under the effective interest method?
      a.   The balance sheet value of the bond increases as the discount on bonds is amortized.
      b.   Cash payments for interest are greater than interest expense.
      c.   Annual interest expense decreases as the discount on bonds is amortized.
      d.   Cash payments for interest increase as the discount on bonds is amortized.

7.   Which of the following interest rates, when used to discount the future interest and principal cash payments, results in a present value that is equal to the amount of cash received by the bond issuer?
      a.   The stated rate
      b.   The coupon rate
      c.   The discount rate
      d.   The effective interest rate

8. Which of the following explains the impact of amortizing a discount on bonds?
   a. Amortization decreases the cash interest payments.
   b. Amortization increases the cash interest payments.
   c. Amortization decreases interest expense.
   d. Amortization increases interest expense.

9. Which of the following statements regarding the recording of a capital lease is true?
   a. The lessor records a capital lease as an asset.
   b. The lessee records a capital lease as an asset.
   c. The lessee records a capital lease as a liability.
   d. All of the above are true statements.

10. Which of the following could be recorded as an operating lease?
    a. The lease transfers ownership to the lessee.
    b. The lease contains an option for the lessee to purchase the property at its fair market value.
    c. The lease term is 75% or more of the useful life of the property.
    d. The present value of the lease payments equals or exceeds 90% of the fair market value of the property.

11. Under which of the following circumstances should a company finance additional assets with long-term debt rather than common stock?
    a. The company has a very high debt-to-equity ratio.
    b. The company has a very high current ratio.
    c. The company has a very low interest coverage ratio.
    d. The company expects the return on the assets purchased to be higher than the interest expense on the debt.

12. Northwestern Corporation borrowed $1,000,000, signing a three-year note payable. The note has a 10% interest rate, compounded annually, and requires payment of principal plus interest at maturity. What is the *total interest* payment on the note?
    a. $ 248,700
    b. $ 300,000
    c. $ 331,000
    d. $1,331,000

Questions 13 through 16 use the following information. On January 1, 2003, Spartan Sporting Goods, Inc. issued $1,000,000 of 5%, five-year bonds payable. The bonds pay interest on January 1 and July 1 each year. Spartan uses the effective interest method to account for bonds.

13. If Spartan issues bonds when the effective rate is 8%, how much cash will Spartan receive?
    a. $ 439,190
    b. $ 878,370
    c. $ 880,240
    d. $1,000,000

14. If the effective interest rate is 8% on the issue date, what amount of interest expense should Spartan record for 2003?
    a. $50,000
    b. $80,000
    c. $70,670
    d. $70,270

15. If the effective interest rate is 8% on the issue date, what is Spartan's balance sheet value on December 31, 2003?
    a. $1,000,000
    b. $ 899,040
    c. $ 979,330
    d. $ 929,330

16. Which of the following is *true*?
    a. Spartan issued the bond at face value.
    b. Spartan issued the bond at a premium.
    c. Spartan issued the bond at a discount.
    d. Spartan's issue price cannot be determined without additional information.

17. Gopher Corporation signed a seven-year lease on equipment. The equipment has a fair market value of $150,000 and the effective interest rate is 6%. Gopher makes annual lease payments. What is the amount of the required annual payment?
    a. $21,428
    b. $26,870
    c. $99,765
    d. $17,870

Questions 18 through 20 refer to the following information. Buckeye Brewing Company issues a ten-year $100,000 bond on January 1, 2003. The bond has a stated interest rate of 10% and pays interest semiannually starting June 30, 2003. Buckeye uses the effective interest method.

18. If Buckeye issues the bond on January 1, when the effective interest rate is 8%, how much cash will Buckeye receive?
    a. $113,592
    b. $116,310
    c. $ 67,952
    d. $100,000

19. If Buckeye issues the bond on January 1, when the effective interest rate is 8%, what amount of Interest Expense should Buckeye record on June 30, 2003?
    a. $10,000
    b. $ 5,000
    c. $ 4,544
    d. $ 4,500

20. If Buckeye issues the bond on January 1, when the effective interest rate is 8%, what is the balance sheet value of the bond on June 30, 2003?
    a. $ 86,864
    b. $100,000
    c. $113,592
    d. $113,136

21. On January 1, 2003, Nittany Enterprises borrowed $42,865 from Joepa National Bank. Nittany gave Joepa a note for $50,000, due December 31, 2004.

    Required:
    a. Compute the present value of the note's future cash flows at the following discount rates:
       (1) 6 percent

       (2) 8 percent

       (3) 10 percent

    b. What is the effective interest rate? Explain your answer.

22. On January 1, 2003, Wildcat Company issued $50,000 of ten-year bonds, with a stated interest rate of 12%, payable semiannually on June 30 and December 31 each year. The effective interest rate was 12% on January 1, 2003.

    Required:
    a. Prepare all entries associated with these bonds during 2003.

    b. Compute the balance sheet value of the bond liability on December 31, 2003. Explain your answer.

    c. Compute the present value of the bond's remaining cash flows on December 31, 2003, using the effective interest rate at the issue date.

23. On January 1, 2003, Badger Corporation issued $50,000 of ten-year bonds, with a stated interest rate of 12%, payable semiannually on June 30 and December 31 each year. The effective interest rate was 10% on January 1, 2003.

    Required:
    a. Prepare all entries associated with these bonds during 2003.

    b. Compute the balance sheet value of the bond liability on December 31, 2003. Explain your answer.

    c. Compute the present value of the bond's remaining cash flows on December 31, 2003, using the effective interest rate at the issue date.

24. On January 1, 2003, Boilermaker, Inc. issued $50,000 of ten-year bonds, with a stated interest rate of 10%, payable semiannually on June 30 and December 31 each year. The effective interest rate was 12% on January 1, 2003.

Required:

a. Prepare all entries associated with these bonds during 2003.

b. Compute the balance sheet value of the bond liability on December 31, 2003. Explain your answer.

c. Compute the present value of the bond's remaining cash flows on December 31, 2003, using the effective interest rate at the issue date.

25. Hawkeye Paving Company leases heavy trucks for its road construction business. On January 1, 2003, Hawkeye leased ten trucks for four years at $20,000 per truck, per year. Payments are to be made on December 31 each year. At the end of the lease, Hawkeye has the option to buy the trucks for a nominal price. The effective interest rate is 6% per year.

Required:
a. Compute the annual rental expense if the lease is treated as an operating lease. Prepare the required journal entries associated with an operating lease for 2003.

b. Prepare all required journal entries for 2003 if the lease is treated as a capital lease. Assume that the trucks are depreciated over a five-year useful life, using the straight-line method, and have no expected salvage value. Compute the total rental expense (interest expense plus depreciation expense) for 2003 if the lease is treated as a capital lease.

c. Prepare all required journal entries for 2004 if the lease is treated as a capital lease. Compute the total rental expense for 2004.

CHAPTER 11 - SOLUTIONS

1.	a	6.	a	11.	d	16.	c
2.	a	7.	d	12.	c	17.	b
3.	c	8.	d	13.	b	18.	a
4.	c	9.	d	14.	c	19.	c
5.	a	10.	b	15.	b	20.	d

21. a. (1) The only cash flow is the repayment of $50,000 at the end of two years. The present value of $50,000, due in two years, discounted at 6% is **$44,500**. The table factor is **.8900**.

     (2) The present value of $50,000, due in two years, discounted at 8% is **$42,865**. The table factor is **.8573**.

     (3) The present value of $50,000, due in two years, discounted at 10% is **$41,320**. The table factor is **.8264**.

    b. The effective interest rate is the rate that, when used to discount the future cash payment, results in a present value equal to the cash received by the borrower. The effective rate is thus *8 percent*.

22. a. 1/1/03   Cash (+A)   50,000
                       Bonds Payable (+L)   50,000
                    Issued bonds.

    6/30/03   Interest Expense (E,-SE)   3,000
                       Cash (-A)   3,000
                    Paid stated interest ($50,000 x 12% x 1/2 year).

    12/31/03 Interest Expense (E,-SE)   3,000
                       Cash (-A)   3,000
                    Paid stated interest.

    b. The bond is issued for its face value of $50,000 since the stated interest rate equals the effective interest rate of 12%. The balance sheet value on December 31, 2003, (and at all other dates) will be equal to the face value of $50,000.

    c. Begin by identifying the remaining future cash flows associated with the bond. There will be a $50,000 outflow at the end of 18 periods for repayment of the principal. There will be semiannual payments of $3,000 each (an annuity) representing the cash payments for interest. This is calculated by multiplying the stated interest rate (12% or 6% per semiannual payment period) times the principal amount of the bond ($50,000). Next, calculate the present value of these future cash flows using the effective interest rate of 12% (6% per semiannual payment period) for the 18 periods remaining until maturity.

The table factor for the present value of a dollar for 18 periods, discounted at 6%, is **.3503**. Multiplying by the principal amount gives the present value of the $50,000 principal repayment as **$17,515**.

The table factor for the present value of an ordinary annuity for 18 periods, discounted at 6%, is **10.8276**. Multiplying by the interest payment amount gives the present value of the $3,000 annuity as **$32,483**.

Adding the present values together gives the total present value of the remaining cash flows as **$49,998**. (There is a $2 difference due to rounding). This amount is equal to the balance sheet value on December 31, 2003.

23. a. 1/1/03   Cash (+A)   56,232

               Bonds Payable (+L)   6,232

               Bonds Payable (+L)   50,000

               Issued bonds.

    6/30/03 Interest Expense (E,-SE)   2,812

               Bonds Payable (-L)   188

                  Cash (-A)   3,000

               Paid stated interest and amortized premium.

    12/31/03 Interest Expense (E,-SE)   2,802

               Bonds Payable (-L)   198

                  Cash (-A)   3,000

               Paid stated interest and amortized premium.

  b. Bonds Payable - principal $50,000

      Plus: Premium on bonds *   5,846

      Balance sheet value $55,846

* The original premium was $6,232. The remaining balance after the two amortization entries ($188 and $198) is **$5,846**.

  c. Begin by identifying the remaining future cash flows associated with the bond. There will be a $50,000 outflow at the end of 18 periods for repayment of the principal. There will be semiannual payments of $3,000 each (an annuity) representing the cash payments for interest. This is calculated by multiplying the stated interest rate (12% or 6% per semiannual payment period) times the principal amount of the bond ($50,000). Next, calculate the present value of these future cash flows using the effective interest rate of 10% (5% per semiannual payment period) for the 18 periods remaining until maturity.

The table factor for the present value of a dollar for 18 periods, discounted at 5%, is **.4155**. Multiplying by the principal amount gives the present value of the $50,000 principal repayment as **$20,775**.

The table factor for the present value of an ordinary annuity for 18 periods, discounted at 5%, is **11.6896**. Multiplying by the interest payment amount gives the present value of the $3,000 annuity as **$35,069**.

Adding the present values together gives the total present value of the remaining cash flows as **$55,844**. This amount is equal to (there is a $2 difference due to rounding) the balance sheet value on December 31, 2003.

24. a. 1/1/03 Cash (+A)   44,265
     Bonds Payable (-L)   5,735
       Bonds Payable (+L)   50,000
     Issued bonds.

 6/30/03 Interest Expense (E,-SE)   2,656
       Bonds Payable (+L)   156
       Cash (-A)   2,500
     Paid stated interest and amortized discount.

 12/31/03 Interest Expense (E,-SE)   2,665
       Bonds Payable (+L)   165
       Cash (-A)   2,500
     Paid stated interest and amortized discount.

 b. Bonds Payable - principal $50,000
   Less: Discount on bonds * (5,414)
   Balance sheet value $44,586

 * The original discount was $5,735. The remaining balance after the two amortization entries ($156 and $165) is **$5,414**.

 c. Begin by identifying the remaining future cash flows associated with the bond. There will be a $50,000 outflow at the end of 18 periods for repayment of the principal. There will be semiannual payments of $2,500 each (an annuity) representing the cash payments for interest. This is calculated by multiplying the stated interest rate (10% or 5% per semiannual payment period) times the principal amount of the bond ($50,000). Next, calculate the present value of these future cash flows using the effective interest rate of 12% (6% per semiannual payment period) for the 18 periods remaining until maturity.

  The table factor for the present value of a dollar for 18 periods, discounted at 6%, is **.3503**. Multiplying by the principal amount gives the present value of the $50,000 principal repayment as **$17,515**.

The table factor for the present value of an ordinary annuity for 18 periods, discounted at 6%, is **10.8276**. Multiplying by the interest payment amount gives the present value of the $2,500 annuity as **$27,069**.

Adding the present values together gives the total present value of the remaining cash flows as **$44,584**. This amount is equal to (there is a $2 difference due to rounding) the balance sheet value on December 31, 2003.

25. a. The rental expense under an operating lease is simply $200,000 ($20,000 x 10).

12/31/03 Rental Expense (E,-SE)	200,000	
Cash (-A)		200,000
Recorded truck rental cost under operating lease.		

No other journal entries are required.

b. 1/1/03

Equipment (+A)	693,020	
Lease Liability (+L)		693,020
Recognized capital lease.		

Annual payments are $200,000. The present value of an ordinary annuity of $200,000 per year for four years, discounted at 6%, is **$693,020**. The table factor is **3.4651**.

12/31/03 Depreciation Expense (E,-SE)	138,604	
Accumulated Depreciation (-A)		138,604
Recognized depreciation ($693,020 / 5 years).		

12/31/03 Interest Expense (E,-SE)	41,581	
Lease Liability (-L) (plug)	158,419	
Cash (-A) (payments)		200,000
Made first annual lease payment.		

Interest expense is calculated by multiplying the lease liability by the effective interest rate ($693,020 x .06). The total rental cost for 2003 is $180,185 ($138,604 plus $41,581).

25. c. 12/31/04 Depreciation Expense (E,-SE)   138,604
                        Accumulated Depreciation (-A)   138,604
                    Recognized depreciation ($693,020 / 5 years).

                    Interest Expense (E,-SE)   32,076
                    Lease Liability (-L) (plug)   167,924
                        Cash (-A) (payments)   200,000
                    Made second annual lease payment.

Interest expense is calculated by multiplying the remaining lease liability by the effective interest rate ($534,601 x .06). The total rental cost for 2004 is $170,680 ($138,604 plus $32,076).

CHAPTER 12

Stockholders' Equity

REVIEW OF KEY CONCEPTS

This chapter initially reviews the similarities and differences among the three major organizational structures of for-profit businesses. The corporation is the focus for the remainder of the review. The major concepts discussed are the structure of corporations, the characteristics of ownership shares, and the rationale behind and accounting for transactions involving the corporation's equity stakeholders. Accounting for the issue and repurchase of preferred and common stock is discussed, including the concept of par value. The review concludes with a discussion of accounting for dividend declaration and payment.

Organizational Structure

The *sole proprietorship, partnership, and corporation* are the three principal organizational forms of for-profit businesses in the United States. When businesses are formed as sole proprietorships or partnerships, owners invest their personal assets in the business. While the business may be known to the public under a different name from its owners, all contracts entered into under the business's name are the personal responsibility of the owners. For example, if for some reason the business's assets are insufficient to satisfy business obligations, the sole proprietor or partner is personally responsible for the shortfall.

Other evidence that businesses established as proprietorships or partnerships are an extension of the owner is that income or losses of such businesses are not taxed under the business's name. Instead, the proprietor and partners report their share of the business's income on their individual tax returns. Their share of business income is taxed as personal income.

In contrast, a **corporation** is a separate legal entity, a status granted to it by the state in which it is incorporated. This status results in significant differences in the legal responsibility of the corporation's owners, the stockholders, compared to sole proprietorships and partnerships.

Stockholders enjoy a **limited liability**. Usually, the most stockholders' can lose is their original investment and any corporate earnings reinvested in the business. If the assets of the corporation are insufficient to satisfy the corporation's debts, the stockholders are not liable for the shortfall. Creditors do not have recourse against the stockholders. Obviously, the limited liability feature of corporations makes this organizational form very attractive to investors.

Since the ownership shares of corporations are usually traded in markets, the potential investor pool is large relative to the other organizational forms. Corporations typically raise large amounts of money from stockholders.

The corporate form of business organization is not without its disadvantages. The cost of applying for corporate status and issuing shares is prohibitive for most small businesses. Usually, businesses begin as sole proprietorships and partnerships and, after reaching a certain size, apply for corporate status. Another disadvantage of the corporate form is *double taxation*. Corporate income is taxed by the government under corporate tax law. The corporation must file annual tax returns and pay taxes on reported corporate income. In addition, cash or property dividend distributions to stockholders are taxable to the owners at an individual level. Potentially, every dollar earned by the corporation can be taxed twice.

Accounting for the Issuance of Stock

Corporations may issue two primary classes of ownership shares, common and preferred stock. Common stockholders are the residual equity stakeholders in the corporation. Ownership of a common share normally includes a right to vote on major corporate issues. While dividends are not guaranteed, common stockholders can share fully in profits earned by the company. Common shareholders are exposed to the most risk compared to any company creditor or other stakeholder because they are the last parties to be paid if the company files for bankruptcy.

Preferred stockholders have rights that common stockholders do not have. Unlike common stock, preferred stock dividends are calculated using a predetermined formula. In addition, preferred stock dividends are required to be declared before common stock cash and property dividends can be declared. If preferred stock is **cumulative**, any preferred stock dividend not previously declared and paid must be declared and paid before common stockholders can receive dividends. The text discusses in detail the different characteristics that preferred stock can possess.

Both preferred and common stock are recorded initially at the price received from the investor purchasing the stock. As mentioned above, corporate status is granted by state governments. At the time the corporation is chartered by the state, the number of shares of preferred and common stock it can sell is specified or **authorized**. **Issued shares** are shares sold previously by the corporation. **Treasury shares** are shares which have been repurchased and retained by the corporation. **Outstanding shares** are shares actually held by investors outside of the business. The total of treasury shares and outstanding shares equals the number of shares issued. Dividends are declared, and earnings per share is calculated using the number of shares outstanding. For example, Hayes Company is authorized to issue 1,000,000 shares of common stock. It has issued and received payment for 600,000 and bought back 25,000 shares. Its shares outstanding would be 575,000, which would be the shares on which it would pay dividends.

Some states require that corporations set **par** or **stated values** when the stock is authorized. The par or stated value sets a minimum per-share amount for which stockholders are personally liable. If the stock initially sells for less than the par or stated value, then the stockholders are personally, contingently liable for the difference between the original market price and the par value. For example, if the par value of the stock is $100 per share and it sells for $90, then the shareholders are contingently liable for $10 per share. If the corporation's assets are insufficient to satisfy its debts, the creditors can require that stockholders pay up to $10 per share to satisfy the debt. While the par or stated value concept was instituted by states to protect creditors, most stock issues are sold at above par or stated value, because today par and stated values are initially set at very low amounts. Par value is used occasionally in the preferred stock dividend formula. For example, 8%, $50 par preferred stock pays dividends of $4 per share, per year.

Accounting for Preferred and Common Stock with Par or Stated Value

When stock has a par or stated value, the Preferred Stock and Common Stock accounts are used to record transactions based on the number of shares issued and the par value. Any difference between the par value or stated value and the issue price is recorded in a separate Additional Paid-In Capital account.

Example. Robbins Construction sells 1,000 shares of its $100 par value, preferred stock for $120 cash per share. Robbins would make the following journal entry.

Cash (+A)	120,000	
Preferred Stock, $100 par (+SE)		100,000
Additional Paid-In Capital - P/S (+SE)		20,000

The par account is increased by $100 x 1,000 shares and the difference between the total amount received and the total par value is recorded in the Additional Paid-In Capital account.

Example. Kane Corporation sells 2,000 shares of its $5 par value, common stock for $25 per share. Kane would make the following entry.

Cash (+A)	50,000	
Common Stock, $5 par (+SE)		10,000
Additional Paid-In Capital - C/S (+SE)		40,000

If a corporation's stock has no par value or stated value, then the entire amount received at issue is recorded in the Preferred Stock or Common Stock account. When there is no par or stated value, no Additional Paid-In Capital account exists.

Example. Clift Corporation sells 2,000 shares of its no par, Common Stock for $25 per share. Clift would make the following entry.

Cash (+A)	50,000	
Common Stock, no par (+SE)		50,000

Treasury Stock

As mentioned in the text, corporations may elect to repurchase previously issued stock. The principal reasons to repurchase shares include fending off take-over attempts and acquiring shares for employee stock option plans. The *cost method* is the most widely used method to account for treasury stock. The following transactions illustrate accounting for treasury stock under the cost method.

Assume that Kane repurchases 200 shares of its $5 par value, common stock for $30 per share on June 1. All transactions are recorded at cost in the Treasury Stock account.

Treasury Stock (-SE)	6,000	
Cash (-A)		6,000

Purchased treasury shares at cost of $30 each.

On July 15, Kane sells 150 of the repurchased treasury shares for $35 each. The excess of the reissue price over the cost of the treasury shares is recorded in a separate Additional Paid-In Capital account.

Cash (+A)	5,250	
Treasury Stock (+SE)		4,500
Additional Paid-In Capital - T/S (+SE)		750

Some shares may be reissued at a price less than cost. Assume Kane sells the remaining 50 treasury shares on July 20, for $27 per share.

Cash (+A)	1,350	
Additional Paid-In Capital - T/S (-SE)	150	
Treasury Stock (+SE)		1,500

Note that the difference between the cost and reissue price is still entered in the Additional Paid-In Capital - Treasury Stock (T/S) account. However, there is a limit to the amount of debits to be recorded in the Additional Paid-In Capital - T/S account. Assume instead that Kane sold the 50 remaining shares for $14 per share. The transaction is recorded with the following entry.

Cash (+A)	700	
Additional Paid-In Capital - T/S (-SE)	750	
Retained Earnings (-SE)	50	
Treasury Stock (+SE)		1,500

As the above example illustrates, if the credit balance in the Additional Paid-In Capital Treasury Stock account is insufficient to absorb the entire difference between the sale price and the repurchase price, the shortfall reduces retained earnings.

Dividends Declaration and Payment

Cash and Property Dividends

Payments to stockholders (either preferred or common) are known as dividends. Normally, dividends are paid in cash, but a corporation may distribute other assets to stockholders. These other asset distributions are called property dividends. If the corporation distributes shares of its own stock, the dividend is called a stock dividend.

The date that the board of directors votes to pay a cash, property, or stock dividend is the **dividend declaration date**. In the case of cash and property dividends, a liability exists at the declaration date because the corporation is now legally obligated to remit assets to the stockholders. The **date of record** is the date that establishes which stockholders will receive the dividend. Stocks are actively traded on stock exchanges. The individual holding stock on the date of record receives the dividend when it is paid. When the payment is made, the liability is settled.

In the case of stock dividends, the corporation is obligated to issue additional shares of its stock to current stockholders. The formula used to determine the number of shares each stockholder receives is a percentage of shares already owned. Since the corporation is not obligated to remit assets to the shareholders, a liability does not exist.

Example. On June 30, 2003, Michaels, Inc.'s board of directors declares a $.50 per share cash dividend on the 100,000 shares of common stock outstanding. The date of record is July 3, 2003. The dividend is scheduled to be paid on July 15, 2003. Michaels would make the following journal entries.

June 30	Cash Dividend (-SE)	50,000	
	Dividends Payable (+L)		50,000
	Declared a cash dividend.		
July 3	*No entry is recorded on the date of record.*		
July 15	Dividends Payable (-L)	50,000	
	Cash (-A)		50,000
	Paid cash dividend previously declared.		
December 31	Retained Earnings (-SE)	50,000	
	Cash Dividend (+SE)		50,000
	To close the Cash Dividend temporary		
	account into retained earnings.		

Example. On September 30, 2003, Pepper, Inc.'s board of directors declares a 10% stock dividend on the 200,000 shares of its $5 par value, common stock. On September 30, 2003, the stock sold for $50 per share. The stock dividend is scheduled to be distributed on October 15, 2003. The stock dividend is recorded based on the market price of the stock at the declaration date.

Stock Dividend (-SE)	1,000,000	
Common Stock Dividend Distributable (+SE)		100,000
Additional Paid-In Capital - C/S (+SE)		900,000
Declared 10% stock dividend.		

Common Stock Dividend Distributable (-SE)	1,000,000	
Common Stock (+SE)		1,000,000
Distributed stock dividend previously declared.		

Retained earnings (-SE)   1,000,000
   Stock Dividend (+SE)   1,000,000
To close the stock dividend account (a temporary account) into Retained Earnings.

QUESTIONS FOR YOUR REVIEW

1. Saban, Inc. is considering declaring a 10% stock dividend. Currently, 200,000 shares of $5 par value, common stock are authorized, 120,000 shares are issued, and 10,000 shares are held in treasury. The total number of shares outstanding after a 10% stock dividend is:
    a. 220,000.
    b. 132,000.
    c. 121,000.
    d. 77,000.

2. Webber is considering a two-for-one stock split of its $100 par value, common stock. Currently, 750,000 shares are authorized, 225,000 shares are outstanding, and 15,000 shares are held in treasury. The total number of shares outstanding after a two for one split is:
    a. 1,500,000.
    b. 1,020,000.
    c. 450,000.
    d. 420,000.

3. Par value is:
    a. the stock's minimum market price.
    b. the stock's initial book value.
    c. the stock's required total yearly dividend.
    d. sometimes used in the preferred stock dividend formula.

4. Nikao repurchases 1,000 shares of its $5 par value, common stock on the market for $25 per share. If Nikao subsequently resells the stock for $35 per share, the $10,000 received above the amount paid to repurchase the stock is recorded as:
    a. a Gain disclosed on the income statement.
    b. a credit to Retained Earnings.
    c. Other Income disclosed on the income statement.
    d. Additional Paid-In Capital - Treasury Stock.

5. In 2000, immediately upon obtaining corporate status, Calgon issued 50,000 shares of 8%, $200 par value, cumulative preferred stock. Through the end of 2002 (three years), no dividends of any type have been declared or paid. In 2003, Calgon's board is considering declaring preferred and common dividends. How much is Calgon obligated to pay the preferred stockholders before paying the common stockholders?
    a. $400,000
    b. $800,000
    c. $1,200,000
    d. $3,200,000

The following information refers to questions 6 through 9.

The stockholders' equity section of Bargain, Inc.'s December 31, 2003, balance sheet appears as follows:

Preferred stock, 15% nonparticipating, noncumulative, $150 par value, 100,000 shares authorized, issued and outstanding	$ 15,000,000
Additional paid-in capital - preferred stock	10,000,000
Common stock, $10 par value, 2,000,000 shares authorized and issued, 100,000 shares held in treasury	20,000,000
Additional paid-in capital - common stock	30,000,000
Total contributed capital	$ 75,000,000
Retained earnings	50,000,000
Total stockholders' equity before treasury stock	$125,000,000
Less: Treasury stock at cost, 100,000 shares	6,000,000
Total stockholders' equity	$119,000,000

6.   How much is Bargain required to pay its preferred stockholders before any common dividends can be paid?
   a. $1,500,000
   b. $2,250,000
   c.   It cannot be determined without information regarding dividends in arrears.
   d.   Since it is nonparticipating, preferred stockholders must be paid the same amount as common stockholders.

7.   Assume the preferred stockholders have not been paid dividends in two years and Bargain's board of directors intends to pay $6,250,000 in total dividends, what is the maximum that common stockholders will receive?
   a. $3,125,000
   b. $4,000,000
   c. $6,250,000
   d.   It cannot be determined without additional information.

8.   The common stock was initially sold for:
   a. $10.00 per share.
   b. $23.16 per share.
   c. $25.00 per share.
   d. $26.32 per share.

9.   Bargain's book value per share of common stock is:
   a. $47.00.
   b. $49.47.
   c. $59.50.
   d. $62.63.

10. Appropriated retained earnings is:
    a. the amount of cash set aside by the board of directors for designated projects.
    b. the amount of reinvested earnings available for dividends during a particular year.
    c. the amount of reinvested earnings not available for dividend declaration at year-end.
    d. the amount that the Internal Revenue Service is entitled to under the Appropriation Act of 1974.

The following information relates to questions 11 and 12.
On January 1, 2004, Duval, Inc.'s Treasury Stock account balance was $6,000,000, representing its purchase of 100,000 shares of common stock in December, 2003. At December 31, 2004, the Treasury Stock account balance was $2,000,000 and the Additional Paid-In Capital Treasury Stock account balance was $2,666,667. Only one treasury stock transaction occurred during 2004.

11. How many shares of treasury stock were sold during 2004?
    a. 33,333
    b. 66,667
    c. 100,000
    d. It is not determinable without par value per share.

12. At what price were the treasury shares sold?
    a. $40
    b. $60
    c. $100
    d. $130

13. Which of the following is not an advantage of the corporate form of organization?
    a. Unlimited life
    b. Limited liability for stockholders
    c. Ease of formation
    d. Ease of transfer of ownership

The following information relates to questions 14 through 17. Consider each question as an independent situation.

On January 1, 2003, Progressive Corporation has 500,000 shares of $10 par value, common stock issued and outstanding. The stock initially sold for $40 per share. Progressive's Retained Earnings account balance is $100,000,000 on that date. Progressive has no preferred stock outstanding. Progressive's total liabilities are $60,000,000.

14. Progressive declares and distributes a 10% stock dividend on January 1 when the market price is $60 per share. What is Progressive's debt to equity ratio after this event (rounded to the nearest thousandth)?
    a. .488
    b. .500
    c. .513
    d. .538

15. Progressive declares and pays a $6 per share cash dividend on January 1. What is Progressive's debt to equity ratio after this event (rounded to the nearest thousandth)?
    a. .488
    b. .500
    c. .513
    d. .538

16. On January 1, Progressive sells 50,000 shares of 10%, $25 par value, preferred stock for $100 per share. What is Progressive's debt to equity ratio after this event (rounded to the nearest thousandth)?
    a. .480
    b. .500
    c. .520
    d. .542

17. On January 1, Progressive signs a 30-year, $5,000,000 note payable which pays interest of 10% annually. What is Progressive's debt to equity ratio after this event (rounded to the nearest thousandth)?
    a. .480
    b. .500
    c. .520
    d. .542

18. An advantage of issuing debt over preferred stock is:
    a. potential dilution of common stockholders' interests is avoided.
    b. the debt to equity ratio is improved when debt is issued instead of preferred stock.
    c. interest is tax deductible, while dividends are not.
    d. interest payments can be delayed while preferred dividends must be declared.

19. From the investor's perspective, an advantage of issuing cash dividends over stock dividends is:
    a. an asset (cash) is distributed to the stockholders while a stock dividend is not a distribution of corporate assets.
    b. cash dividends are not taxable to the stockholder while stock dividends are taxable.
    c. the total economic resources of the company are unaffected by cash dividends.
    d. the book value per share is unaffected by cash dividends.

20. An advantage of the partnership form of organization over the corporate form is:
    a. partners' liability is unlimited.
    b. partners can withdraw assets from the business more freely than can stockholders.
    c. partnership interests are easily transferred compared to stock investments.
    d. corporations are subject to less regulation than partnerships.

21. Nance, Inc. incorporated on January 1, 2003 and was authorized to issue 200,000 shares of $10 par value, common stock and 50,000 shares of $50 par value, 8% noncumulative preferred stock. The following stock-related transactions occurred during 2003:
    1. On April 1, Nance sold 150,000 shares of common stock for $25 per share.
    2. On July 1, Nance sold 30,000 shares of preferred stock for $80 per share.
    3. On August 1, Nance repurchased 10,000 shares of preferred stock for $70 per share.
    4. On October 30, Nance sold 6,000 of the preferred shares repurchased on August 1 for $75 per share.
    5. On December 1, Nance sold 3,000 shares of the preferred shares repurchased on August 1 for $65 per share.
    6. Net income for 2003 is $40,000.

    Required:
    a. Prepare the journal entries for each of the transactions.

    b. Prepare the stockholders' equity section of the balance sheet at December 31, 2003.

22. The board of directors of Rankin, Inc. is considering paying a $3 per share cash dividend. Rankin is authorized to issue 100,000 shares of common stock. 80,000 shares have been issued to date and 10,000 reacquired. All of the reacquired shares are held in treasury. Rankin has no preferred stock outstanding.

   Required:

   a. Compute the total cash dividend that Rankin will pay.

   b. Prepare the required journal entries at:

      (1) the declaration date.

      (2) the date of record.

      (3) the payment date.

23. Cochran, Inc. has 100,000 shares of $30 par value, 8% cumulative preferred stock issued and outstanding. Cochran also has 500,000 shares of $5 par value, common stock issued and 25,000 shares repurchased for $20 per share held in treasury. Cochran has not paid dividends in 2001 or 2002. Cochran has $1,000,000 available for dividends in 2003.

    Required:
    a. Determine how much Cochran will pay its common and preferred stockholders, respectively.

    b. Determine how these amounts will change if the preferred stock is noncumulative rather than cumulative.

24. The Arledge Company's September 30, 2003, balances in its no par value Common Stock, Retained Earnings, and Treasury Stock accounts are $100,000, $500,000 and $25,000, respectively. Arledge has 20,000 shares issued and 2,000 shares held in treasury. The market price of common stock on September 30 is $30 per share. Arledge's board of directors is considering the following options:

    Option 1: A five percent stock dividend
    Option 2: A fifteen percent stock dividend
    Option 3: A 2 for 1 stock split

    Required:
    a. Compute the number of shares that Mochrie would issue under each option.

b. Prepare the journal entries for each of the options.

c. How does total stockholders' equity change under each option?

d. How does the amount available for future cash dividends change under each option?

25. The Bohop Company has the following stockholders' equity balance at the end of 2004 and 2003, respectively:

	2004	2003
Preferred stock ($50 par value)	$ 62,500	$ 43,750
Common stock (no par)	100,000	80,000
Additional paid-in capital:		
Preferred stock	16,250	8,750
Treasury stock	3,000	-
Less: Treasury stock	10,000	25,000

a. Provide the journal entry to record the issuance of preferred stock during 2004.

b. Provide the journal entry to record the issuance of common stock during 2004.

c. Provide the journal entry to record the sale of treasury stock during 2004.

CHAPTER 12 - SOLUTIONS

1.	c	6.	b	11.	b	16.	a
2.	c	7.	b	12.	c	17.	d
3.	d	8.	c	13.	c	18.	c
4.	d	9.	b	14.	b	19.	a
5.	d	10.	c	15.	c	20.	b

21. a.

1. Cash (+A)   3,750,000
   Common Stock (+SE)   1,500,000
   Additional Paid-In Capital - C/S (+SE)   2,250,000

2. Cash (+A)   2,400,000
   Preferred Stock (+SE)   1,500,000
   Additional Paid-In Capital - P/S (+SE)   900,000

3. Treasury Stock (-SE)   700,000
   Cash (-A)   700,000

4. Cash (+A)   450,000
   Treasury Stock (+SE)   420,000
   Additional Paid-In Capital - T/S (+SE)   30,000

5. Cash (+A)   195,000
   Additional Paid-In Capital - T/S (-SE)   15,000
   Treasury Stock (+SE)   210,000

6. Income Summary (-SE)   40,000
   Retained Earnings (+SE)   40,000

21. b.

Nance, Inc.
Partial Balance Sheet
Stockholders' Equity Section
December 31, 2003

Preferred stock (8%, $50 par value, 50,000 shares authorized, 30,000 shares issued, 1,000 shares held in treasury)	$1,500,000
Additional paid-in capital - preferred stock	900,000
Common stock ($10 par value, 200,000 shares authorized, 150,000 shares issued and outstanding)	1,500,000
Additional paid-in capital - common stock	2,250,000
Additional paid-in capital - treasury stock	15,000
Total contributed capital	$6,165,000
Retained earnings	40,000
Total stockholders' equity before treasury stock	$6,205,000
Less: Treasury stock, 1,000 shares of preferred stock held in treasury	70,000
Total stockholders' equity	$6,135,000

22. a. $3 per share x 70,000 (shares outstanding, 80,000 - 10,000)
= $210,000.

b. 1. Cash Dividends (-SE)   210,000
      Cash Dividend Payable (+L)   210,000

2. No entry

3. Cash Dividend Payable (-L)   210,000
      Cash (-A)   210,000

23. a. Since the preferred stock is cumulative, all the previously undeclared preferred dividends must be paid before the common stockholders can receive their dividends.

Annual preferred dividends = 100,000 shares x $30 par value x .08 = $240,000 per year.

Total to be declared: $240,000 x 3 = $720,000.

Common stockholders will receive: $1,000,000 - $720,000 = $280,000.

b. Annual preferred dividend = $240,000.
Common stockholders will receive: $1,000,000 - $240,000 = $760,000.

24. a. Option 1: .05 x 18,000 (shares outstanding) = 900
         Option 2: .15 x 18,000 (shares outstanding) = 2,700
         Option 3: 2 x 18,000 old shares = 36,000 totally outstanding after the split. Thus, 18,000
         new shares must be issued.

     b. 1. Stock Dividends (-SE)   27,000
             Common Stock (+SE)   27,000

         2. Stock Dividends (-SE)   81,000
             Common Stock (+SE)   81,000

         3. No entry.

         The stock dividend is valued using the common stock price at the date of declaration, $30
         per share.

     c. Total stockholders' equity is unchanged in all three scenarios.

     d. Less is available for dividends in the stock dividend scenarios since the dividends represent
         a permanent capitalization of earnings.

25. a. Cash (+A)   26,250
             Preferred Stock (+SE)   18,750
             Additional Paid-In Capital - P/S (+SE)   7,500

     b. Cash (+A)   20,000
             Common Stock (+SE)   20,000

     c. Cash (+A)   18,000
             Treasury Stock (+SE)   15,000
             Additional Paid-In Capital - T/S (+SE)   3,000

CHAPTER 13

The Complete Income Statement

REVIEW OF KEY CONCEPTS

Transactions included in the income statement are discussed in detail in this chapter. The format used to organize income statement transactions within the body of the income statement is also presented. After completing this chapter, you will be able to distinguish between financing and investing and operating transactions and describe the circumstances under which they are included in the income statement.

While Chapters 6 through 12 have examined accounting for various balance sheet accounts, many of the transactions analyzed also affected income statement accounts. The transactions in which a business engages can be sorted into five categories:

1. Revenues and expenses
2. Purchases, sales, and exchanges of assets
3. Issues and payments of debt
4. Exchanges of liabilities and stockholders' equity
5. Exchanges with stockholders

Revenues and Expenses. Revenues are inflows of net assets (assets minus liabilities) from providing goods or services to customers. Expenses are outflows of net assets from providing those goods or services. Revenues and expenses represent the transactions directly involved in the ongoing operations of the business. They form the core of the transactions included in the income statement.

Purchases, Sales, and Exchanges of Assets. Assets are the economic resources in which capital contributed by creditors and stockholders is invested. The purpose of these investments in economic resources is to establish a wealth-generating structure. These resources are used up or converted into other resources that are eventually used up in order to earn revenues.

Occasionally, long-lived assets and investments in bonds or stocks are sold. These sales are not directly part of the ongoing transactions of the business. Instead, the company's management may decide to rebalance its portfolio of investments into one that is expected to result in larger increases in wealth in the future. Companies may sell plant and equipment that is not consistent with the company's evolving strategy. Gains or losses on the sale of assets are included in the income statement since these transactions relate to the operating strategy of the company.

Issues and Payments of Debt. One reason a company incurs debt instead of issuing additional shares of stock is that the expected return on the project the money is invested in exceeds the after-tax cost of the debt. Stockholders' wealth is increased by this difference. To measure the change in wealth because of operations, the cost of debt (i.e., interest expense) is included on the income statement. Usually, interest expense is reported as a separate line item after all of the operating expenses.

Debt may be retired early by the company. For example, if the market price of bonds is less than the maturity value, companies may elect to repurchase bonds payable in the bond market. The retirement price is likely to differ from the book value of the bond (principal plus premium on bonds payable or, less discount on bonds payable). This difference is included in the income statement as a gain or loss.

Exchanges of Liabilities and Stockholders' Equity. These exchanges involve replacing a liability with another liability (debt refinancing) and conversion of convertible bonds and preferred stock into common stock. Usually, these transactions are not reported in the income statement because they are removed from the ongoing operating activities of the business. These transactions affect the capital structure of the business which is the relative proportion of assets claimed by creditors and stockholders.

Exchanges with Stockholders. These exchanges involve selling stock, distributing dividends, and treasury stock transactions. According to GAAP, these transactions are not reported in the income statement. Even though net assets can change because of these transactions, they are considered activities so far removed from the normal ongoing operating activities of the business that they are excluded from income.

For example, if treasury stock is resold at a different price than the corporation initially paid to repurchase it, the difference is not reported as a gain or loss on the income statement. If the resale price is higher than cost, Additional Paid-In Capital - Treasury Stock is increased by the difference. If the resale price is lower than cost, Additional Paid-In Capital - Treasury Stock is decreased. If Additional Paid-In Capital-Treasury Stock's balance becomes zero, then Retained Earnings is decreased when treasury stock is resold at less than the purchase price. In any event, Stockholders' equity increases (decreases), but the increase (decrease) is not disclosed on the income statement.

Revenues and expenses are called operating transactions because they involve the actual conduct of operating activities. Categories 2 through 5 (above) are capital transactions because they involve acquiring resources to conduct business and investing those resources in productive assets to allow the company to conduct operations.

A Complete Income Statement: Disclosure and Presentation

The accounts listed in the income statement are organized in a manner that reflects the categories of transactions described above. The sale of goods or services is the activity that the business was formed to conduct. Investors base investment decisions on the expectation that the business's primary operations will result in the growth of wealth invested in the business. Accordingly, **operating revenue and expense transactions** are listed in a separate section of the income statement. These transactions are the normal, recurring operating transactions of the business. Investors analyze changes in these revenue and expense categories to determine how the business is performing its primary activity.

As mentioned above, certain capital transactions are also included in the income statement, and are listed after operating income items. Most of these transactions are included in the *other revenues and expenses* section. Common examples of these transactions are interest expense, interest and dividend revenue from investments, and gains and losses on disposal of assets. After the net of other revenues and expenses is deducted from operating income, income tax expense is presented.

While most nonoperating transactions are included in the other revenues and expenses section, GAAP requires the disclosure of three types of events in a special section of the income statement. These events are *disposal of a business segment, extraordinary items,* and *changes in accounting principle*. These events are reported after operating items and other revenues and expenses. If these special items exist, the income tax effect for these items is presented separately from the income tax expense related to the income determined from operating items and other revenues and expenses. **Intra-period tax allocation** is the process of separating the tax effect of the special items from the tax related to income from operations and other revenues and expenses. The accounting and disclosure of each of these items is briefly described below.

Disposal of a Business Segment

GAAP defines a **business segment** as a separate line of business, product line, or class of customers involving an operation independent from other company operations. The disposal of a segment represents a major shift in the strategy of the business, which warrants this additional disclosure.

Since the segment is discontinued, operating income of the segment is backed out of the operating income from continuing operations to enable the investor or creditor to develop expectations regarding the company in the future. The operating income of the discontinued segment is computed from the beginning of the fiscal year to the disposal date.

Usually, a company will attempt to sell the segment to another company. Occasionally, the segment's assets may be sold separately. In any event, the book value of the segment is likely to differ from the selling price received for the segment or its assets. This results in a gain or loss on the disposal. Both the operating results of the segment and the gain or loss on disposal are presented in the discontinued operations section, net of their specific tax effect.

Example. Chique, Inc., a cosmetics manufacturer, decides to discontinue sales to beauty salons and focus on department stores only. This constitutes discontinuing a major line of customer. During the year, Chique, Inc.'s net income before tax is $300,000, which includes the loss on salon operating activities for the year, $25,000, and the gain on sale of the assets of the beauty salon division, $60,000. The assets' book value was $200,000. Chique is subject to a 30% income tax rate.

Net income before tax on continuing operations for the year is $265,000 ($300,000 + Loss on salon operating activities, $25,000 - Gain on sale of the assets, $60,000). The income tax on continuing operations income is $79,500 ($265,000 x .30). Income from continuing operations is $185,500 ($265,000 - $79,500).

The information regarding the discontinued segment is presented after income from continuing operations on the income statement. The loss on salon operating activities after tax is $17,500 [$25,000 - (.30 x $25,000)], and the after tax gain on the sale of salon assets is $42,000 [$60,000 -

(.30 x $60,000)]. The partial income statement for Chique follows:

Chique, Inc.
Partial Income Statement
For the Year Ended December 31, 2003

Income from continuing operations before tax	$265,000
Income tax	79,500
Income from continuing operations	$185,500
Discontinued operations:	
Operating loss on salon division	$(17,500)
(net of $7,500 tax benefit)	
Gain on disposal of salon division assets	42,000
(net of $18,000 tax expense)	
Income from discontinued operations	$ 24,500
Net income	$210,000

Extraordinary Items

GAAP defines **extraordinary items** as material events which are *both unusual* and *infrequent* in nature. These events must differ from the business's normal operating and capital transactions. They must be nonrecurring as well, since investors' predictions of future performance are likely to exclude such events. If they are recurring, investors should factor them into predictions. For example, damage resulting from a tornado in Kansas is clearly not a usual operating or capital transaction. However, tornados occur in certain regions, including Kansas, on a regular basis. The investor may wish to factor the cost of the damage into future performance projections, since this is an additional risk due to operating in Kansas. This loss would be disclosed in the other revenue and expense section with accompanying footnotes describing the damage.

In addition to applying the unusual and infrequent criteria to transactions, certain events are required to be disclosed as extraordinary by specific GAAP pronouncements. For example, the gain or loss from early retirement of long-term debt and the gain or loss from pension plan terminations must be disclosed as extraordinary items.

Extraordinary items are disclosed in the same manner as discontinued operations. For example, assume that Chique, Inc. retired $100,000 face amount of bonds payable, with a book value of $100,000, for $98,000. The gain on retirement is $2,000 before tax. The tax expense associated with the gain is $600, and the gain is reported as an extraordinary item, net of tax, for $1,400 in the income statement. Revising Chique's income statement:

Chique, Inc.
Partial Income Statement
For the Year Ended December 31, 2003

Income from continuing operations before tax	$265,000
Income tax	79,500
Income from continuing operations	$ 185,500
Discontinued operations:	
Operating loss on salon division	$ (17,500)
(net of $7,500 tax benefit)	
Gain on disposal of salon division assets	42,000
(net of $18,000 tax expense)	
Income from discontinued operations	$ 24,500
Extraordinary item:	
Gain from the early extinguishment of bonds payable	
(net of tax expense, $600)	$ 1,400
Net income	$211,400

Changes in Accounting Principle

Because of operating environment changes, companies occasionally decide that their current methods of calculating particular revenue or expense accounts and the related balance sheet accounts are no longer effective. If the company can convince its auditors that a new method better reflects the economic condition of the company, a change in accounting principle is enacted.

The financial statements are in a sense converted to the new method. For example, assume Chique, Inc., decides to change its depreciation method from an accelerated method to straight-line for its ongoing operating assets. The balance sheet account affected by this change is Accumulated Depreciation. Assume that at the beginning of the year accumulated depreciation balance was $75,000, reflecting the use of the accelerated method. If straight-line had always been used, accumulated depreciation's balance would have been $60,000. 2003 income already reflects straight-line. To convert Accumulated Depreciation to straight-line basis, $15,000 is backed out of the account. Clearly, if straight-line had been used all along, reported income would have been higher by $15,000 before tax and $10,500 after tax since depreciation expense would have been lower in past years. After-tax income is closed each year into retained earnings. Thus, in some way, retained earnings must also reflect the change.

For most accounting principle changes, the cumulative effect of the change (in this example, $15,000 before tax and $10,500 after tax) is disclosed in a special section of the income statement as the very last item before net income on the statement. Since net income is closed into retained earnings after the financial statements are prepared, retained earnings will reflect the change to straight-line on the balance sheet and the general ledger.

Chique made the following entry to record the cumulative effect of the accounting principle change:

Accumulated Depreciation (+A)   15,000
    Cumulative Gain from Accounting Change (Ga,+SE)   10,500
    Income Tax Liability (+L)   4,500

Chique's revised income statement is:

Chique, Inc.
Partial Income Statement
For the Year Ended December 31, 2003

Income from continuing operations before tax	$265,000
Income tax	79,500
Income from continuing operations	$185,500
Discontinued operations:	
Operating loss on salon division	$(17,500)
(net of $7,500 tax benefit)	
Gain on disposal of salon division assets	42,000
(net of $18,000 tax expense)	
Income from discontinued operations	$ 24,500
Extraordinary item:	
Gain from the early extinguishment of bonds payable	
(net of tax expense, $600)	$ 1,400
Cumulative gain from accounting change:	
Accelerated depreciation to straight-line	
(net of tax, $4,500)	$ 10,500
Net income	$221,900

Comprehensive Income

The FASB issued a new standard in 1997, which will require companies to disclose **Comprehensive Income**. This is a broader concept than net income, and includes all changes in equity arising from transactions with nonowners. The most significant differences from net income are likely to arise from unrealized market value gains and losses on available-for-sale securities and foreign currency translation adjustments. (Foreign currency translation adjustments are beyond the scope of the introductory course. They arise from investments in foreign subsidiary companies and changes in relative currency values over time.) Comprehensive income may be disclosed in a separate statement of comprehensive income, as an adjustment on the income statement, or as a part of **the statement of stockholders' equity.**

Assume Chique, Inc. has a foreign currency translation gain of $10,000 and unrealized losses on available-for-sale securities of $4,000 during 2003. Both are items subject to a 30% effective tax rate. If Chique chooses to prepare a separate statement, it would appear as follows:

Chique, Inc.
Comprehensive Income Statement
For the Year Ended December 31, 2003

Net income (from the income statement)		$221,900
Other comprehensive income:		
Foreign currency translation adjustment	10,000	
Tax effect	(3,000)	7,000
Unrealized losses on		
available-for-sale securities	(4,000)	
Tax effect	1,200	(2,800)
Comprehensive income		$226,100

The comprehensive income amount also requires earnings per share disclosure effects.

QUESTIONS FOR YOUR REVIEW

1. The capital maintenance approach to measuring income involves:
    a. determining the change in total assets during the year and backing out additional stockholder contributions and dividends.
    b. determining the change in net assets during the year and backing out additional stockholder contributions and dividends.
    c. determining the change in productive capital (inventory and plant and equipment) during the year and backing out additional stockholder contributions and dividends.
    d. determining the change in the total market value of stock (shares outstanding times market price) during the year and backing out additional stockholder contributions and dividends.

2. An example of a transaction which is not reported on the income statement is:
    a. the sale of equipment at a price above its book value.
    b. the sale of treasury stock at a price below its cost.
    c. the sale of inventory at a price above its book value.
    d. the change in accounting for inventory from the FIFO cost flow assumption to average cost flow assumption.

3. An example of a capital transaction is:
    a. issuance of common stock.
    b. sale of inventory at a price above its cost.
    c. payment for utilities expense.
    d. recognition of depreciation expense on machinery.

4.   An example of an operating transaction is:
     a.   declaration of a stock dividend.
     b.   purchase of machinery.
     c.   purchase of inventory on account.
     d.   recognition of depreciation expense on machinery.

5.   Net assets are:
     a.   total assets less related contra accounts such as Accumulated Depreciation.
     b.   current assets net of current liabilities.
     c.   the total assets contributed by stockholders during a period less dividends distributed during the period.
     d.   total assets less total liabilities.

6.   David, Inc.'s beginning and ending total stockholders' equity are $400,000 and $500,000, respectively. During the year, stock dividends of $40,000 and cash dividends of $66,667 were distributed. David purchased 3,000 shares of its own stock for $26,667 which are still held as Treasury Stock at year-end. David's net income for the year is:
     a. $166,667.
     b. $193,333.
     c. $206,667.
     d. $233,333.

7.   An example of an operating transaction is:
     a.   collection of an account receivable.
     b.   recognition of prepaid rent used during the period.
     c.   purchase of inventory for cash.
     d.   purchase of equipment using a long-term note payable.

8.   The category of transactions whose results are never reported on the income statement is:
     a.   operating transactions.
     b.   issues and payments of debt.
     c.   purchases, sales, and exchanges of assets.
     d.   exchanges with stockholders.

9.   The category of transactions whose results form the core of the transactions reported on the income statement is:
     a.   operating transactions.
     b.   issues and payments of debt.
     c.   purchases, sales and exchanges of assets.
     d.   exchanges with stockholders.

10. A transaction reported under other revenues and expenses in the income statement is:
     a.   the sale of inventory at below its cost.
     b.   the sale of equipment at above its book value.
     c.   the recognition of depreciation expense on machinery.
     d.   the recognition of supplies used during the period.

11. Woods, Inc.'s total income before tax is $400,000. Included in this amount is a $100,000 loss from the disposal of a business segment. Woods is subject to a 30% tax rate. What is Woods' income tax expense for the year?
    a. $90,000
    b. $120,000
    c. $150,000
    d. $0, since a loss has been incurred.

12. Refer to question 11. What is Woods' income after tax from continuing operations?
    a. $210,000
    b. $280,000
    c. $350,000
    d. $0, since a loss has been incurred.

13. Refer to question 11. What amount is reported as discontinued operations for Woods?
    a. $100,000 loss
    b. $70,000 loss
    c. $100,000 gain
    d. $0, since this is a financing and investing, not an operating transaction.

14. The correction of an error detected in prior years' reported income is:
    a.   ignored, since investors' decisions are primarily based upon current year's income.
    b.   reported in current year's income as an extraordinary item.
    c.   recorded directly in retained earnings, bypassing the current year's income statement.
    d.   reported in current year's income as other revenue and expense.

15. Which of the following is likely to be reported as an extraordinary item in the income statement?
    a.   Switch from accelerated depreciation method to straight-line
    b.   Loss from a hurricane in Tampa, Florida
    c.   Loss from an earthquake in Los Angeles
    d.   Loss from a blizzard in Hawaii

16. Smith, Inc. switches its inventory method from FIFO to LIFO at the beginning of 2003. 2003 inventory and cost of goods sold are accounted for using LIFO. Beginning inventory is $40,000 under FIFO and $35,000 under LIFO. Smith has always been subject to a 30% tax rate. Where, and at what amount, is the change reported in the 2003 income statement?
    a.   Inventory is an operating item, the $5,000 extra expense is included in cost of goods sold.
    b.   Since prior years' income would have been $3,500 ($5,000 - (.3 x $5,000)] lower, retained earnings is reduced by $3,500. The item is not presented on the income statement.
    c.   The cumulative effect of the accounting change, a $5,000 deduction, is reported in its own special section just before net income.
    d.   The cumulative effect of the accounting change, net of tax, a $3,500 deduction, is reported in its own special section just before net income.

17. Comprehensive income is to be reported:
    a.   in a separate statement of comprehensive income.
    b.   as a component of the statement of stockholders' equity.
    c.   as an additional component of the income statement.
    d.   All of the above are acceptable alternative disclosures.

18. The denominator in computing diluted earnings per share is:
    a.   the average number of preferred and common shares outstanding during the year.
    b.   the average number of common shares outstanding adjusted for shares held in treasury.
    c.   the average number of common shares outstanding plus the number of additional shares outstanding if options and securities which are convertible into common shares were exercised.
    d.   the authorized number of common shares since this is the maximum number of shares that could be issued.

19. The transactions approach for presenting income is preferred over the capital maintenance approach because:
    a.   income is more accurately measured under the transactions approach.
    b.   the transactions approach is less costly to apply than the capital maintenance approach.
    c.   the transactions approach allows the investor to more fully examine the reasons behind a company's performance during the year than the capital maintenance approach.
    d.   for most companies, the accounting system can produce only the transactions approach income statement.

20. The group of transactions disclosed in the income statement which are expected to be the most persistent in the future is:
    a.   operating revenues and expenses.
    b.   other revenues and expenses.
    c.   disposal of segments.
    d.   extraordinary items.

21. The Tuller Company's December 31, 2002, balance sheet is presented below.

Assets	$100,000	Liabilities	$ 60,000
		Stockholders' equity	40,000
		Total liabilities and	
Total assets	$100,000	stockholders' equity	$100,000

During 2003, the following transactions occurred:
1.   Land was purchased for $20,000 by issuing a long-term note payable.
2.   Common stock was issued for $50,000 cash.
3.   Dividends of $15,000 were declared and paid.
4.   Services were performed for $45,000. $20,000 cash was received, the remainder was on account.
5.   Cash expenses of $45,000 were incurred.

21. **Required:**

    Classify each transaction as operating or financing and investing and prepare an income statement.

22. Gilder, Inc. decides to sell its mainframe computer division, retaining its personal computer division. On June 1, 2003, the division is sold for $500,000 cash. The following mainframe division financial information at June 1, 2003, was pulled from the books (all numbers are before tax):

Sales (January 1 through June 1, 2003)	$ 700,000
Operating expenses	730,000
Operating loss	$ (30,000)
Assets	$ 3,000,000
Liabilities	$ 2,800,000

    At December 31, 2003, Gilder's personal computer division reports income before tax of $500,000. Gilder's corporate tax rate is 30%.

22. Continued
    Required:

a. Prepare the journal entry (entries) to record the sale of the mainframe division.

b. Prepare Gilder's income statement beginning with income from continuing operations before tax.

23. The following is from Archival's adjusted trial balance at December 31, 2003.

	Debit	Credit
Retained Earnings, January 1, 2003		1,000,000
Sales Revenue		400,000
Gain from Sale of Equipment		3,000
Cost of Goods Sold	190,000	
Salaries Expense	30,000	
Depreciation Expense	50,000	
Interest Expense	25,000	
Interest Revenue		10,000
Loss from Early Extinguishment of Debt	45,000	
Income Tax Expense	35,400	
Dividends	75,000	

Archival's corporate tax rate is 30%. The loss from the early extinguishment is already recorded net of its tax effect.

Required:

a. Determine the income tax liability for Archival for the year.

b. Prepare a multi-step income statement for Archival.

c. Prepare the statement of retained earnings for Archival.

24. Hotspot, Inc.'s manager's bonus is 5% of pre-bonus income from continuing operations after tax. During 2003, Hotspot sold a plant in Europe, but continues to produce the product in its remaining plants and sell it worldwide. The plant lost $100,000 from operations in 2003 before it was sold. The plant was sold at a loss of $300,000. Both losses are before tax. Hotspot's other operations earned $2,000,000 before tax. Hotspot is subject to a 30% tax rate.

Required:

a.   Compute the manager's bonus if the sale is not considered a disposal of a segment.

b.   Compute the manager's bonus if the sale is considered a disposal of a segment.

c.   Assuming the manager is primarily concerned about his or her take-home pay, which classification would he or she prefer? Why?

d.   What do you believe should be the appropriate classification of the disposal? Why?

25. CT Specialties, a producer of fine teas and coffees, decides to switch its depreciation method from straight-line to an accelerated method. Its auditors concur with the change. On January 1, 2003, accumulated depreciation is $50,000. If the company had used an accelerated method all along, accumulated depreciation would have been $80,000. Depreciation expense is recorded using the accelerated method during 2003. The company is subject to a 30% tax rate.

Required:

a. Prepare the journal entry (entries) to record the change in depreciation method.

b. Prepare the income statement section which discloses the change, if income before the cumulative effect of the accounting change is $200,000 (net of tax).

CHAPTER 13 - SOLUTIONS

1.	b	6.	b	11.	c	16.	d
2.	b	7.	b	12.	c	17.	d
3.	a	8.	d	13.	b	18.	c
4.	d	9.	a	14.	c	19.	c
5.	d	10.	b	15.	d	20.	a

21. Classification of transactions:

1. Financing and investing, purchase of an asset
2. Financing and investing, exchange with stockholders
3. Financing and investing, exchange with stockholders
4. Operating
5. Operating

Tuller Company
Income Statement
For the Year Ended December 31, 2003

Service revenue	$45,000	
Expenses	45,000	
Net income	$ 0	

22. a.

Cash (+A)	500,000	
Liabilities (-L)	2,800,000	
Assets (-A)		3,000,000
Gain on Disposal of the		
Mainframe Division (Ga,+SE)		300,000
Gain on Disposal of the		
Mainframe Division (-Ga,-SE)	90,000	
Income Tax Payable(+L)		90,000

22. b.

Gilder, Inc.
Income Statement
For the Year Ended December 31, 2003

Income from continuing operations before tax	$500,000
Income tax expense	(150,000)
Income from continuing operations	$350,000
Discontinued operations:	
Operating loss from mainframe division	
(net of $9,000 tax benefit)	$(21,000)
Gain on sale of mainframe division	
(net of $90,000 tax expense)	210,000
Income from discontinued operations	$189,000
Net income	$539,000

23. a. Archival's total income tax expense:

Income before tax and extraordinary loss:
$400,000 + 3,000 - 190,000 - 30,000 - 50,000 - 25,000 + 10,000
= $118,000 x .30 = $ 35,400
Tax benefit from the extraordinary loss:
$45,000 = Pretax Loss - Pretax Loss x .30
$45,000 = Pretax Loss (1 -.30)
$64,286 = Pretax Loss

Tax benefit = .30 x 64,286 = $19,286

Total income tax liability = $35,400 - $19,286 = $16,114

23. b.

Archival, Inc.
Income Statement
For the Year Ended December 31, 2003

Sales		$400,000
Less: Cost of goods sold		190,000
Gross profit		$210,000
Less operating expenses:		
Salaries	$30,000	
Depreciation	50,000	80,000
Operating income		$130,000
Other revenues and expenses:		
Gain on equipment sale	$ 3,000	
Interest revenue	10,000	
Interest expense	(25,000)	(12,000)
Income before tax and extraordinary loss		$118,000
Income tax expense		35,400
Income before extraordinary loss		$ 82,600
Extraordinary loss from early extinguishment of debt		
(net of $19,286 tax benefit)		(45,000)
Net income		$ 37,600

c.

Archival, Inc.
Statement of Retained Earnings
For the Year Ended December 31, 2003

Retained earnings, January 1, 2003	$1,000,000
Add: 2003 net income	37,600
Less: Dividends declared	(75,000)
Retained earnings, December 31, 2003	$ 962,600

24. a. His bonus based upon income from continuing operations after tax including the loss on the plant asset is:

Income from continuing plants - Loss from discontinued plant operations - Loss on discontinued plant sale.
$2,000,000 - $100,000 - $300,000 = $1,600,000

$1,600,000 - $480,000 (tax at 30%) = $1,120,000

The bonus is: $1,120,000 x .05 = $56,000

24. b. If the sale is considered a segment disposal, the basis for the bonus is: $2,000,000 - $600,000 (tax at 30%) = $1,400,000

    The bonus is: $ 1,400,000 x .05 = <u>$70,000</u>

   c. Clearly, the manager would prefer the discontinued segment designation because his/her bonus is higher under that accounting treatment.

   d. Discontinued segment designation is inappropriate because the company's remaining plants absorb the discontinued plant's production and the entire world continues to be served. The plant's operating loss should not be separated from the continuing plants. The loss on the plant disposal should be reported in the other revenue and expense section of the income statement.

25. a. Accumulated depreciation is higher under accelerated than under straight-line. The change increases accumulated depreciation. The cumulative effect, $21,000 after tax, is a reduction of income.

Cumulative effect of an accounting principle change:		
Straight-Line to Accelerated Depreciation (-SE)	21,000	
Income Tax Receivable (+A)	9,000	
Accumulated Depreciation (-A)		30,000

   b.

CT Specialties
Partial Income Statement
For the Year Ended December 31, 2003

Income before the cumulative effect of accounting principle change	$200,000
Cumulative effect of an accounting principle change: Straight-line depreciation method to accelerated depreciation (net of $9,000 tax benefit)	(21,000)
Net income	$179,000

CHAPTER 14

The Statement of Cash Flows

REVIEW OF KEY CONCEPTS

This chapter focuses upon the preparation and use of the *statement of cash flows*. The review of key concepts focuses primarily upon the preparation of the statement. The text's discussion on interpretation of the statement is excellent. Questions emphasizing the preparation of the statement are included at the end of this study guide chapter for your review.

The statement of cash flows provides information about transactions that resulted in the change in the cash balance over a period of time. A business's ability to generate adequate amounts of cash from operating activities is critical to its long-run success. Eventually, most assets used to produce the services or products sold by the business are paid for with cash. Some assets are purchased directly with cash, others are purchased with short-term or long-term notes which are subsequently retired with cash. Investors usually receive a portion of the earnings of the business in dividends..

Preparation of the Statement of Cash Flows

Activities that provide or use cash are included in one of three categories in the statement: *operating activities, investing activities,* and *financing activities*. Transactions directly related to the sale of products or services are categorized as operating activities. Investing activities involve the purchase and sale of the company's noncurrent assets. Financing activities involve cash receipts from, and payments to, the providers of capital, creditors and stockholders. The income statement and balance sheet of Sommers, Inc., presented below, are used to illustrate the preparation of a statement of cash flows.

Sommers, Inc.
Income Statement
For the Year Ended June 30, 2003

Sales	$1,000,000
Gain from land sale	10,000
Total revenues and gains	$1,010,000
Cost of goods sold	$ 700,000
Salaries expense	150,000
Depreciation expense	50,000
Utilities expense	20,000
Total expenses	920,000
Income before taxes	$ 90,000
Income taxes	36,000
Net income	$ 54,000

Sommers, Inc.
Balance Sheet
June 30, 2003 and 2002

	2003	2002
Cash	$ 40,000	$ 60,000
Accounts receivable	260,000	250,000
Inventory	160,000	175,000
Land	100,000	125,000
Building	520,000	375,000
Less: Accumulated depreciation	(210,000)	(160,000)
Total assets	$870,000	$825,000
Accounts payable	$ 50,000	$ 57,000
Salaries payable	15,000	10,000
Utilities payable	1,000	0
Income tax payable	2,000	5,000
Total liabilities	$ 68,000	$ 72,000
Common stock, no par value	$400,000	$400,000
Retained earnings	402,000	353,000
Total stockholders' equity	$802,000	$753,000
Total liabilities and stockholders' equity	$870,000	$825,000

Additional Information: All sales and merchandise purchases are on account.

Cash Provided (Used) by Operating Activities - the Direct Method

   The same types of transactions are included in cash provided by operating activities as are included in net income. The income statement is prepared under the accrual basis of accounting. The revenue realization and matching rules are used to determine when operating transactions are included in income. The timing of the related cash receipt or payment determines when a transaction is included in cash generated from operations. By examining the income statement, the types of transactions included in the cash provided (used) by operations section are identified for Sommers.

Income Statement Account	Comparable Cash Transaction Category
Sales	Cash collections from customers (either through cash sales or collections of accounts receivable).
Cost of Goods Sold	Cash paid for merchandise (either through cash payments or payments of accounts payable).
Salaries Expense	Cash paid for salaries (either through cash payments or payments of salaries payable).
Depreciation Expense	The purchase of long-lived assets is included in the investing activities section. No comparable cash transaction is included for depreciation expense.

Utilities Expense	Cash paid for utilities (either through cash payments or payments of utilities payable).
Gain on Land Sale	Cash received from the sale of land is included in the investing activities section. No comparable transaction for gains or losses on sales of assets is included here.
Income Tax Expense	Cash paid for income taxes (either through cash payments or payments of income taxes payable).

The income statement accounts are separated into two categories. The Gain on Land Sale and Depreciation Expense are excluded from the cash provided (used) by operating activities section because the related cash flows are located elsewhere in the statement of cash flows. In particular, the cash received from the sale of land is included in the *investing activities* section because land is a long-lived asset. While depreciation expense represents the allocation of a long-lived asset's cost over time, the cash paid to acquire the asset was reported in the *investing activities* section when the asset was acquired. Thus, depreciation expense is not included in the computation of cash from operations. Goodwill amortization and losses on long-lived asset sales are other examples of income statement items excluded from cash from operations.

The second category of income statement accounts are items with comparable operating cash flow transactions. The relation between the accrual and cash bases is used to identify the balance sheet accounts, aside from the cash account itself, which involves both the accrual and cash items listed above. From analyzing changes in the current asset and liability accounts, the cash received or paid related to each of these items can be identified as illustrated below, using Sommers, Inc.'s information.

Cash provided (used) by operations computed using the direct method is:

[a]Cash collections from customers	$990,000
Cash payments for:	
[b]Merchandise	692,000
[c]Salaries	145,000
[d]Utilities	19,000
[e]Income taxes	39,000
Total cash payments	$895,000
Cash generated from operations	$ 95,000

The T-account analysis of Sommers's balance sheet accounts is presented on the following page. Use the superscripted cross-references from above to determine how these numbers were computed (B.B. - beginning balance, E.B. - ending balance).

Accounts Receivable

B.B.	250,000	Cash	
Sales	1,000,000	Collections ?	
E.B.	260,000		

B.B. + Sales - Cash Collections = E.B.
250,000 + 1,000,000 - ? = 260,000
? = 990,000 = Cash Collections from Customers[a]

Inventory

B.B.	175,000		
Pur.	?	CGS	700,000
E.B.	160,000		

B.B. + Purchases - CGS = E.B.
175,000 + ? - 700,000 = 160,000
? = 685,000 = Purchases

Accounts Payable

Cash		B.B.	57,000
Payments ?		Pur.	?
		E.B.	50,000

B.B. + Pur. - Cash Payments = E.B.
57,000 + 685,000 - ? = 50,000
?= 692,000 =Inventory Payments[b]

Salaries Payable

Cash		B.B.	10,000
Payments ?		Sal. Exp.	
			150,000
		E.B.	15,000

B.B. + Exp - Cash Payments = E.B.
10,000 + 150,000 - ? = 15,000
? = 145,000 = Salary Payments[c]

Utilities Payable

Cash		B.B.	0
Payments ?		Util. Exp.	
			20,000
		E.B.	1,000

B.B. + Exp. - Cash Payments = E.B.
0 + 20,000 - ? = 1,000
? = 19,000 = Utility Payments[d]

Income Tax Payable

Cash		B.B.	5,000
Payments ?		Income Tax	
		Exp.	36,000
		E.B.	2,000

B.B.   + Expense - Cash Payments = E.B.
5,000 + 36,000 - ? = 2,000
? = 39,000 = Income Tax Payments[e]

Reconciling Net Income to Cash Provided (Used) by Operating Activities - the Indirect Method

An alternative approach to computing cash provided (used) by operating activities is the **indirect method** which some companies use instead of the direct method. The difference between the methods is a procedural one since they result in the same cash provided by operating activities. The reasoning behind the indirect method is presented below.

The direct method's T-account analysis can be organized as follows:

Cash received from customers	= Sales + Beginning A/R - Ending A/R = Sales - (Ending A/R - Beginning A/R) = Sales - Change in Accounts Receivable
Purchases **Cash paid to vendors**	= Cost of Goods Sold + Change in Inventory = Purchases - Change in Accounts Payable = Cost of Goods Sold + Change in Inventory - Change in Accounts Payable
Cash paid for salaries	= Salaries Expense - Change in Salaries Payable
Cash paid for utilities	= Utilities Expense - Change in Utilities Payable
Cash paid for income tax	= Income Tax Expense - Change in Income Tax Payable

You'll notice that each of the formulas above contains an income statement account (such as sales, cost of goods sold and salaries expense) and the change in a balance sheet account from the beginning of the year to the end. The indirect method uses net income (the net of all of the income statement accounts) as a starting point to compute cash from operations. Net income is then adjusted for the changes in account balances and for income statement accounts that have the cash consequence reported elsewhere in the statement of cash flows. An example is a gain or loss on an asset sale, the proceeds of which are reported in the investing activities section, or depreciation expense, where the cash paid to originally acquire the asset is included in the investing activities section in the year of acquisition.

The following formula can be used to compute cash provided by operations under the indirect method for Sommers, Inc.:

Cash provided (used) by operations =
   Net Income + Depreciation Expense - Gain on Land Sale - Change in Accounts Receivable - Change in Inventory + Change in Accounts Payable + Change in Salaries Payable + Change in Utilities Payable + Change in Income Tax Payable

Notice that the items that are not related to cash from operations are backed out of net income: Depreciation Expense and Gain on Land Sale. The other adjustments involve the change in the current asset and current liability accounts. Increases (decreases) in current asset accounts are subtracted (added) and increases (decreases) in current liabilities are added (subtracted) to arrive at cash provided from operations.

This alternative approach can be applied to the Sommers example, as follows.

54,000 (Net Income) + 50,000 (Depreciation Expense) - 10,000 (Gain) - 10,000 (Increase in Accounts Receivable) + 15,000 (Decrease in Inventory) - 7,000 (Decrease in Accounts Payable) + 5,000 (Increase in Salaries Payable) + 1,000 (Increase in Utilities Payable) - 3,000 (Decrease in Income Tax Payable) = 95,000.

Since the difference between the direct and indirect methods is a procedural one, they yield the same amount of cash provided by operating activities.

Cash Provided (Used) by Investing Activities

The cash transactions related to the purchase and sale of noncurrent assets are summarized here. Referring to the Sommers balance sheet, the only long-lived asset accounts are Land and Building. The income statement reports a gain on land sale of $10,000. This means that the land was sold for $10,000 more than its cost. Changes in the Land account are examined to determine the cost of the land sold. Land decreased by $25,000 (125,000 B.B. - 100,000 E.B.). No other transactions affected the Land account during the year. Thus, the land was sold for $35,000 ($25,000 + $10,000).

The Building account increased by $145,000 ($520,000 E.B. - $375,000 B.B.). No sales occurred during the year. Thus, a building was acquired for $125,000.

Cash Provided (Used) by Financing Activities

Cash transactions related to receiving capital or making payments to capital sources, long-term creditors and stockholders, are presented in this section. Referring to the Sommers balance sheet, Sommers has no long-term liabilities. Sommers's common stock balance is unchanged. Retained earnings increased by $49,000. Net income is $54,000. Sommers must have paid $5,000 in dividends to explain the $49,000 increase ($54,000 - $5,000).

The statement of cash flows for Sommers is presented using the indirect method to compute cash provided by operating activities.

Sommers, Inc.
Statement of Cash Flows
For the Year Ended December 31, 2003

Cash provided (used) by operating activities:

Net income	$ 54,000
+ Depreciation expense	+ 50,000
- Gain on land sale	- 10,000
- Increase in accounts receivable	- 10,000
+ Decrease in inventory	+ 15,000
- Decrease in accounts payable	- 7,000
+ Increase in salaries payable	+ 5,000
+ Increase in utilities payable	+ 1,000
- Decrease in income tax payable	- 3,000
Net cash provided by operating activities	$ 95,000

Cash provided (used) by investing activities:

Proceeds from land sale	$ 35,000
Purchase of building	-145,000
Net cash used by investing activities	-110,000

Cash provided (used) by financing activities:

Cash dividends paid to stockholders	$- 5,000
Net cash used by financing activities	- 5,000

Net change in the cash balance	$ -20,000
Beginning cash balance	60,000
Ending cash balance	$ 40,000

QUESTIONS FOR YOUR REVIEW

The following information relates to questions 1 through 3.

All of Sandburg, Inc.'s sales and merchandise purchases are on account. Sandburg, Inc.'s records reveal:

	2003	2002
Prepaid rent	$ 12,000	$ 14,000
Wages payable	0	7,000
Rent expense	15,000	13,000
Wages expense	75,000	72,000
Accounts receivable	150,000	170,000
Sales	800,000	750,000

1. During 2003, cash collected from customers is:
   a. $780,000.
   b. $800,000.
   c. $820,000.
   d. $970,000.

2. During 2003, cash paid for rent is:
   a. $13,000.
   b. $15,000.
   c. $17,000.
   d. $27,000.

3. During 2003, cash paid for wages is:
   a. $67,000.
   b. $75,000.
   c. $79,000.
   d. $82,000.

4. Woolf Corporation's 2003 cost of goods sold is $700,000. Beginning inventory is $50,000. Ending inventory is $40,000. Beginning accounts payable is $70,000 and ending accounts payable is $75,000. Cash paid for merchandise during 2003 is:
   a. $685,000.
   b. $690,000.
   c. $695,000.
   d. $700,000.

5. A purchase of land in exchange for a corporation's common stock is disclosed:
   a. in the operating activities section of the statement of cash flows.
   b. in the investing activities section of the statement of cash flows.
   c. in the investing and financing activities sections of the statement of cash flows.
   d. in the footnotes to the financial statements.

6. Net income can be less than cash provided (used) by operating activities if:
   a. land is sold at a gain.
   b. the balance in Accounts Receivable increases.
   c. the balance in Accounts Payable increases.
   d. the balance in Income Taxes Payable decreases.

The following information relates to questions 7 and 8.
Wharton, Inc.'s books revealed the following:

	2003	2002
Equipment	$ 50,000	$ 40,000
Accumulated depreciation	10,500	10,000
Depreciation expense	5,000	5,000
Loss on equipment sale	2,000	1,000

Additional information: Equipment which originally cost $8,000 was sold during 2003.

7. How much cash was collected on the sale of the equipment in 2003?
    a. $1,500
    b. $2,000
    c. $5,500
    d. $6,000

8. How much equipment was purchased in 2003?
    a. $9,500
    b. $10,000
    c. $18,000
    d. $20,000

9. Which of the following transactions is not a financing activity disclosed on Chandler, Inc.'s statement of cash flows?
    a. Repurchased 10,000 shares of 10% preferred stock at $20 per share.
    b. Declared and paid a $2 per share cash dividend on common stock.
    c. Sold 25,000 shares of Raymond, Inc.'s common stock for $30 per share.
    d. Retired $100,000 of bonds payable by paying them off.

10. Which of the following is not an investing activity disclosed on McGuire, Inc.'s statement of cash flows?
    a. Sold land which cost $30,000, originally, for $30,000. $20,000 cash and $10,000 long-term notes receivable were received in exchange.
    b. Purchased Arkansas Sports, Inc.'s bonds for $70,000 cash.
    c. Purchased Dixie Ale Company stock.
    d. Declared and paid a dividend to common stockholders.

The following information relates to questions 11 and 12. Hammerstein, Inc.'s books reveal the following:

	2003	2002
Accounts receivable	$400,000	$410,000
Allowance for doubtful accounts	20,000	28,000
Bad debt expense	70,000	80,000
Sales	1,400,000	1,300,000

11. The accounts written off during 2003 totaled:
    a. $8,000.
    b. $10,000.
    c. $70,000.
    d. $78,000.

12. Cash collected from charge customers totaled:
    a. $1,332,000.
    b. $1,340,000.
    c. $1,400,000.
    d. $1,410,000.

The following information relates to questions 13 through 15. Syracuse, Inc.'s stockholders' equity section is:

	2003	2002
Common stock, $5 par value	$ 700,000	$ 650,000
Additional paid-in capital	300,000	200,000
Retained earnings	500,000	560,000
Less: Treasury stock	(80,000)	(90,000)
Net stockholders' equity	$1,420,000	$1,320,000

Additional Information:

a. The 2002 treasury stock which cost $90,000 was sold for $85,000 on January 15, 2003. The ending 2003 treasury stock was purchased for $80,000 on December 12, 2003. 8,000 shares were purchased on that date. No other treasury stock transactions occurred during the year.

b. Additional common stock was issued on December 20, 2003.

c. A 5% stock dividend was declared and issued on October 15, 2003, when the stock price was $10 per share.

d. 2003 net income is $40,000.

13. The number of shares issued through the common stock dividend is:
    a.   3,500.
    b.   6,500.
    c.   10,000.
    d.   30,000.

14. Total cash received through the common stock sale is:
    a. $60,000.
    b. $85,000.
    c. $90,000.
    d. $150,000.

15. Cash dividends declared total:
    a. $30,000.
    b. $50,000.
    c. $60,000.
    d. $100,000.

16. Which of the following is added to net income to arrive at cash provided (used) by operating activities?
    a.   Gain on land sale
    b.   Increase in accounts receivable
    c.   Increase in interest payable
    d.   Decrease in accounts payable

17. Which of the following decisions might improve the appearance of reported cash provided (used) by operating activities, temporarily?
    a. Purchase long-lived asset with a long-term note payable.
    b. Delay declaring and paying preferred dividends.
    c. Delay paying a long-term note payable.
    d. Delay paying accounts payable.

The following information relates to questions 18 and 19.

	2003	2002
Sales	$1,350,000	$1,125,000
Accounts receivable	225,000	240,000
Allowance for doubtful accounts	22,500	21,000
Bad debt expense	82,500	60,000

All sales are on credit.

18. Accounts receivable written off during 2003 total:
    a. $1,500.
    b. $15,000.
    c. $81,000.
    d. $82,500.

19. Collections on accounts receivable total:
    a. $1,200,000.
    b. $1,284,000.
    c. $1,590,000.
    d. $1,671,000.

20. Net income can be greater than cash provided (used) by operating activities if:
    a. accounts receivable decrease.
    b. premium on bonds payable decreases.
    c. accounts payable increase.
    d. prepaid rent decreases.

21. Twins Enterprises engaged in the following transactions during 2003:
    1. Sold 20,000 shares of preferred stock ($50 par value) for $75 per share.
    2. Purchased $100,000 of Jefferson Company's 10%, 20-year bonds for $92,000. Twins intends to hold the bonds until maturity.
    3. Paid $48,000 for four years of rent in advance.
    4. Purchased equipment for $500,000: $50,000 cash down payment and the balance financed through a 20-year mortgage.

    Required:
    a. Prepare the journal entries to record each of the above transactions.

   b. What is the cash effect of each item, and in which section of the statement of cash flows does the item appear and at what amount?

22. Compute the cash outflows associated with interest and rent during 2003, using the following information:

	2003	2002
Interest expense	$ 20,000	$ 15,000
Interest payable	5,000	8,000
Discount on note payable	48,000	50,000
Prepaid rent	60,000	68,000
Rent expense	300,000	312,000

Additional information: No notes were issued during 2003.

23. Fisher, Inc.'s statement of cash flows calculated under both the direct and indirect methods is presented below. Prepare an income statement from this data.

Direct Method

Customer collections	$70,000
Payments to vendors	(40,000)
Payments for operating expenses	(36,000)
Cash provided (used) by operations	$(6,000)

Indirect Method

Net income	$12,000
Noncash charges to noncurrent accounts:	
Depreciation	10,000
Gain on equipment sale	(6,000)
Changes in current accounts other than cash:	
Increase in accounts receivable	(9,000)
Decrease in inventory	5,000
Decrease in accounts payable	(20,000)
Increase in accrued payables	2,000
Cash provided (used) by operations	$(6,000)

The following information relates to questions 24 and 25.

The following are the balance sheets and income statement of Burnett Corporation.

Burnett Corporation
Balance Sheets
December 31, 2003 and 2002

	2003	2002
Cash	$ 23,000	$ 16,000
Accounts receivable	300,000	325,000
Inventory	400,000	390,000
Prepaid rent	12,000	16,000
Plant equipment	500,000	450,000
Less: Accumulated depreciation	(225,000)	(200,000)
Total assets	$1,010,000	$997,000
Accounts payable	$ 200,000	$195,000
Bonds payable	300,000	300,000
Premium on bonds payable	20,000	22,000
Common stock - no par	300,000	300,000
Retained earnings	190,000	180,000
Total equity	$1,010,000	$997,000

Burnett Corporation
Income Statement
For the Year Ended December 31, 2003

Sales	$600,000
Less expenses and losses:	
Cost of goods sold	(450,000)
Rent expense	(25,000)
Depreciation expense	(50,000)
Interest expense	(40,000)
Other expenses	(5,000)
Loss on plant equipment sale	(5,000)
Net income	$ 25,000

24. Prepare the statement of cash flows for Burnett Corporation using the direct method to compute cash provided (used) by operating activities.

25. Prepare the operating activities section of Burnett Corporation's statement of cash flows using the indirect method.

CHAPTER 14 - SOLUTIONS

1.	c	6.	c	11.	d	16.	c
2.	a	7.	a	12.	a	17.	d
3.	d	8.	c	13.	b	18.	c
4.	a	9.	c	14.	b	19.	b
5.	d	10.	d	15.	a	20.	b

21. a. Cash (+A)   1,500,000
     Preferred Stock $50 par (+SE)   1,000,000
     Additional Paid-In Capital - P/S (+SE)   500,000
  Sold preferred stock.

    Investment in Jefferson Co. Bonds (+A)   92,000
     Cash (-A)   92,000
    Purchased bonds.

    Prepaid Rent (+A)   48,000
     Cash (-A)   48,000
    Prepaid rent.

    Equipment (+A)   500,000
     Cash (-A)   50,000
     Mortgage Payable (+L)   450,000
    Purchased equipment with cash and debt.

b.   1. Cash increased by $1,500,000. This item is reported in the financing activities section since capital is being contributed by the preferred stockholders.

     2. Cash is decreased by $92,000. This item is reported in the investing activities section since a noncurrent asset is being purchased with cash.

     3. Cash is decreased by $48,000. This item is reported in the operating activities section since rent is an operating expenditure.

     4. Cash is decreased by $50,000. This item is reported in the investing activities section since a long-lived productive asset is purchased. The mortgage payable portion of the transaction is disclosed in a footnote since it does not involve the receipt or disbursement of cash.

22. **Interest:** From Chapter 11, the entry to record interest expense when a note payable is issued at a discount is:

Interest Expense (E,-SE)	xxx	
Discount on Notes Payable (+L)		xxx
Cash (-A) or Interest Payable (+L)		xxx

The payment of the note's face amount at maturity will include a portion of the interest expense accumulated over the note's duration. The total amount of interest included in the face amount is the original balance in Discount on Notes Payable. This account is amortized as interest accumulates over time.

In this problem, Interest Expense ($20,000) - Change in Discount on Notes Payable ($2,000) = Current Year's Increase in Interest Payable ($18,000).

The Interest Payable account decreased from the beginning of the year by $3,000. This means that $3,000 of last year's accrued interest was paid this year.

Total cash paid for interest = $18,000 + $3,000 = $21,000.

Rent: The Prepaid Rent account is increased by prepayments of rent and decreased as the rented space is used. During the year, Prepaid Rent balance decreased by $8,000 (E.B., $60,000 - B.B., $68,000). This means that rent expense exceeded cash payments by $8,000. Total Cash rent payments = Rent Expense Payments ($300,000) - Decrease in Prepaid Rent ($8,000) = $292,000.

23. To construct the income statement, the revenue and expense balances are determined by using the relation between cash collections and cash payments and current asset and liability account balance changes. These relations are summarized in the review of key concepts.

Cash received from customers $70,000	= Sales + Beginning A/R - Ending A/R = Sales - (Ending A/R - Beginning A/R) = Sales - Change in Accounts Receivable = Sales - ($9,000) **= Sales = $79,000**
Purchases **Cash paid to vendors** **Cash paid to vendors** $40,000	= Cost of Goods Sold + Change in Inventory = Purchases - Change in Accounts Payable = Cost of Goods Sold + Change in Inventory - Change in Accounts Payable = Cost of Goods Sold + $5,000 + $20,000 **= Cost of Goods Sold = $25,000**

Cash paid for operating expenses $36,000	= Operating Expenses - Change in Accrued Payables = Operating Expenses - ($2,000) **= Operating Expenses = $38,000**

These items are combined with the noncurrent items backed out of income in the indirect method, Depreciation Expense and Gain on Equipment, to prepare the income statement.

Sales	$79,000
Gain on equipment sale	6,000
Total revenues	$85,000
Less: Cost of goods sold	25,000
Accrued expenses	38,000
Depreciation expense	10,000
Net income	$12,000

24. Direct method: Using the current account and revenue and expense account relations, cash receipts and disbursements due to operations are determined. Then the noncurrent accounts are examined to determine the investing and financing activities.

Cash received from customers	= Sales + Beginning A/R - Ending A/R = Sales - (Ending A/R - Beginning A/R) = Sales - Change in Accounts Receivable = $600,000 - ($300,000 - $325,000) **= $625,000**

Purchases
 	
Cash paid to vendors
 	
Cash paid to vendors
	= Cost of Goods Sold + Change in Inventory
	= Purchases - Change in Accounts Payable
	= Cost of Goods Sold + Change in Inventory
	  - Change in Accounts Payable
	= $450,000 + ($400,000 - $390,000)
	  - ($200,000 - $195,000)
	= $455,000

Cash paid for rent	= Rent Expense + Change in Prepaid Rent = $25,000 + ($12,000 - $16,000) **= $21,000**
Cash paid for accrued expenses	= Accrued Expense - Change in Accrued Payable = $5,000 - ($0 - $0) **= $5,000**

Interest Payable. From Chapter 11, the entry to record interest expense for a bond issued at a premium is:

Interest Expense (E,-SE)	xxx	
Discount on Notes Payable (+L)		xxx
Cash (-A) or Interest Payable (+L)		xxx

In this example, interest payable has a zero balance at the end of 2002 and 2003. Thus, the total of interest expense and the decrease in the Premium on Bonds Payable account equals the cash paid for interest during 2003.

Interest Expense ($40,000) + Decrease in Premium on B/P ($2,000)
= $42,000 Cash Paid for Interest.

Investing Activities. The Plant Equipment account is the only noncurrent asset on the balance sheet. During the year, the company sold an asset that cost $50,000 originally, had accumulated depreciation of $25,000, and realized a $5,000 loss according to the income statement. The cash received on the sale is $25,000 (asset book value) - $5,000 (loss) = $20,000.

The Plant Equipment account increased by $50,000 over the year. A purchase of $100,000 must have occurred after the sale is considered. $50,000 = $100,000 (purchase) - $50,000 (sale).

Since no information is provided to the contrary, the purchase is made with cash.

Financing activities. The bond payable is unchanged. Common stock is unchanged. Retained earnings increased by $10,000.

    B.B. + Net Income - Dividends = E.B.
    Dividends = Net income - (E.B. - B.B.)
 = $25,000 - ($190,000 - $180,000)
 = $15,000

Burnett Corporation
Statement of Cash Flows
For the Year Ended December 31, 2003

Cash provided (used) by operating activities:		
Customer collections	$625,000	
Payments to suppliers	(455,000)	
Payments for other expenses	(5,000)	
Payments for interest	(42,000)	
Payments for rent	(21,000)	
Cash provided by operations		$102,000
Cash provided (used) by investing activities:		
Proceeds from equipment sale	$ 20,000	
Equipment purchase	(100,000)	
Cash used by investing activities		(80,000)
Cash provided (used) by financing activities:		
Payment of cash dividends	$(15,000)	
Cash used by financing activities		(15,000)
Net increase in cash balance		$ 7,000
Beginning cash balance		16,000
Ending cash balance		$ 23,000

25. Indirect method.

Cash provided (used) by operating activities:	
Net income	$ 25,000
Add: Loss on equipment sale	5,000
Depreciation expense	50,000
Decrease in accounts receivable	25,000
Decrease in prepaid rent	4,000
Increase in accounts payable	5,000
Less: Increase in inventory	(10,000)
Decrease in premium on bond payable	(2,000)
Cash provided by operations	$102,000

Note: The investing and financing activities sections of the Statement of Cash Flows are the same as under the direct method.

Notes

Notes

Notes

Notes

Notes

Notes

Notes

Notes

Notes